TWO ROADS *To* AUGUSTA

The Inspiring Story of How Two Men From Different Backgrounds
Grew to Become Best Friends *and* Capture the Biggest Prize in Golf

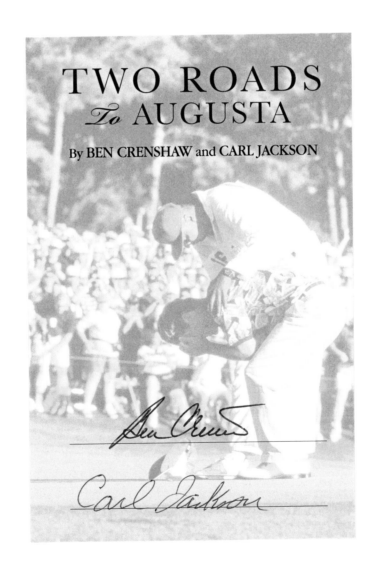

American Golfer titles may be purchased for business or promotional use for special
sales. For information, please write to: The American Golfer Inc., 87 Greenwich Avenue,
Greenwich, Connecticut 06830.

SECOND EDITION

ISBN 1-888-531-19-3
ESN 978-1888531190

Published by:
The American Golfer
87 Greenwich Avenue
Greenwich, Connecticut 08630
TEL: (203) 862-9720
FAX: (203) 862-9724
E-MAIL: imd@aol.com

Art Direction by:
Joe Caputo
J. See Design
Green Brook, New Jersey
TEL: (973) 610-5668
E-MAIL: joesee@optonline.net

ACKNOWLEDGEMENTS
Grateful acknowledgments to the Augusta National Golf Club for helping set the record
straight and especially to the following individuals: Warren Stephens, Julie Crenshaw,
Scott Sayers and Melanie Hauser. From an editorial perspective, this book could not have
been done without the considerable research and editorial talents of Peter Kollmann of
The American Golfer staff. And kudos to our superb art director Joe Caputo.

Photos courtesy of Augusta Country Club, Ben Crenshaw and family, Scotty Sayers,
Carl Jackson, The American Golfer, National Baseball Hall of Fame, USGA, Ralph Barrera/
Austin American-Statesman, and Julius Morck/ZUMA Press

Dedicated to
Bob Jones, Jack Stephens
and the Masters' patrons.

TWO ROADS
To AUGUSTA

The Inspiring Story of How Two Men From Different Backgrounds
Grew to Become Best Friends *and* Capture the Biggest Prize in Golf

by **Ben Crenshaw and Carl Jackson**
with Melanie Hauser

Edited by Scotty Sayers and Martin Davis

The American Golfer, Inc. • 87 Greenwich Avenue • Greenwich, Connecticut 06830
tel 203-862-9720 • fax 203-862-9724 • www.theamericangolfer.com

CHAPTER 1

AND IN THE BEGINNING

"[My grandfather] instilled traditional family values in me: worship God, say your prayers, respect all elders ..."
– Carl Jackson, on the strong influence of his grandfather

It was one of those icy gray mornings when all you want to do is pull the covers over your head and try your best to stay warm. And fall back to sleep.

Carl Jackson rolled over, pulled the quilt tighter and burrowed a little bit deeper under the covers. Lord, it was cold.

Outside a few flakes were still dancing in the wind, slowly falling toward the blanket of snow covering the yard and the dirt road in front of the tiny wooden house at 2439 Mt. Auburn Ave.

The Sand Hill was starting to stir. Another winter morning, another day filled with more challenges than most folks could imagine.

Mothers headed to their kitchens to fire up the wood stoves. Breakfast would come later. If at all.

First things first. Those stoves had to start take the chill off the house.

There was no central heat or air conditioning on the Sand Hill. Fans would move the air during the summer, and windows and doors stayed propped open to catch what breeze there was on a stifling afternoon. Neighbors gathered on porches and sipped cold drinks in hopes of finding a bit of relief from the relentless Georgia sun at the end of another long week.

In the winter, the cold wind would whistle through the cracks around the windows and doors; the only way to stay warm was to pile on an extra quilt or two. And hope your brother or sister didn't pull them all over to their side of the small bed.

Like most deep Southern towns, Augusta in the 1950s was still segregated. Colored-only water fountains, theaters, schools and neighborhoods. Lines that couldn't be seen, but simply weren't crossed. Ever.

Carl's neighborhood was originally called Elizabethtown, but it was now known simply as the Sand Hill, a poor, predominantly African-American community of carpenters, painters, cooks, maids, brick masons, laborers and caddies. They didn't own cars, but they didn't have to. It was only a short walk – a few blocks – to work for the wealthy Augustans who lived just up the road.

The Sand Hill was surrounded by the Summerville District, which, from the 1890s through the early 1930s, was one of the

*A sign of the times, not just in the Sand Hill where **Carl** grew up, but throughout the Deep South from Reconstruction through the mid-1960s.*

As a youngster, Ben's first sports love was baseball.

South's biggest resort areas. Presidents, business magnates and captains of industry like the Vanderbilt family came to relax at the Partridge Inn or Bon Air Hotel, built across from each other on Walton Way, and spend their days on the gracious nine-foot wide wooden hotel porches or at the Savannah River a few miles away. It was also a summer haven for Augusta's rich and famous, who would pack up their downtown houses and move four miles or so to homes off Wheeler Road or Walton Way – the highest ground in the city where breezes tempered the suffocating heat.

> It was never a surprise to come home and have the lights or telephone turned off because there simply wasn't enough money to pay the bills.

Eventually, Augusta's influential families left downtown for good – some because of a fire in 1912 that swept through the business district, others downsized to just one house – and moved to stately permanent homes in neighborhoods that surrounded Augusta Country Club and Augusta National. Sand Hill was a mile walk or so from the Partridge Inn, where people could find good, steady jobs. The walk was even less to Augusta National or Augusta CC, where there were caddie jobs or to those stunning homes that were always in need of a painter, a cook, a maid or a yardman. Downtown was just a four-mile bus ride.

People in the Sand Hill didn't have much, but they shared what they could and watched over each other. The Chinese families who ran Low Bow's and Woo Dunn, two grocery stores in the neighborhood, lived behind their stores and would let you buy on credit – balance due when the paychecks came at the end of the week. Even two-income families were hurting.

It was never a surprise to come home and have the lights or telephone turned off because there simply wasn't enough money to pay the bills. Sometimes not even for that coal or wood to heat the house. It was a harsh reality in Carl's world, something unimaginable to the Augusta society who lived a few blocks – but a world – away.

Ten-year-old Carl could hear his mother rattling around in the kitchen. The two youngest children – Jane and Willie – were fast asleep. Austin, the oldest, rolled over and pretended not to hear a thing.

"Tweet. Tweet, you get up now," Margie Jackson's tone meant business. "I need you to get over to the wood yard. Can't cook without wood. Can't get warm without coal."

Woo Dunn was one of the neighborhood grocery stores that let families like the Jacksons buy on credit and pay up when the checks came at the end of the week.

She waited a few minutes.

"Tweet! Now!"

Austin Jackson was three years older than Carl and a whole lot bigger and stronger. No one ever called him Austin. Just Tweet, the name he'd earned in the caddie yard. Or Tweety.

He just flipped over and closed his eyes. It was his way of saying no. Forget it. Not getting up.

Margie sighed.

"Carl Jackson. Get your skinny tail out of bed. Your brother won't go. You're gonna have to go get some wood."

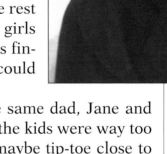

Margie Jackson, Carl's mother.

It wasn't the first time Tweety had pushed something off on his younger brother. It wouldn't be the last either. Tweety was all about Tweety. He wasn't too worried about his mom or the rest of his siblings. He had black curly hair the girls loved and a way of twisting folks around his finger. He'd move on soon enough. The work could get passed around. Mostly to Carl.

Their fathers – Tweety and Carl had the same dad, Jane and Willie another – weren't in the picture and the kids were way too young to handle this chore. So at 10 and maybe tip-toe close to 5-feet tall and 70 pounds, Carl Jackson was becoming the man of the house.

He pulled on the warmest clothes he could find and headed out the door to Charlie Jackson's – no relation – wood yard about 250 yards up the road. Not a bad walk on a good day, but on this morning the surface turned from rock-hard dirt to a mixture of slush and rocks overnight.

Carl knocked on the door.

"Get whatever you need," the wood merchant said. "I'll bill you later."

Later was good. A necessity really. It was the way folks did business on the Sand Hill, where rent in the late 1950s was $15-$20 a month, $1 would get you breakfast and $5 worth of groceries from Low Bow's would feed a family for a day. Maybe two or three.

Carl grabbed the creaky old wheelbarrow with a heavy iron wheel and started stacking up the wood. That done, he struggled to throw a sack of coal on top. Took him five tries. The first four he turned the wheelbarrow over and had to stack it all again. The fifth was the charm.

It was really too much for him to handle. Too heavy. Too unbalanced. Especially on the bumpy, messy road.

"I got it balanced and I went down the street," he said. "The wheelbarrow threw me three or four more times trying to get back to the house."

He sighed. "I get back home and I'm frozen and I can't pick

up a piece of wood. That got me a little bit bitter with my older brother."

Or maybe just a little more bitter.

Tweety had that way about him. He could sweet talk just about anyone and the uncles and aunts from his mother's side loved him. Treated him so special, in fact, it wasn't long until he moved downtown and lived with them.

> The Jackson house was one of the smallest on the block. A wooden porch in the front, a front room, a bedroom and a kitchen. The house was raised up a yard or so off the ground on concrete blocks …

"We'd have been better off if he'd have been the older brother he needed to be," Carl said.

But he wasn't, so Carl stepped in.

Someone had to take care of the younger kids and that, too, fell to Carl. He was a good student, but there were times when Margie had no one else to watch the children, so Carl stayed home from school.

"I'd look out the window and see all the kids going to school," he said, "and I knew I was losing something."

Most of the houses on the Sand Hill were three- to five-room narrow wooden shotgun houses. They were easy to build, the breeze flowed through them and you could build a lot of them on a plot of land. So why call it a shotgun house? You open the front and back doors of these simple homes – a front room, a bedroom or two, a kitchen, no hallway and one bathroom – and you could shoot a shotgun round straight through the house.

When it rained, the drops danced on the Jackson's tin roof.

"I loved it when it rained," Carl said. "It was so peaceful and calm."

The Jackson house was one of the smallest on the block. A wooden porch in the front, a front room, a bedroom and a kitchen. The house was raised up a yard or so off the ground on concrete blocks, providing the perfect place for kids to play or, in the late 1940s and early 1950s, a place to hide when racially motivated hate groups swept through the neighborhood.

For the most part, the Jackson kids slept in the bedroom unless, of course, one of them decided to snuggle with their mother in her bedroom, which also served as the living room. It was crowded, but it was home.

A homemade kitchen table seated six, which, seeing as how a few someones always seemed to be coming or going, was always enough. That morning as Carl, the second of what would eventually be nine children, struggled back from the wood yard, Margie was getting about her day.

For years, Carl's only pictures of his mother were in his mind. Any photographs he had were destroyed in two fires and too many moves. But in late 2012, his little brother Romeo found one lone photo of Margie – she's dressed in a wool coat and simply staring into the camera lens – and made copies to share.

Margie was a handsome woman. She was 5-foot-10 with long, jet black hair, a loving heart and bad luck with men. She had nine children by five different boyfriends and none of the men hung around, leaving her to shoulder the financial burden.

When Carl was younger, Margie worked just across the street for a while at Brown's Snack Bar. They served beer, hot food and sandwiches, and Margie waitressed and ran the cash register.

"It was at 1 o'clock from our front door," Carl said. "I guess that's where she met my old sorry daddy and the other men in her life.

"We were allowed to sit on the steps until 10 o'clock, then Mother usually get off about midnight. "It was less than 20 yards before she'd be in the door."

But Brown's closed before Carl entered the fifth grade and Margie went to work as a maid for several different families. The $5 a day she made cleaning and ironing when she could find work had to cover rent, utilities and food.

"When Brown's closed down, that's when the really hard times came," Carl said.

By 11, Carl was working after school or skipping it completely to shag balls at Augusta Country Club. The extra $1.25 or so he would make – it was 50 to 75 cents per shag bag – made the difference between a real trip-to-the-grocery-store meal and making do by frying rice in butter.

"We was pretty poor ... Some nights, that's all we had," Carl said. "She fed all the kids and she went to bed without eating. So, yeah, we were hungry."

But lord, when Margie had groceries in the house, she could cook on that old two-burner stove where the cooking temperature was centered in the middle and dropped to cool if you got too close to the edge. Not the easiest way to cook, but the neighborhood did more than cope. The smells of good down-home Southern cooking wafted through the yards, and someone was always willing to share with those down on their luck.

Carl's favorite? Without a doubt, burgers smothered in gravy with rice, corn and vegetables. Smothered chicken too. And true Southern fried chicken and grits, which sometimes served as breakfast too.

"The aromas were great," he said. "They just made your stomach growl."

But sometimes those meals came with collateral damage.

Carl had a pet duck when he was in second or third grade. Usually the duck lived in a pen in the yard, but sometimes he'd follow Carl around in the yard. One day, Carl came home from school and the duck was gone.

"I went up the back steps and found what looked like a chicken all cooked up for dinner," Carl said. "It wasn't a chicken. Come to find out, it was the duck. I cried so hard."

Bootlegging – producing illegal whiskey – was often a way of life for lower-income whites and blacks in the rural South.

Some folks in the neighborhood were a little better off than the Jacksons – if only by an extra bedroom or two and maybe a hallway. But almost everyone struggled, which meant entertainment was often just time on the front or back porch.

The Jackson house and those surrounding it backed up to a huge common yard. The kids would play baseball there most afternoons and evenings, but on Saturday night and Sunday morning, the area belonged to Uncle Bam, Pretty Pop, Peg and the other "businessmen" in the Sand Hill.

The kids called them businessmen, but they were really bootleggers. They didn't run the stills; they just bought the moonshine from the distillers who operated down quiet country roads. They'd load it up in gallon jugs and sell it for 50 cents or a dollar a glass to whoever could pay.

And, they drank a bit of their wares along the way.

One day Pretty Pop drank so much it knocked him out. "They had to rush him to the hospital and the doctors had to pump his stomach," Carl said. "Once he got better, the doctors came back and said what he drank was 1500 proof or some ridiculously high number."

Peg's right leg had been amputated, but he still zipped around in a car with standard transmission. He'd accelerated with this crutch and use his left leg for the clutch.

But that wasn't the most mindboggling part of the story. "The most amazing part is he amputated his other leg and he still drove," Carl said. "With both crutches."

Uncle Bam lived around the corner on Fleming Avenue and had two sons older than Carl. Pretty Pop – "I guess the women thought he was a handsome guy," Carl said – stayed down on Gardner Street, a little closer to the entrance to Augusta Country Club.

They had a time of it on weekend nights. Margie's brothers came over to sample the latest batch of moonshine, play cards and dominos and tell stories long into the night.

"You wake up on Sunday morning and they'd been out on the porch and you could smell that moonshine," Carl said. "I'm blessed that I survived."

> "My granddaddy was the first strong male influence in my life. He instilled traditional family values in me: worship God, say your prayers, respect all elders and listen to what they are trying to tell you."   – Carl Jackson

He said early on that wasn't the life he wanted, but that didn't mean he didn't sample a bit of moonshine from time to time.

Carl and his friends knew Uncle Bam didn't keep his product anywhere near his house. He'd hide his wares in thick stands of trees or bushes and, late one night when Carl was about 13 or 14, curiosity got the best of him and a handful of friends and they stole a jug. Then took a swig.

"Oh my god. It was like pure alcohol," Carl said.

It wasn't the last time they went looking, either. "Uncle Bam was pretty sneaky," Carl said. "He'd walk up on us and we'd have to scatter like chickens."

It was easy to get caught up in the moonshine business. Or a few other shady jobs that paid. Easier than becoming a brick mason or a painter. So much less backbreaking than working in the fields. So much more likely to take kids down the road to jail. Or worse.

Saturday mornings the cotton truck would be parked in the neighborhood to pick up folks to work in the cotton fields all day in North Augusta. At night, the truck would rumble down the street to bring home mothers, fathers and children with $2 or $3 – payment for the full day – stashed in their pockets.

The Wallace House served as the first golf shop at Augusta Country Club.

When he was old enough, Carl did the math. Pick cotton for $2 or caddie and shag balls at Augusta CC for the same amount. It wasn't even close. Caddying was one done deal.

Lewis Jackson was a painter by trade. He married Anna Romeo and they had 10 children before Anna died in 1937, when his son

Romeo was born. In all, Lewis raised 14 kids, including Margie, then helped raise his grandchildren. Three children – Lillie, Albert and Romeo – moved to Oregon in the late 1940s – and four sons went into the military (Albert, Austin, George and Romeo).

He lived in the house with Margie and kids on and off for years and worked for some of the wealthy folks in Augusta who had built houses an easy walk away on Walton Way or Monte Sano Avenue. Lewis painted for his poorer neighbors, too, when people needed a hand.

Now the caddie master at Alotian Club in Little Rock, Carl tries to channel his grandfather's wisdom every day. "His spirit stays with me today, always trying to get the best deals for my caddies at Alotian. The many people I managed for Jack Stephens, I tried to get the best for them, too."

His mother – Carl's great grandmother – lived in the house next door. Mamie Jackson was a tiny woman, but a strong one. Mammo, as Carl called her, was born in 1850, raised during the Civil War and Reconstruction and couldn't read or write. She must have had some stories to tell, but Carl doesn't remember her ever talking about any of those days or her ancestors. In fact, he didn't even know how old she was until he saw the obituary.

She raised three children and dozens of grandchildren and great-grandchildren before she died in 1959 at the age of 109.

Carl, who couldn't go to the funeral because he was home taking care of the younger children, remembers his great grandmother shuffling around the yard looking for kindling. And, there was her passion for sweet rolls.

"She loved those things," he said. "And she was always sharing one with me."

Mamie shared plenty more too, since she raised Lewis, and Lewis, in turn, helped raise Carl.

Carl's first job was to tag along with Lewis and, since he wasn't much of a painter and was scared silly of heights, he'd do the yard work. The combination worked pretty well. Plus, it gave Lewis time to make sure his grandson knew there was a better life out there.

Lewis wasn't a big man – maybe 5-8 – but when he spoke, people listened. He wasn't afraid to raise his hoarse voice or hand when need be and Carl got a more than bit of both growing up. Yet he was really the first of what could only be described as a series of angels that helped Carl find his way.

"He would give me that talk about staying away from trouble, always worshipping God, taking care of your mother, respecting your elders," Carl said. "No matter where he went, he was Mr. Jackson. People around there today refer to me as Mr. Jackson. I just say, that's my granddaddy.

"He only knew to give an honest day's work for an honest

day's pay. ... My granddaddy was the first strong male influence in my life. He instilled traditional family values in me: worship God, say your prayers, respect all elders and listen to what they are trying to tell you. He also taught me many lessons about life in general: finish what you start, work hard, take care of your family."

Lewis was poor, but determined. He didn't own a car, so when he'd finish for the day, he grabbed the back of his paint ladder and Carl or one of his uncles took the front and they headed toward home.

It was a moving carnival. Everyone popped their head out to say hello and chat a minute.

By the time Carl went to work at Augusta National at 13, Lewis had moved downtown, but that didn't stop him from worrying. He'd catch a bus and make his way to the house every morning to make sure Carl had lunch money for the day. Then he'd head off to work.

And the one day Carl did paint with him? Lewis put him in charge of the trim. Lewis had two coats of paint on the house before Carl had trimmed out half the windows, so Lewis stepped in and helped his grandson finish.

"The man paid him and we walked back toward Weed Elementary School," Carl said. "He was going to cut through the school yard and I had to cut the other way. He said, 'Here, let me pay you.'"

He made $600 on the job and gave Carl $300.

"I really was no help to him," Carl said. "I know he was trying to help me and I was his partner on that job. It was my last painting job for him."

Carl paused.

Now the caddie master at Alotian Club in Little Rock, Carl tries to channel his grandfather's wisdom every day.

"His spirit stays with me today, always trying to get the best deals for my caddies at Alotian. The many people I managed for Jack Stephens, I tried to get the best for them, too."

And it wasn't without sacrifice.

Carl was 13 when Lewis sat him down and told him he hated to say it, but it was time. Carl needed to start contributing more money every month. Margie couldn't make ends meet on what she brought home and Carl's smaller contributions.

He didn't go to Tweety. He went to Carl.

"You gotta go do it or you and your brothers are going to be orphans," Lewis said.

Carl nodded.

"It made me determined ... determined to do something," he said. "The choices – for me, it came down to the golf course or the cotton truck.

"I went to the golf course."

*   *   *   *

Ben Crenshaw must have been about six when he decided his future was behind home plate.

It was a done deal. His dad had been an All-Southwest Conference (SWC) catcher at Baylor University, after all, and his older brother was blossoming into one heck of a Little League pitcher.

> The [Crenshaw] boys played football and a little golf, too, but baseball? That was the game they loved, the one that captured their imagination and took up most of their time during the season. It was a passion they shared with their dad.

Problem was, Ben thought that deep tight pocket of catcher's mitt – the hole – would just catch the ball by itself. He was thumbing through a catalog one day when it caught his eye. And his imagination.

He was playing with a tiny old worn mitt that was perfect for playing catch, not so much for climbing up the ranks of his Little League roster. So what's a guy to do? Wear out his father about a new glove. For close to two years.

Big Charlie Crenshaw was a blend of discipline and a tender heart. He was tough when he had to be, which was pretty often with two rambunctious boys who were born 15 months apart and competed in just about everything they did. But he was a softie, too. He'd always find a way for them to get what they wanted – but he made them work for it.

So when Ben kept pushing for that glove, he said yes. But only when Ben could catch Charlie. Charlie wanted no part of it, but he finally agreed.

They marked off the distances in the front yard and went at it.

"He threw balls at me into the dirt, over my head," Ben said. "Anything but a strike.

"He tried to make it tough on me and that little itty bitty glove I had that couldn't catch a thing. That's just what a big brother does to irritate you. And he leaves a few bruises while he's at it."

*Ben, left, and big brother **Charlie**.*

After a few months, Ben figured it out, starting catching those ridiculously crazy pitches from his brother, and Big Charlie took him down to Rooster Andrews Sporting Goods and bought him the real catcher's mitt.

Back in those days, the Crenshaw boys came in a pair. No matter what the sport, they were playing it – usually together. They were best friends.

Every so often, Ben would have to wait a year to step up the same level in Little League or graduate from Casis Elementary to O'Henry Junior High or O'Henry to Austin High, but that didn't matter. Sharing the sports was.

The boys played football and a little golf, too, but baseball? That was the game they loved, the one that captured their imagination and took up most of their time during the season. It was a passion they shared with their dad.

Ben, far left, **Bonnie,** **Charlie** *and* **Donnie** **Kirkland.**

It was also, at times, a battle of wills. Ben learned to catch Charlie really well and they were good together. Until Ben got a little hot at his big brother.

"I'd be so mad at him when he'd throw a ball instead of a strike," Ben said. "I'd throw it back so hard at him it would almost knock him down. We'd get mad and keep doing that. People used to laugh at it when we'd go at it."

Big Charlie started coaching Ben and Charlie in Little League when Ben was seven and spent the next six years coaching their team. An attorney, he represented big firms like 3M in the state legislature during the day, but couldn't wait to get out of the office and get to his all – not just Ben and Charlie – his boys.

They couldn't get enough of him, either.

Decades later, Houston attorney Jerry Bell, who played on

those teams, wrote Big Charlie a note. Ben saw it in Big Charlie's coat pocket a few months before his dad died in 1999.

"It was a beautiful, sweet little letter," Ben said. "It was remembering those years and telling Dad that as he coached his daughter and her softball team, all he could think about was wanting to coach like Dad."

> Learning the game from Harvey was learning life – you played by the rules, worked hard and valued things like kindness, respect and compassion.

Yes, Big Charlie had a way about him. He was only 6-1, but owned the room when he walked in the door. He owned the mornings at the old Commodore Perry Hotel coffee shop downtown, too. There he'd have breakfast with the other downtown attorneys – basically everyone who was anyone in Texas politics – and chew over the issues of the day.

He had a stunning circle of influential friends around the country, including old law school buddy Stone Red Wells, who was key in what turned out to be the best trip ever for Ben and Charlie when they were in grade school. What else can you say about meeting Stan Musial, Ernie Banks and taking in a St. Louis Cardinals-Chicago Cubs game?

Big Charlie and the boys – dressed in their good clothes because that's what you traveled in during the 1950s and '60s – took the train up from Austin and Wells took care of them. In addition to meeting Banks and Musial and shaking their hands, they ate at Musial's restaurant – Biggie's – outside the stadium and went to the zoo. They had, quite simply, a blast.

"We thought we were in heaven for those five days," Ben said. "The whole trip back, Charlie and I ran all over the train. We wore Dad out. I think he was glad to get us back home."

Ben might have seen a baseball future, but that didn't stop him and Charlie from playing a little golf on the side. Which brings us to another man in Big Charlie's world, a man who would nurture Ben's talents for almost four decades – Harvey Penick.

Penick grew up caddying at Austin Country Club, took the assistant's job at 17 and became the club's head pro in 1923. He was only 19. At the time, no one knew the soft-spoken gentle man who was content with three meals a day and a place to teach would become a legend.

*Ben and his brother Charlie met **Ernie Banks,** top, and **Stan Musial** at a Cubs-Cardinals game.*

Harvey knew golf and he knew people. He wasn't about immediate results or instant success. He knew golf, like life, was a journey and he just wanted to help you on your way. He never raised his voice, never spoke a harsh word. Learning the game from Harvey was learning life – you played by the rules, worked hard and valued things like kindness, respect and compassion.

Harvey always considered himself the lucky one for taking the assistant's job at Austin CC when he 17 and never leaving. He did coach the Texas team from 1931-63, but that was a little add-on, another avenue to share his love for the game.

His students knew deep down they were the lucky ones.

Every year the sun baked a little more character into a face that always seemed a decade older than it was.

"He had so many wrinkles," the legendary Jimmy Demaret once said, "his face could hold a seven-day rain."

Big Charlie would take the boys to Austin Country Club when he'd play 18 and Harvey would send them – and the other kids their age – over to a little practice hole and let them chip and putt.

Harvey Penick went to work at Austin Country Club at 17 and never left.

"Harvey had a way of keeping the kids off the big course and knowing when a kid was ready to go to the big course," Ben said.

"He gave us the three little excursions – putting on the putting green, chipping around the green and then we had one little practice hole that was alongside No. 1. He'd tell us, 'If y'all want to go practice, go down there by the tree and play that hole."

Ben's first lesson? Big Charlie took him to the tee and Harvey placed his hands on a little mashie – a 5-iron. "Now keep them there," he said.

Simple, to the point. One that's Ben's never forgotten.

Once Ben found that grip, the golf balls started coming through the windows of the house and Pearl Crenshaw laid down the law with her boys – whiffle balls only in the yard.

Not long afterward, Wilmer Allison, the former Texas tennis coach, had gifted him with a putter he claimed had been given to him by Bobby Jones. It didn't have a gooseneck like Jones' beloved Calamity Jane, a Winton that was given to Jones by a member at Nassau Country Club, but it worked.

At the time, it was all just another diversion for the boys – another sport to challenge them. Little did anyone know how much Harvey or Jones' legacy would eventually mean to Crenshaw.

The Crenshaw house was tucked on the corner of Bridle Path and Elton Lane, smack in the middle of a quiet little neighborhood in west Austin called Tarrytown. A little wall bordered the property and it came with a daily admonishment – don't go into the street and watch for cars.

To a bunch of kids, that was, quite simply, a dare. One of those lines your toes just can't stop themselves from touching. And usually crossing.

Charlie and Ben didn't need too much prodding. Charlie tossed a broken bat at a car one day and got worn out. Another time, Ben decided it would be fun to use a bat as a golf club and hit rocks with it instead of golf balls. Again, they got worn out.

> The boys didn't really pay much attention to politics or the influential people in Big Charlie's circle until Nov. 22, 1963 – the day President John F. Kennedy was assassinated.

There was always a game going in the front yard. Depending on the season, it was football or baseball – the two best sports in the world to a six-year-old. Especially a couple of them who were growing up with University of Texas coaches' kids and trying to keep up with guys like future major leaguer Don Baylor, who lived across town and was a couple years older and way better than they were.

Their two-story home, where the boys shared a bedroom, was comfortably middle class, and Bridle Path was just like the other streets in Tarrytown – all lined with sprawling oak and pecan trees, all with freshly mowed, perfectly landscaped lawns.

Families went to church on Sundays and sat down to dinner together – moms rang dinner bells to get the kids inside – around a big table every night.

Some moms worked, others didn't. Dads hustled off to their offices in the morning and got home in plenty of time to coach Little League or play a little catch. There was love, laughter and warmth up and down the streets, and no one wanted for anything.

Trouble? It was there if you really wanted to find it but, for the most part, the Crenshaw boys and their friends didn't even look. They weren't, however, above a little mischief. Or wearing out a lawn.

The trees in the Crenshaws' front yard were placed in what could only be called the perfect spots to open up an area just large enough to walk off a baseball diamond. The boys used the trees as bases until one day when neighbor Andy Loudermilk knocked himself out on the third base tree. After that, they threw down towels to use as bases and left them there, which pretty much killed the grass underneath. Football games took care of the rest.

*Big sister **Bonnie** holding baby Ben.*

Big Charlie was always bringing someone to the house for dinner. One night it was a politician or elected official, the next a coach or businessman. Always someone with influence.

He'd grown up in Alabama and was Bear Bryant's suitemate his freshman year and Sigma Nu fraternity brother. He and Bear looked so much alike that when, years later, Big Charlie would put on a houndstooth hat, people had trouble telling them apart.

He transferred to Baylor his second year, was All SWC and, after getting his law degree, he met the reason he never moved back to Alabama – elementary school teacher Pearl Vail Johnson. The two lived in the same boarding house in Houston and, after some prodding from friends, fell in love and got married – at that boarding house. Daughter Bonnie came along first, then, a decade later, Charlie and Ben.

Bonnie and Pearl with Charlie and Ben as they wait for the train to St. Louis, where the boys and Big Charlie took the trip of a lifetime and met Stan Musial and Ernie Banks.

As with Southern tradition, their first son was named for Big Charlie – Charles Edward V – while Ben Daniel is named for one of Pearl's brother Ben and former Texas Gov. Price Daniel. When Daniel ran for Texas attorney general, Big Charlie was Daniel's Harris County campaign manager. When he won, he lured Big Charlie, who had roomed with Daniel's brother at Baylor, to work on his staff in Austin. The Crenshaws never left.

Although he eventually went into private practice, Big Charlie had friends all around the State Capitol and the circle expanded with the boys, who grew up with the sons and daughters of politicians and University of Texas coaches.

And Pearl? She taught more than a few of those kids in sixth grade at Brykerwoods Elementary.

"I run into people all the time who she taught," Ben said. "They loved her. She had such a kind, sweet spirit."

Big Charlie was a Texas Democrat to the core until, of course, his friend Gov. John Connally, who had run Lyndon Johnson's campaigns, changed parties in the early 1970s and took the balance of power in the state with him. One minute The Lone Star State was blue, the next it was red.

Texas Gov. John Connally, far left, with President John F. Kennedy in Dallas on that fateful day of Nov. 22, 1963.

The boys didn't really pay much attention to politics or the influential people in Big Charlie's circle until Nov. 22, 1963 – the day President John F. Kennedy was assassinated. Kennedy, who started the day in Houston, was due to fly from Dallas to Austin that night for a fundraising dinner.

Suddenly, Ben's friends Mark Connally and Scotty Sayers – Connally was the son of the then-Texas Governor and Sayers' father was in charge of the dinner – were whisked out of their sixth grade classroom at Casis by Texas Department of Safety troopers.

Later, they found out what happened.

"Those days were as solemn and hurtful," Ben said. "I just remember the nation being crippled with grief that a young president was killed. It was so shocking."

> The Crenshaws were comfortably middle class, not rich. Ben and Charlie didn't get allowances, but didn't have to work, either.

Almost three years later, they were stunned once more. On Aug. 1, 1966, former marine and architectural engineering student Charles Whitman killed 16 people and wounded 32 more in a lunchtime shooting rampage from the top of the Tower on the University of Texas campus.

Ben was standing in the parking lot across from Casis Elementary – the same parking lot where, today, he goes for a Starbucks every morning – seeing his girlfriend Margaret Kreisle off to Camp Longhorn when the shooting started.

It was several miles away, so he was oblivious until he got home and his mother was watching it unfold on Austin's only local station at the time – KTBC, which ironically, was owned back then by President Lyndon Johnson.

He stayed clear of the horrific scene, but Charlie and his friend Ed White drove over to Memorial Stadium and scrambled to the top – there was no upper deck at the time – and watched it unfold. They were lucky. Whitman's rifles had the range to reach the stadium, but Whitman, a former Marine who was killed that day, never aimed their way.

Equally as lucky was Ben's older sister Bonnie, who was working on her master's degree in library science that summer. Normally she would have been walking by the Tower around that time. Instead, she had stayed home to study.

*Former **President Lyndon Johnson**, right, congratulates Texas coach **Darrell Royal** and quarterback **James Street** after the Longhorns' win over Notre Dame in the 1970 Cotton Bowl.*

"The most amazing thing, when people knew he was starting to shoot, it was like the whole community went home, got their guns and they were returning fire," Ben said. "They were keeping him pinned down. They weren't going to let that happen to their community."

One of the boys killed in the 96-minute rampage was 18-year-old Paul Sonntag, whose younger brother George was a friend of Ben and Charlie's.

"Those were two very shocking events in someone's life," Ben said. "The whole nation who was that age could tell you where they were when Kennedy was assassinated. And, equally, the people in Texas who were living through that horrific event could tell you where they were, too."

It took a long while for the city to heal from the Tower shootings, but a month later, the boys were – along with the rest of Austin – cheering for the Texas Longhorns football team. They had won a national football championship in 1963 when Ben was 10, and folks like Darrell Royal and his staff were welcome at the Crenshaw home anytime.

And, of course, they didn't know who some of their guests were.

One night Big Charlie came home and called the boys away from whatever game was going on in the front yard to introduce them to a short, balding older gentleman he had in tow.

"Boys," he said, "I want you to meet D.X. Bible."

Bible handed the boys a football – a Wilson J5V1 college football with The University of Texas stamped on it – and told them to scuff the heck out of it. They did. He came by a few more times, too, each time with a new football.

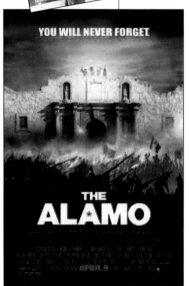

A favorite of the Crenshaw boys was the movie "The Alamo," starring John Wayne.

Charlie and Ben thought of him as the guy with the footballs. Years later they'd find out he was one of UT's legendary football coaches, a World War I pilot and one of the creators of the T-formation.

Growing up, the boys were inseparable. They shared an endless supply of friends and athletic talent too, although Charlie always seemed to be a head taller and a tad better. That only drove Ben a little harder.

And they could wheel and deal. When "The Alamo," the epic movie starring John Wayne, came out in 1960, the boys turned to one of their friends whose uncle was the manager of both the Paramount and State theaters down on Congress Avenue.

"A lot of people there trying to get in," Ben said. "Mr. Root saw us, pulled us under the usher's ropes and got us a seat. John Wayne at the Alamo. I wanted to see that because of (Wayne) and because Gov. Price Daniel's brother Bill had a bit part in the movie. He played Sam Houston's – he was played by Richard Boone – scout."

The Crenshaws were comfortably middle class, not rich. Ben and Charlie didn't get allowances, but didn't have to work, either. And their part-time maids – at different times, Pearlie Mae and Manya – were around to help Pearl when she needed it.

She taught. She played bridge. She cooked. And she was never thrown by her husband calling late and saying he was bringing someone – or a few someones – home for dinner.

Pearl was sweet, kind and a bit devilish at times. When Ben's lunch was stolen out of his locker the first three days his freshman year at Austin High, Pearl had the answer – a Thor sandwich.

Ben was not just learning from Harvey. He was also watching some of the best players in Austin.

Thor was the family dog – a Norwegian elkhound – and left presents in the yard. Pearl scooped up one of the presents, added a little lettuce, tomato, cheese and other things and made quite an inviting Dagwood sandwich.

"I took it to school the next day and it was stolen," Ben said. "But it was the last time it was stolen."

Pearl stepped in, too, one day when Ben was down. There was no one to do anything with, so he grabbed his clubs and walked six blocks for a solitary round at Lions Municipal Golf Course, known simply as Muny.

Ben had just teed off on the fourth hole when he saw Pearl walking over the hill. She figured he could use a little company.

"I remember, she said, 'I knew that you would be alone and I just wanted to be with you,' " Ben said. "It was the sweetest, sweetest thing. I was so disappointed and then she appeared."

Pearl had that way about her. One word, one touch. It was all the reassurance Ben and Charlie seemed to need growing up.

"I still remember the house," he said. "There were such great smells in it. I can still smell those turnip greens. Dog smells. Cats running around. And Mom's cooking. I loved her chicken and rice, but her tuna casserole was a staple. I can still taste it."

As for special breakfasts? Big Charlie had that covered. His specialty was Andalusia sausage, eggs and pancakes with ribbon cane syrup.

"Dad used to stop in Louisiana to get the syrup every time he drove to Mississippi or Alabama," Ben said. "The sausage was from Alabama and would make a popping sound when you broke it open. And the syrup was thick and dark. It was like molasses. The whole breakfast was incredible."

Most kids mowed the lawn or did chores around the house. Not Ben and Charlie. They were on a field or a diamond or a course.

Their little neighborhood had everything. West Enfield Park was a quick bike ride away for a pickup game or an afternoon at the pool. Little League games were at Knebel Field, right across Enfield Road from Muny, where golf was something fun to do if you couldn't field enough kids for a baseball game. And even the baseball games had a tie-in to Muny – Danay Covert once launched a home run at Knebel that landed on the second green at Muny.

There was an empty lot down the way, too. The perfect place to build forts out of discarded Christmas trees in January and boards and boxes in the summer. The end game? Almost always a world-class dirt-clod war.

But the most inviting spot had to be the big old mulberry tree in the Crenshaw's backyard. The boys would stuff their faces until they were purple – or until someone failed to inspect a berry and bit into a worm.

One day Big Charlie came home with gifts from Harvey – a little 5-iron for Ben and a 3-iron for Charlie. He told them to take them out into the yard and start swinging. Once they did, they didn't stop. They'd go to Austin Country Club and play for a while, then swim for a while.

Sometimes they'd follow Big Charlie and his group and hit a few shots. His favorite partners were Jimmy Connolly and Walter Benson, two of the best amateur players in Austin.

Ben was not just learning from Harvey. He was also watching some of the best players in Austin. His father played with the likes of Connolly and Benson, two of Austin's top players. Former UT player Billy Penn, an Austin attorney and family friend who became executive director of the Texas Golf Association, was another big-name player Ben would watch at Austin CC.

He just kept watching shots. It was all starting to sink in.

"He just wanted us to learn how to compete," Ben said.

Harvey was a man of few words. He figured students didn't need a treatise every time he worked with them on the tee. A golf swing was complex enough. Let one lesson settle in at a time.

People would walk away from the tee wondering how in the heck a nice thought would be enough to straighten them out. It would take a few weeks, but it eventually sunk in and, like everyone else before them, they'd understand.

Top photo: **Ben** *putting at Lions Muny at age 15.*

Above: **Austin Country Club** *was the other course where* **Ben** *played most of his childhood golf.*

Big Charlie had joined the club in 1954 and by the late 1950s, he had already served on both the greens and junior golf committees. He wasn't just an active member, either. He was one of the club's better golfers. At one point, he worked his way from a 4-handicap down to scratch, but it didn't last. He went back up to a 4.

But like everyone else, Big Charlie needed a few lessons from Harvey now and then. In fact, one time Big Charlie had a case of the shanks and went to the tee with Harvey. He pulled a 7-iron and shanked 17 shots in a row.

Harvey didn't say a word until Big Charlie stopped and looked at him. "Mr. Crenshaw," Harvey said, "I think we'd better tackle this tomorrow.' "

> The turning point came two years later, when (Ben) read Charlie Price's *The World of Golf* and qualified for the 1968 U.S. Junior Amateur at The Country Club in Brookline, Mass.

He was gentle and patient and somehow all-knowing. He used to encourage Ben and Charlie to play with someone older. It was a chance to see someone a bit mature, as well as someone who had a lot more shots in their bag.

One of the players Ben watched was Lester Lundell. Lundell later got the nickname Lumpy because he didn't have any corners on his body, was four years older than Ben and he was the guy to beat as a junior player in Austin.

"He was a beautiful player," Ben said. "He was a good athlete and he hit some beautiful shots. Watching his shots and how he could play fascinated me. Everyone had eyes on Lester because he was such a good player."

Ben played in his first Texas Junior Amateur at Brackenridge Park in San Antonio when he was 13. It was his first "who's who" statewide competition, his first chance to tee it up with future tournament champions like Midland's Terry Jastrow, who went on to become an Emmy award-winning producer for ABC Sports, and Beaumont's Bruce Lietzke. Ben shot 70 to qualify for the Championship Flight that first time out, but lost on the 18th hole in the quarterfinals. Sandy Adelman, who played college golf at Stanford and is now a doctor in San Antonio, won that 1965 tournament.

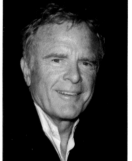

Terry Jastrow, later an award-winning producer for ABC Sports, was a stellar junior golfer from Midland, Texas.

Ben was dangerously close to working the counter and cutting greens at Muny that next summer of 1966, but he was far too busy for golf, let alone work. Too busy hanging out at Margaret's house, swimming and doing nothing.

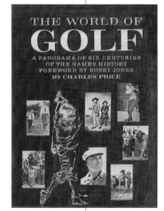

*Ben read Charlie Price's book, **The World of Golf**.*

"My dad was really not happy with me," Ben said. "He always said I left a lot of golf in that girl's living room."

The turning point came two years later, when he read Charlie Price's *The World of Golf* and qualified for the 1968 U.S. Junior Amateur at The Country Club in Brookline, Mass. There was, indeed, a whole new world opening up – one that spread far beyond the comfortable confines of Muny and Morris Williams and Austin Country Club.

Ben won the first of his two state junior titles at 15, beating Brownsville's Wayne Fenack in the match play finals in 1967. Two years later, Ben won the title again, this time in medal play.

But even at 15, Ben was slowly figuring out his future wasn't behind the plate. It was on the golf course.

He had been splitting time between the two sports – Charlie also added football to his list – and it was working. But Ben, along with Tom Kite, another of Harvey's students, was making an impact on Austin golf, and people around him were already wondering what was ahead.

Then, a year after winning that first State Junior, one at-bat against future major leaguer Bill Greif changed everything.

Greif, who played at Reagan, was one of the top high school pitchers in the country. The 6-5 right-hander was drafted by Houston and played for the Astros, San Diego Padres and St. Louis Cardinals. Ben found himself overmatched in an American Legion game.

"I'd fouled off a couple toward our dugout," Ben said. "Then he threw me a slider. I whiffed. I looked over and Charlie was there with Doug Baylor, Don's little brother, laughing at me.

"I stepped out of the batter's box, put my bat down. That's it. It's over.

"It was a pretty easy decision."

* * * *

Weed Street was a great place to ride bikes.

The street started at Mt. Auburn Avenue and dead-ended at the ditch bordering the Augusta Country Club's fence. The road was 350 yards – all downhill. An exciting racetrack for a bunch kids looking for a few thrills. A great spot, when you weren't busy on your bike or skates, to "people watch."

Carl would pause every so often and study the impeccably dressed club members putting out on the 16th green and enjoying a lifestyle that was beyond his imagination. He watched them swing away on the immaculate fairways and hand their clubs to their caddies, most of whom lived within a par 5 of his house.

That old chain link fence was all that separat-

Caddies at Augusta National Golf Club watch other players finish at the end of a long day.

ed the Sand Hill from Augusta CC, yet it felt like so much more.

On hot summer mornings, they'd head for the woods near the club to pick up golf balls to sell to golfers on the course or at a store. A good morning meant they could buy a sandwich from the store counter.

But more times than not, the neighborhood boys used to sneak under the fence near the ninth hole so they could float down Rae's Creek and come up near the 13th tee at Augusta National, which backed up to Augusta CC at that point. They swam, they fished. Most of the time they didn't get caught. Sometimes they did.

Augusta CC had a security guard the caddies named Nubby ... "One evening, Nubby caught us and we just ran for the woods across the 11th fairway toward the cemetery," Carl said. "Nubby was chasing us in the cart and, for some reason, he started to shoot."

"We'd get a frying pan, used cooking grease, sandwich bread, mustard, hot sauce and our fishing poles," Carl said. "We'd catch fish, cook and eat, and then we would swim for a while until the horse flies got us. They could bite harder than a bull dog."

As he stood there, Carl wouldn't think about the creek or the fish or the grease sandwiches or the day Tweety dove off the bridge at 13 on Augusta National's course and came up with a bloody head. He'd imagine another life – one where he'd be walking those fairways too.

Then, one morning in 1958, he followed a couple of the older boys over to Augusta Country Club and got put to work.

Tweety was already caddying there, but none of his pay was going toward the Jackson's household expenses. It was going in his pocket.

Carl started off like everyone else. He shagged balls for 75 cents on the range. On a good day, a guy could walk away with $1.50. After spending $1 combined on breakfast and lunch, he'd net 50 cents.

It was hard work, not to mention dangerous. This was in the days before you sat in a cage and drove a golf ball picker around the range. These guys wrapped their hands in towels and ran out onto the range and caught the balls. Or let them drop and then pick 'em up.

It was heads-up time all the time. Someone else's player might hook or slice one in your direction without you knowing.

The caddie master over there was Big Henry Avery, an imposing 6-4, 300-pound man who pretty much taught, raised and nicknamed just about every caddie at Augusta National. Henry, whose older brother Nathaniel – a.k.a. Iron Man – was on Arnold Palmer's bag for all four Masters wins, would get them started at Augusta CC. Those who showed talent like Carl would graduate to the caddie shack at Augusta National.

Every morning the caddies gathered in a field the other side of the 18th green and waited. The oldest, most experienced guys like Tweety got called first.

"One day he called for Little Tweet," Carl said. "And we all said 'Who is Little Tweet?' Finally, I figured out he was talking about me and I got to caddie my first 18 holes."

He was 11.

Carl spent as much time as he could in the pen. He learned the game and learned people. On slow days, they'd hit balls in the field.

The caddies had a collection of clubs that had found their way into the pen and they came in pretty handy on the days they'd sneak onto the course. Of course, they played at Fort Gordon and a little place near the airport too. But Augusta CC was just a hop over or a squeeze under the fence.

Somebody had a 4-iron, a 6-iron and a wedge. Someone else had an 8-iron and a 5-iron.

"We learned how to play by sneaking out on the Augusta Country Club," Carl said. "There were times when we'd be playing a 15-some."

After a good rain, they'd sneak over and play the holes closest to the fence. It was something to watch as they tossed clubs from player to player so everyone could hit their shots.

But Augusta CC had a security guard the caddies called Nubby because he'd had one hand amputated. Nubby carried a gun, but, according to local legend – and the caddies all bought into it –

*Carl and friends learned to play by sneaking onto **Augusta Country Club**, a fine Donald Ross design that abuts Augusta National Golf Club.*

that gun was loaded with blanks.

"One evening, Nubby caught us and we just ran for the woods across the 11th fairway toward the cemetery, near the intersection of Berckmans and Wheeler Roads," Carl said. "Nubby was chasing us in the cart and, for some reason, he started to shoot.

"I hid behind a big oak tree. I'm nearly off the property. He shot one more time and that bullet hit that tree. That was enough to stop me from sneaking over there ever again. He wasn't shooting blanks. He was shooting.

"I'm scared of the police and I don't like jail. Never did it again."

What he did do was soak up all he could. He learned about grass and clubs and eyeballing yardages and started to realize he had a pretty good feel for everything, including one of the toughest challenges – reading greens. He even learned a little about competing from Avery, who was a pretty good player in his own right.

"I used to go watch them play on Monday mornings," Carl said. "He and his club repair guy took on all comers and he gave Jim Dent and any partner he brought all the trouble they wanted.

"That guy could play some golf."

But more about that later.

Wednesdays and Thursdays were good days to skip school. All the doctors and businessmen took off early and played an afternoon 18. You could take a double, but Carl never did. He concentrated on one loop, which, with a tip, was a good day.

Two years after stepping into the pen at Augusta Country Club, Freddie Bennett came driving around the Sand Hill looking for caddies. The Augusta National caddie master had been watching Carl for a while and stopped to ask if he'd like to caddie at The National.

"I jumped in the car," Carl said.

Carl is a lanky, imposing 6-5 today, but back then he was a squirt. By the time he got to eighth grade he was 5-9, about 100 pounds and played fullback for Weed Elementary School.

Like the Crenshaw boys, he never met a sport he didn't like. Football was fun, but he was on a city-wide all-star basketball team and he played city league baseball until he was 15. After that, he pitched in a semi-pro baseball league. He always thought his future would be in baseball, but like Crenshaw, fate had another plan.

"We had some good athletes," he said. "I would caddie all day and we'd all get home in time to play some basketball at night. And we had a serious baseball league.

"People would pay us to play. Went to different counties and people could come out of the woods to see us play."

*Carl's friend **"Hop" Harrison** caddied for Raymond Floyd when he won the Masters in 1976.*

They didn't make much. Just enough to cover the cost of uniforms and a party at the end of the day, but some players got looks from Major League Baseball teams. Carl wasn't one of them.

When Carl was 16, he and Fred "Hop" Harrison, who caddied

for Raymond Floyd when he won in 1976, pulled together $600 and bought a '53 Ford. They called it "The Rust Out" because there was rust everywhere. It had even eaten away at the right headlight, which hadn't fallen out yet, but was swinging loose.

Half the Augusta Hawks team would pile into that old thing and head to a game. One day they were driving down a dirt road near Lincolnton and the car filled up with dust.

> "Many times I've said Jack Stephens saw in me what my mother and granddaddy saw in me. The day he hired me full-time to be his caddie, I was only 14 years old. And he *fired* another caddie, a man about 30 years old, in order to hire me." – Carl Jackson

"Everyone was 'Roll up the windows, roll up the windows,' " Carl said. "We did and dust was still coming in the car. When we pulled up to the field, we found out why – the bottom was rusting out and we could see the highway through the floor."

The Hawks were one of the better collection of players in the league. One weekend, Calvin Robinson went out and struck out 13 to win the Saturday game. On Sunday, they drove to Waynesboro and Carl pitched. He was working on a no-hitter and the Hawks were so far ahead going into the ninth – they had a 9-0 lead – that Carl demanded his outfield sit down. They did and he got his no-hitter.

Carl wasn't one of those guys who threw fastballs, but he always found a way to get his opponents out. So they gave him a nickname – Skillet.

"I couldn't throw the power," he said. "I threw junk. I couldn't throw hard enough to break an egg. That's why they called me Skillet.

"But I'd gotten in their heads."

Carl might have been a good high school player, but he never got the chance to find out.

When he wasn't earning money at Augusta Country Club or watching his toddler siblings at home, Carl was one of those kids everyone liked. He studied, was a mostly high-B student and took his responsibilities seriously. In seventh grade, he was patrol boy captain, helping kids cross the streets and get into the school, and lunchroom captain.

But by eighth grade, Margie's financial situation was precarious at best, there were more mouths to feed and Carl was a part-time student. He'd skip Wednesday and Thursday, for sure, to pick up extra money caddying and sometimes a few more days. On the way home, he'd get his friends to fill him in on what he'd missed in class so he could study and show up for the tests.

It wasn't the best solution, but it was the only one he had. And he dealt with it pretty well until the last day of class.

Walking to school, he just knew he was going to be held back because he'd missed so much school. He understood, of course, but deep down he was taking it hard. He was caught between supporting his family and getting an education that, no matter how you looked at it, wasn't fair. Especially not for a 14-year-old.

Racial tensions were flaring everywhere in the late '50s and early '60s as the Civil Rights Movement sparked sit-ins, marches and even riots in the Deep South.

"When I got there, I saw my teacher, Albert Greenleaf, and he beckoned for me to come over to him," Carl said. "He proceeded to give me the speech that I had missed exactly half of the school year."

At then end of his speech scolding me, he said: "I'm probably going to get into trouble but there's – and he named a few kids – who were here every day and they got Ds and Fs on their cards and I passed them on. You missed half the year and you didn't get a D or an F and I've got to pass you on. I was excited. That's how much I wanted to be in school. I wanted to be there."

The following fall, life threw another curve at Carl when A.R. Johnson High School and the entire Richmond County system started a dress code, requiring all the boys to wear dress pants.

"I had clothes, but didn't have dress pants that fit," Carl said. "I had one pair and they were worse than high-waters. I didn't have the money to buy another pair so I wore them to school and the kids laughed at me. It looked like I had a pair of Buckwheat hand-me-downs."

He decided that day to drop out of school and caddie full-time.

Carl was already making his way at Augusta National. He had put his mind to learning the course. He watched, he asked questions. He learned the good and the bad from the caddie shack and legends like Thor "Stovepipe" Nordwall, Willie "Cemetery" Perteet, Nathaniel "Ironman" Avery, Willie "Pete" Peterson and Ernest "Snipes" Nipper.

But it was Willie "Pappy" Stokes who had the most influence. Stokes was raised on the grounds at Fruitland Nurseries before it became Augusta National and won five Masters with four champions: Jackie Burke Jr., Ben Hogan (twice), Claude Harmon and Henry Picard.

"I've said before that I love golf enough that when I showed up at Augusta National, I was going to make that my diploma," Carl said, "and I was going to be a good caddie at this course."

Bennett said he turned out to be one of the best.

It wouldn't have happened, though, had Arkansas investment banker and influential member Jack Stephens, who served as Augusta's Chairman for eight years, not been there to watch over him.

"Many times I've said Jack Stephens saw in me what my mother and granddaddy saw in me," Carl said. "The day he hired me full-time to be his caddie, I was only 14 years old. And he *fired* another caddie, a man about 30 years old, in order to hire me.

"Now Mr. Jack was a fair man, but he was a disciplined man and he had high expectations for the all people who worked for him."

He also took on anyone – including Clifford Roberts and President Dwight Eisenhower – who didn't like his decisions. Carl was one of them. He was 14 and a high school dropout when Stephens hired him. The other caddies were either way older or were, at the very least, 18 or 19.

"Clifford Roberts and General Eisenhower knew that I was working at the Club and that I was underage," Carl said. "They were both very concerned about that fact, and they wanted me to leave the Club because they knew I should be in school since I was a juvenile.

"If he got the chance, General Eisenhower would say 'Son, why are you not in school?'"

Carl smiled.

"Mr. Jack had a way of taking care of things," he said. "When he heard the problem that had always dogged me, he saw to it that problem went away. He encouraged me to find a way to complete my education. And I did."

Stephens promised Roberts and Eisenhower that he would make sure Carl finished school or got his GED. Carl enrolled in a correspondence course and earned his GED a year before his classmates graduated from high school.

Henry "Leven" Williams, an early caddie master at Augusta National Golf Club.

"I am quite certain that any education I would have received in a public high school pales in comparison to the life lessons that were in my future," he said. "Who would have ever known in those early days of working for Mr. Jack that I would meet presidents and heads of state, people like former Presidents Bill Clinton and Jimmy Carter, former Vice President Dan Quayle, and Sen. Fulbright, to name a few.

"Here I was, a skinny kid from the Sand Hill neighborhood in Augusta, Ga., and I am now working together with some of the most famous people in the world."

Carl's job with Stephens was seasonal. If the Club was open, he worked. If not . . . there wasn't any money coming in. One day, Stephens asked Carl if he wanted to go into business with his absentee father Alvin Britt. Britt was a partner with Charlie

Reed in one of the two major cab companies in Augusta – Harlem Cab Company, which had the contract at Fort Gordon. Stephens could make that happen.

Carl's answer? A quick, sharp no.

He declines to go into the details, but said, "I'll tell you this much, I've forgiven my father in my heart because of my beliefs in God . . . Later in life, I knew why my mother got away from him."

If Stephens was in Augusta, Carl was with him. At 15, he was mixing drinks for Mr. Stephens and his guests in one of the cabins he used until the Stephens Cabin – the last members' cabin built at Augusta – was ready. He was running errands, laying out clothes and attending to every detail, large and small.

During the summers, he would work a bit with Charlie Jackson, the wood and coal man who was also a professional mover.

"He had the big trucks," Carl said. "You could work with him and make some money. Go to work early, then you were on the playground practicing baseball or basketball."

But it wasn't always enough.

Carl always considered the Mt. Auburn house home, but the reality is Margie and the kids had moved half a dozen times before he was 15. They lived in that same house twice, lived a year downtown at Sunset Homes near the Medical College of Georgia, stayed with Margie's family a few times and rented two different houses on Wheeler Road. Each move, it seemed, was temporary – "Until," Carl said, "we could do better."

One day when funds were low, Carl was in the front yard of one of the Wheeler Street houses when a private plane buzzed low over the golf course. Carl recognized the plane and knew Mr. Stephens was in town. There was no phone in the house, so Carl hustled over to Augusta National and found Mr. Stephens, who wanted to play a quick nine.

The money was a blessing, but it was getting harder for Carl to make ends meet when the Club was closed.

> The world has come a long way in the last four decades – and so have barriers at Augusta National. Lee Elder broke the color barrier, as it was called, back in 1975 when he was the first African-American to play in the Masters…

Stephens found the first of two solutions to the off-season dilemma by sending Carl a check from time to time. That way he could play basketball and baseball to earn a little money.

It was enough to pay the bills and have a little left over. A little to head downtown with a few friends, chase a few girls and try to stay out of trouble. It wasn't always easy, but Carl did his best.

Racial tensions were flaring everywhere in the late '50s and early '60s as the Civil Rights Movement sparked sit-ins, marches and even riots in the Deep South. While so much was focused on President Eisenhower calling out the National Guard in 1957 to protect nine African-American students, who were enrolling in a previously segregated high school in Little Rock, and Kennedy calling out the Guard when James Meredith became the first African-American to enroll at the University of Mississippi, there were issues everywhere. Even Augusta.

Two events that rocked young Carl's life were the assassinations of **President John F. Kennedy** *and, later,* **Martin Luther King Jr.**

Carl's great grandmother Mamie was, he said, of Native-American descent and had two daughters by a previous relationship before she had Lewis. The girls were blonde and light-skinned and, according to Carl's uncle George, had a number of white suitors, which they rejected. That didn't sit well with some folks and when members of the Ku Klux Klan would ride by on horseback, the family snuck out the back door and into the woods or hid in the crawl space under the house.

"It got so bad that my great aunts had to slip out of town under the cover of rain and darkness," Carl said. "They went to California and we never heard from them again."

The corner of Wheeler Road and Fleming Avenue was the place to hang out at night if you were from the Sand Hill, and Carl's group was no exception. Low Bow's was there, so was Tate's Grill, a barber shop, a washateria and a cleaners.

"It was the place to be for anything you might be looking for in Augusta – legal and illegal," Carl said. "Trouble and fights were a daily occurrence."

Carl carried his anger over the battle for civil rights inside. It burned deep down, knowing that he couldn't sit at the counter at Woolworths down on Broad Street. And when he and some buddies were about 16, they tried to play Augusta Municipal Golf Course, a public course by the airport, but were turned away.

"They told us blacks couldn't play," Carl said. "It really did something to me. I thought it was such a mean thing. Later, when things changed, I wouldn't even go there when my buddies wanted to go there. They had to beg me."

Through all the trouble that went on at Wheeler and Fleming, Carl said there really wasn't any racial violence, but there were a group of white kids who would drive through the area and try to stir things up.

"They would come down Highland Avenue, turn up Wheeler, get in that curve, call us the N-word then speed away," Carl said. "Sometimes, when we were alerted they were coming, we'd pick up bricks and throw them at them."

One night when he was 16, the kids drove through again. They were headed just a few blocks over to Monte Sano where there was a dance at Teen Town.

"We headed over there on foot and when we got there, it

looked like 1,000 people came out of there," Carl said. "The next thing you know, the police are on the way and we're scattering and running through backyards. A buddy and I jumped a fence and the next thing you know, a horse was chasing us."

The police were waiting when the kids got back to the Sand Hill, but no one went to jail.

Another night, a car sped through and turned down Weed toward that dead end. One of Carl's cousins saw it and knew they were trapped.

"He jumped and ran across the school yard and came up Montgomery Street, and when they went by, he threw a slab brick at the back window of the car," Carl said. "It shattered the window, but no one was hurt. And those boys had to go home and explain to their parents what happened."

Two of the regular officers patrolling the corner were known as Snag and Stone. Snag, who was named because of his crooked teeth, was the mean one. Also called "Big Red," Snag was about 6-5, 255 pounds and angry. Stone was nicer, not as intimidating.

One night, everyone was scattering and running home. Stone recognized Carl and chased him back to the Mt. Auburn house. By the time the officer got there, Carl had jumped in bed with his clothes on and sweat was pouring down his face.

"All he did," Carl said, "was yell at me a bit."

Big Red was a different story. He was a piece of work, always trying to intimidate whoever passed by. One night, he parked in front of Tate's, just daring someone to step across a line or look at him the wrong way. He irked a few regular customers in the process and, the next thing you know, someone went behind Tate's and launched a brick over the roof.

"It landed smack dab in Big Red's windshield," Carl said, chuckling. "He's screaming and suddenly there is a self-imposed curfew. We knew what was coming next – the police."

Not long after that, Big Red was disciplined for harassing the corner and was put on traffic duty on Walton Way. "The school bus went that way and everybody saw him," Carl said. "The next morning . . . well, nothing was planned, but seemed like everyone had an egg in their hand and they just tore him up. It was a love-hate relationship."

Most of the riots and violence seemed to be in Mississippi or Alabama, or even Macon, which was pretty far away. Augusta had its share of protests, but only one riot.

In May 1970, an African-American was killed in jail, sparking a riot near downtown that left six people dead. Although there was no problem at Augusta National, where caddies and staff parked their politics at the gate, the Club members and their guests left town.

The mayor sat down with civil rights leaders and hammered out what was at the time a progressive program for change. Racism began – very slowly – to fade away.

Carl still recalls getting the news of Kennedy's assassination – actually overhearing it – at Augusta National. He was caddying for Mr. Stephens and they were by the bunker on the third hole when another member walked over to tell them what happened.

"It wound up being a very sad week watching all of that on TV," Carl said.

And it wasn't the last.

On April 4, 1968, Martin Luther King was assassinated in Memphis, Tenn. Two months later, presidential candidate and former Attorney General Robert Kennedy was assassinated in Los Angeles.

"I cried my eyes out when Martin Luther King was killed and the same for Kennedy," Carl said. "They represented hope."

So did his relationship with Stephens and Augusta National.

The world has come a long way in the last four decades – and so have barriers at Augusta National. Lee Elder broke the color barrier, as it was called, back in 1975 when he was the first African-American to play in the Masters, but the Club didn't admit its first African-American member until 1990, when TV executive Ron Townsend slipped on a member's jacket.

When Carl started there, the caddie pen was all African-American, as was the wait staff in the Clubhouse. But, despite that unseen line, it didn't feel the way it did when you drove out the Magnolia Lane gate.

"Inside those gates it was like family," Carl said. "People like Jack Stephens and Dick Knight . . . they all had personal caddies, and those members took really good care of us. They came, we gave them great service and they showed their appreciation.

"I couldn't tell you how many caddies whose members helped their kids go to college."

* * * *

Three states away, Ben was looking up to Don Baylor, who was a born leader. He didn't see black or white; he saw talent, grace and drive. Baylor and his brother Doug were two of a handful of African-Americans to break the color barrier: first, at O'Henry Junior High, then at Austin High.

Don went on to become a great baseball player, playing for the Boston Red Sox, California Angels and New York Yankees, to name a few, then transitioned into coaching and managing the Colorado Rockies and Chicago Cubs. He still ranks fourth overall – and second among modern era players behind Craig Biggio – on the all-time hit-by-pitch leaders.

*Don Baylor was the athlete everyone looked up to in Austin. The future major league player and manager was a few years ahead of **Ben** and **Charlie** at Austin High School. The boys were teammates and friends with Baylor's younger brother, Doug.*

"He'd just turn his shoulder," Ben said. "He wouldn't look at the pitcher. He'd just go down to first base.

" ... Everyone admired Don. I'll never forget I got to play a charity golf tournament in New York and I happened to play with (then Major League Baseball commissioner) Peter Ueberroth. I told him my claim to fame, growing up with Don Baylor."

(Ben) and Charlie would go at it with their friends on the golf course, but this was the summer a whole lot changed. A kid named Tom Kite moved to town and started working with Harvey, too.

Ueberroth chuckled and told Ben he'd basically do anything for Baylor.

Baylor's presence helped ease any racial tensions when he was in high school. Instead of picketing, people lined up to watch him play. He would have been the first African-American football player at Texas – Julius Whittier earned that distinction in 1969 – but he turned down a scholarship to play for Darrell Royal and played baseball at Blinn Junior College instead.

Carl was hoping the kind of change that Baylor was forcing by being a star would heal the hurt Carl and others were feeling.

"You never get used to it," he said. "It burns in your memory to be denied common things. As you get older, you forgive, but you don't forget."

Carl getting his GED was just the first step of his journey. In 1969, Stephens made an even sweeter offer to Carl – move to Little Rock and work for him. Full-time. As his right-hand man.

"I worked at his house, traveled with him and ran his staff," Carl said. "My title was Get the Job Done."

He coordinated dinners, planned menus, worked on travel arrangements and took care of the stream of guests that came and went. He was always within earshot of Stephens' business meetings and was privy to discussions over some pretty big deals Stephens put together.

"Mr. Jack trusted me," he said. "Can you imagine the education I was getting? Can you imagine the life lessons I was learning? It was a world-class education.

"I can say without hesitation, the work I did on and off the golf course taught me more than any school book or any class lecture could have ever given me. I 'grew up' watching these captains of industry play golf with honesty and integrity and with complete respect for their opponents, who often were their guests ...

"I witnessed business deals being made and political leaders discuss matters of national importance. It was a world-class education."

And an incredible journey.

* * * *

It's hard to tell what made the biggest impression. Mike Souchak's snarly lined face, his powerful linebacker build or the big black-faced MacGregor 1-iron he whapped off the first tee at Oak Hills Country Club.

Ben was 10, Charlie 11 when Big Charlie drove them an hour or so down I-35 to San Antonio to watch their first professional golf tournament. They'd seen some players in Austin, mind you. Some tournaments too – but only amateur events, the kind they were already playing in and winning.

This was golf's version of The Show. The major leagues. Like meeting Musial and Banks and watching batters launch pitches out of the stadium.

Souchak had been on a Ryder Cup team. He'd won 13 tournaments, including the Houston Open, Texas Open and Colonial National Invitation. At the time, he held the PGA Tour record for the lowest 72-hole score in history – 257 – which he shot to win the 1955 Texas Open at Brackenridge Park. He held that record for 46 years, until Mark Calcavecchia shot 256 at the 2001 Phoenix Open.

But hearing the wins and records was nothing compared to seeing him stroll onto the first tee.

"He buzzed his tee shot past Charlie and me," Ben said. "That was a hell of an impression."

One of many that day.

Ben was a budding prodigy at 10. It all began the day Harvey put the mashie in his hands and marveled about how good his hands looked on the club.

It grew when Harvey asked him to chip the ball onto the green. That done, Ben asked, "What now?" Harvey said, "Putt the ball in the hole."

Ben just looked up and said, "Why didn't you say you wanted the ball in the hole in the first place?"

He and Charlie would go at it with their friends on the golf course, but this was the summer a whole lot changed. A kid named Tom Kite moved to town and started working with Harvey, too.

The first time Ben and Charlie saw Tom, he was dressed as well as any Tour player – right down to the slacks – and was carrying a big Wilson bag. Ben and Charlie, of course, were in T-shirts and cutoffs and had small carry bags slung over their shoulders.

Kite, who was 12, introduced himself – his family had just moved down from Dallas – and asked if he

Ben showed a natural, fluid swing at a young age.

Tom Kite, left, and Ben both honed their games under Harvey Penick's watchful eye, but Harvey always worked with each player separately. All three of them are now in the World Golf Hall of Fame.

Ben and *Tom* were prepared for a playoff when the NCAA declared they would share individual honors at the 1972 NCAA Championship.

could join them for the back nine at old Austin Country Club – the one that was off Riverside Drive. They said fine and teed off. Then Kite stepped to the tee with a humongous driver. He wound up and hit the ground about two feet behind the ball.

"Charlie and I stared at each other in amazement," Ben said. "We didn't know what to say."

By the time they all walked off 18, though, the boys had a pretty good idea they'd be seeing at lot of Kite on the junior circuit. And at the club since both were Harvey's pupils. Ben just didn't know that before they were 20, it would be almost impossible to hear someone mention one without mentioning the other.

And he had no idea the stars he was seeing that day in San Antonio would become friends, captains and playing partners, and a select few would join him at Augusta National every year for the Champions Dinner. Nor did he know that 11 years later, he would win the first of his 19 Tour events – and in fact his first Tour event as a professional – at Woodlake Country Club, about 20 minutes away from Oak Hills.

They caught up with Arnold Palmer on the third hole. It was Arnie!!! The hottest player in the game, the guy with so much charisma was changing the face of the game and ushering in the era of televised golf. He had won two Masters, a U.S. Open and was in the middle of what would be an eight-win, two-major year. He would go on to win his third Texas Open that week in 1962 and head to the British Open, where he would win the third leg of the career Grand Slam.

The boys' heads were on a swivel. Charlie was brave enough to ask temperamental Tommy Bolt for an autograph and got it!! They were amazed how nice he was – almost as amazed as they were with the giant tee Bobby Nichols was using.

"It was about four inches high, I swear," Ben said. "We'd never seen a tee that high. It was a higher tee than anyone else was using."

Demaret, a friend of Big Charlie and Pearl's from Houston, gave them a golf ball – a professional steel-center First Flight ball. He was a colorful, gregarious guy who never met anyone he didn't like. Or a tune he couldn't sing.

Demaret was the life of the party in the old days, holding court in the hotel lobbies where players gathered at the end of the day, and he made sure the party went long into the wee hours of the next morning. The tradition continued at the old Odessa Pro-Am in west Texas. Big Charlie was always on the guest list, and Demaret and Pearl were quite the combination each night when she played the piano and he sang.

Demaret co-founded Champions Golf Club with Jackie Burke Jr.

During the two years their collegiate careers overlapped, (Ben and Tom) shared the top spot on the roster and led the Longhorns to NCAA titles in 1971 and '72.

back in the late 1950s – a club that hosted the 1967 Ryder Cup and 1969 U.S. Open – and they were as different as day and night. Burke grumbled at folks and Demaret followed behind, soothing any hurt feelings. They were characters, lifelong friends of Big Charlie's and eventually wound up being friends of Ben's too.

Ben played in tournaments at Champions and would just drop by, at times, for a dose of Jimmy and Jackie. Demaret won three Masters, but never got the chance to share that dinner – or the World Golf Hall of Fame – with Ben. He passed away in 1983, but Burke, who won there in 1956 and is also a Hall of Famer, was a regular at the Masters until the past few years.

That '62 Texas Open is still one of Ben's fondest memories. He loved the course, the competition, the people and, of course, the shots.

"It was unbelievable," he said. "The first day watching professional golf – at Oak Hills, which I dearly love and seeing all those guys for the first time in my life."

But hardly the last.

Jimmy Demaret, a three-time Masters champion, was a friend of Ben's parents and later Ben.

Harvey's golf shop at Austin CC was tucked down under the main part of the clubhouse. It was dark and smelled like golf clubs and old worn gloves. He wasn't much on inventory, either. If you wanted a club or a certain shoe, he'd order it. It was simple and to the point – just like Harvey.

Most of those guys of Harvey's generation were professionals who knew a lot about club-making. They didn't just give lessons and sell shirts. And they didn't just repair clubs. They built them.

Ben and Charlie used to sit and watch Harvey re-wrap those old leather grips and listen to stories. Ben didn't realize it at the time, but he was absorbing so much about the game's history and roots.

"Harvey used to tell us, in hickory shaft days, he would try to be the first person at the train station down by Lake Austin," Ben said. "He wanted to be there when the actual shipment of hickory shafts were coming in on an order, so he could pick out the best

*Even at a young age, **Ben** exhibited textbook form.*

shafts for his clubs."

Ben doesn't remember ever getting a formal lesson from Harvey. It was more like an ongoing conversation. He put Ben's hands on the club that day, then let things percolate. He kept an eye on Ben – just like he did with all his pupils – and made suggestions. Yes, he checked on grips and stances, but the game wasn't just fundamentals. It was learning to play shots and compete. About not just playing, but also loving the game.

When Kite came to town, things started to get interesting. Harvey taught both boys, but never worked with them at the same time. Different swings, different people. Tom was the kid on the range. Ben was either on the putting green, the course or in the swimming pool.

"It always seemed strange to me that we never worked with him together," Ben said, "but that defines the beauty of Harvey's teaching in attempting to handle us both."

Tom and Ben started competing against each other in junior events, but didn't really face each other that often in high school. Ben was two years younger and played for Austin High; Tom, who grew up a few miles north of Ben's neighborhood, went to McCallum.

Still, they're names were synonymous. From their early teenage years on, you heard one name, you heard them both.

*Betsy Rawls, left, and **Kathy Whitworth** were two leading players in LPGA history and also students of Harvey's at Austin Country Club.*

Crenshaw and Kite. Ben and Tom. Tom and Ben.

"I knew I was going to stack up pretty good if I beat him and he probably thought the same," Ben said. "All I know is we were pretty good for each other."

And Harvey was pretty darn good for both of them. Even as teenagers, you knew Ben and Tom were special players. And their bond with Harvey? They both put their careers in those old weathered hands and it all turned out pretty well. Ben and Harvey were inducted into the World Golf Hall of Fame in 2002, while Tom was elected in 2004.

To have three careers like that intersect the way they did produced a unique moment in history, but so did Harvey's career. His list of pupils is a "who's who" of Texas golf and includes two

other Hall of Famers – Kathy Whitworth and Betsy Rawls. Rawls graduated Phi Beta Kappa from Texas with a degree in physics and math and may be the only one of Harvey's pupils who gave him a lesson.

One day, Harvey was trying to teach Rawls two or three things at the same time and she stopped him. How about just working on two things this week and worrying about the third next week, she suggested. Harvey agreed. If a Phi Beta Kappa couldn't handle all that, what about your average golfer. From then on, Harvey stuck to one thing at a time.

Harvey used to put a bench down between a student and the green and ask them what he wanted them to do. They'd all say chip over it. Harvey would shake his head and tell them to chip the ball under it. It was all about the position of a player's hands and creativity.

Tom signed with Texas in 1968, Ben in 1970. They had grown up in Austin and it made perfect sense to stay right there. During the two years their collegiate careers overlapped, they shared the top spot on the roster and led the Longhorns to NCAA titles in 1971 and '72. Ben won the NCAA individual title all three years, but shared the '72 title with Tom.

The highly successful Texas golf team. **Tom Kite** *is fifth from right on bottom row.* **Ben** *is second from right, next to* **Brent Buckman**, *on far right.*

Ben and Tom still scratch their heads over that day at the NCAA Championship in Cape Coral, Fla. Tom was finished and Ben needed a desperate par at the 18th to force the tie. He'd put his drive behind a tree, chipped out and had 20 yards left to the flagstick. He didn't hit a good chip and left himself 20 feet – uphill on a grainy green – to tie.

"I hit it so hard, it bounced off the back of the hole, flew up and fell into the hole," Ben said.

Tom had his head down; he didn't want to watch. A few minutes later, they thought they were headed to a playoff, but officials declared them co-champions.

"We were bewildered," Ben said. "We wanted the playoff."

Ben's first win came at Muny – the Casis fourth-grade tournament. His first big win was at 15, when he won Austin City Men's Championship at Morris Williams, beating family friend

> (Ben's) first memories of the Masters? Sneaking into the 19th hole at Austin CC to watch Arnold Palmer win his third and fourth Masters in 1962 and 1964.

Billy Penn, who was 36 and already a two-time city champ, in the finals. Penn would win two more city titles in the '70s and was influential in Austin golf until he passed away in 2003. Ben won three in a row – 1967, '68 and '69.

"Billy was part of my dad's circle of friends, and I watched him play many, many times when I was younger," Ben said. "That win gave me a lot of confidence. And it gave me a lot of confidence to go down to San Antonio and win the state junior."

He paused and chuckled.

"You know, Billy called me 'Little Punk' from then after."

To everyone else, he became Gentle Ben – but not for the reason you might think.

Ben had a temper. Too many bad shots and a club would take a beating. Or a tee marker. Or, in 1980, a toe.

After three-putting the par-3 16th at Colonial that year, Crenshaw was frustrated. He was in contention and a three-putt on a course he knew that well was unacceptable. So, walking off the green, he kicked one of those oil drums they used to use as garbage cans. The next day he cut a hole in the top of his shoe and limped along.

*Amateur **Francis Ouimet**, middle, defeated Brits **Harry Vardon**, left, and **Ted Ray** in an 18-hole playoff for the 1913 U.S. Open. Vardon and Ray were the best players in the world at the time.*

Years later, he found he'd broken the sesamoid bone on the bottom of his right foot and eventually – in 1997 – doctors removed the bone and calcium deposits surrounding it. It bothers him to this day.

When Ben's temper would get the best of him growing up, Big Charlie was there with a reprimand. Or two. Or three. And a bill for the repair. A shaft would cost him $1.

Austin sportswriter Dick Collins saw enough over the years and one day – sarcastically – called him Gentle Ben in print. It stuck.

Harvey saw it and heard about, too. He watched, he listened. He told Ben that a little temper was good. "If you don't have a temper," Harvey said, "you're not going anywhere."

But too much temper could cost you your career.

The late Dave Marr used to tease Ben that he was going to get called up on child abuse charges for chastising his putter – a $15 Wilson 8802 found at Muny one day – that everyone called "Little Ben."

Dave Marr, right, *a fellow Texan and good friend of* **Ben's**, *was captain of the 1981 Ryder Cup team, perhaps the strongest team ever.*

Ben chuckles that Little Ben is on life support these days. He's tired. He was stolen a couple times, stepped on and beaten on concrete bridges and greens. But what started as an average putting partnership wound up years later turning Ben into one of the best putters in the game.

The year Ben turned 15, so much changed. Big Charlie brought home Price's book that summer and Ben was hooked. He was learning about the history of the game, letting Price take him to incredible courses continents away and introducing him to Bobby Jones and the Masters.

"I became fascinated by Jones," Ben said. "I'd seen his name on clubs and Harvey talked about him – but just enough for me to know who he was as a player. The first time I heard him referred as Emperor Jones was in Price's book.

"Not too long after that, I remember Harvey told me to stick with Bobby Jones, that whatever he writes is great.

"That stuck with me."

The following summer, Ben's world got a whole lot bigger. He qualified for the U.S. Junior Amateur at The Country Club in Brookline, Mass., where 20-year-old Francis Ouimet upset legends Harry Vardon and Ted Ray in a playoff to win the 1913 U.S. Open.

Everything tumbled together from there.

He and Big Charlie flew up, took in a Red Sox game at Fenway Park, toured historic Boston, and Ben threw his game on center stage. He was one of the new kids challenging the likes of Billy Harmon, Bobby Wadkins, Billy Kratzert, David Eger, Eddie

Pearce and Gary Koch. Koch, who played at the University of Florida and is now an NBC announcer, was low qualifier. Harmon, the youngest son of 1948 Masters champ Claude Harmon, was one of the men to beat, but it was Pearce, one of the most supremely talented junior players ever, who won it all.

Ben lost in the quarterfinals to New Orleans amateur Larry Griffin, but he walked away with so much more. He was already close with Texas juniors like Bruce Lietzke, who lost to Pearce in the semifinals, but now he was getting to know players he would compete against for decades and forging strong friendships with players like Harmon. In fact, Ben became friends with his father Claude and Billy's brothers Butch, Craig and Dick, all teaching pros. To this day, Ben misses his strong friendship with Dick, who passed away in 2006.

Herbert Warren Wind, one of America's greatest golf writers, encouraged Ben in his writing and architecture.

"I came away with the love of national competition, in a completely different place, on a vastly interesting golf course – none of which the likes I'd ever seen," Ben said. "And my love of golf history started there.

"I came back and thought, 'Whoa. Oh my Lord, this is a completely different world.' "

He explored the clubhouse and the course and met legendary writer – and another Hall of Fame member – Herbert Warren Wind, who would much later become a friend.

"I remember thinking we're in a magical place here and on an unbelievably historic golf course," Ben said.

Later that summer, Ben beat a field that included Pearce and Kratzert to win the 1968 National Jaycee Tournament in Tulsa, Okla. Four years later, he won his first NCAA title and qualified for the Masters by virtue of making the semifinals of the U.S. Amateur.

Suddenly, he wasn't just a floppy-haired kid from Austin. He was one of the best amateurs in the game – a player with a golden touch.

"The first realistic notions of getting to Augusta came when I started to travel to a few more amateur tournaments on a national scale," Ben said. "We'd hear what the qualifications were and players like Downing Gray, Steve Melnyk and Vinny Giles would talk about the Masters."

His first memories of the Masters? Sneaking into the 19th hole at Austin CC to watch Arnold Palmer win his third and fourth Masters in 1962 and 1964. As Ben admits, he was more interested in the cheese and jalapenos on crackers they served to the members.

Ben hasn't always been the most consistent ball-striker, but for one round in 1969, he was truly amazing. He hit driver, then 5-iron to reach a par-5 at Muny in two, then either drove or just missed the green on the next four 350-yard plus par 4s. Shot 64 that day to win Austin's annual Fourth of July Firecracker Open.

More than four decades later, it remains the best ball-striking round of his career.

One of the "luckiest days in his life" – his words – had nothing to do with a golf club or golf course. Instead, it was the draft and the Vietnam War.

In 1969, the Selective Service instituted a draft lottery and all men over the age of 18 were required to report and undergo physicals. Anyone with a lottery number below 198 (out of 365) and a 1-A status was possibly going to Vietnam to fight.

The Main and West Malls on the Texas campus were filled with protesters and anti-war demonstrations and marches. Some headed to Canada or overseas to avoid the draft. Ben and Charlie went through the process.

Charlie was the starting right fielder for the Texas baseball team and was supposed have a student deferment, but a glitch during UT registration – he signed up for 12 hours, but only got 9 – left him three hours short of full-time status needed for a student deferment. To make a long story short, Darrell Royal made a few calls and everything worked out.

On the day he was supposed to be bussed to San Antonio for his physical, Ben reported to the Travis County Courthouse. His number was 90, certainly low enough to be worrisome.

"We're standing there and this little old lady came out and said, 'Boys, this is your lucky day. We're not taking anyone today. They're going to sign the peace treaty.' Ben said.

"I don't remember who was with me, but I think we immediately went over and had a few beers. And it was like 9:30 in the morning."

Fortunate? Blessed? Ben will tell you he has been both.

"How many kids make a decision at 16 to play golf instead of baseball?" he said. "I'll tell you what it is. I just fell in love so early with the game . . . the progression to where it's gone started early and it's just stayed on the path.

"I'm still fascinated with how to play the game. It's still a great object of desire to still play. And not many people can say that through their whole life, no matter what they pursue. You have to have a thirst for it.

"To me, the fascination and the mystery of it is you never know what's going to happen."

Or who'll be walking alongside you when it does.

CHAPTER 2

GETTING TO AUGUSTA AND A PARTNERSHIP

"By the time Ben was 14, there wasn't anybody on the Texas team who could beat him. He was remarkable. He's that gifted."
– Bill Munn, Ben's longtime friend

The place to be on Monday mornings in the Sand Hill – even during the school year – was Augusta Country Club. And not for the dice games going on in the caddie pen.

It was the one day a week when Henry Avery stepped away from his duties as caddie master and onto the golf course. He usually teamed up with Roy Garnett, the club repairman, and they took on any and all comers, which, more often than not, meant Jim Dent and his assortment of partners.

Dent grew up in the Sand Hill, an easy pitching wedge across Wheeler Road from the Mt. Auburn house Carl called home. He had played football at all-black Lucy Laney High School and even stole a little limelight from teammate and future NFL star Emerson Boozer one Friday night. Dent, just this side of 6-foot-3, 200 pounds, was the Wildcats' starting tight end and he caught a pass over the middle and took it to the house for a big win.

Carl was in the stands that night watching in awe. He didn't get many chances to go to Laney football games when he was 10, so this was more than a big deal. He was friends with Dent's youngest brother Tom – the boys lost their parents at a young age and were raised by an aunt – and Jim, who was eight years older than Carl. Tom and Jim were becoming more than just football heroes around the Sand Hill.

"In hindsight, I was watching two black men from my home town (at that football game) who would become millionaires the hard way," Carl said.

Back then, though, they were just the big men in the Sand Hill and downtown, the two large African-American communities in Augusta.

Most afternoons, the kids would be hanging out on Weed Street when Dent would walk by with a handful of clubs and a shag bag and head to the playground or the Weed Elementary campus to hit balls. He, too, had started out shagging balls and caddying for Big Henry and had worked at Augusta National. He caddied in about a half dozen Masters in the late 1950s and early '60s for Bob Rosburg and Bob Goalby.

Dent had his eye on playing, not caddying. He had a powerful,

*Left: The 6-foot-5 **Carl Jackson** has caddied in 52 Masters, including the 2013 Tournament.*

***Ben** wasn't looking for a new caddie, but Augusta National members John Griffith and Jack Stephens thought Ben and Carl would make a good team and put them together in 1976.*

elegant swing and Big Henry, who shot in the low 70s, was a handful. Dent's best friend Charlie Choice was a cross-handed player who could play Dent straight up and often rounded out an entertaining foursome. Other Monday players included Augusta

Bobby Jones and Clifford Roberts wanted everything to be a cut above at Augusta National – and it was. From the service to the decorum to the private members' cabins to the names on the roster, the Club exuded the best.

caddies Johnny and Leon McCladdie and Henry Brown. Leon was on Tom Watson's bag for both Masters wins, and Brown caddied for Roberto De Vicenzo the year he signed the incorrect scorecard.

It wasn't Hogan vs. Nelson or Snead at the Masters, but those caddies could play. And Dent was at the top of the list.

Carl just watched and learned.

Jim Dent, an Augusta native, caddied at Augusta National but never played in the Masters. He did, however, win 12 times on the Champions Tour.

No question Boozer was *the* hero for everyone from the Sand Hill – not just young black athletes – in the late '50s. Heck, he was a star in the city, period. He played at Maryland State and went to the AFL's New York Jets, where he played on the Super Bowl III championship team with Joe Namath.

Dent played wherever he could before getting his Tour card in 1971, and inspired the neighborhood kids, too. He never won on the PGA Tour – he finished second to Jack Nicklaus at the 1972 Walt Disney World Classic – and never played in the Masters, but, when he turned 50, his career blossomed on the Champions Tour, where he won a dozen times.

"I've always marveled at his athletic ability," Ben said years later after the two had competed on the Champions Tour. "You cannot swing at the ball like that unless you're an athlete and you can tell by the way he walks. He's got the most beautiful swing. It's like a ballet – powerful, but synchronized."

Dent was the star, but it was his oldest brother Sugar Pie – his given name was Lipot – who really touched Carl's heart a number of years later.

Sugar Pie lived two doors south of Low Bow's with his wife and children. "As he was getting home from work one day his house was engulfed in flames and his children were inside, and they said several men tried to restrain him from going into that house because it was already too late," Carl said. "But Sugar Pie won that battle and went into those flames to save his babies. He did save them, but he died later that day (from smoke that brought on a heart attack). I'll never forget his courage as long as I live."

Every day was an education at Augusta Country Club. If Big Henry wasn't telling tales, the dice were flying in the pen. Or the caddies were working on their games.

Carl was taking it all in. He was only 11, but he figured the more he could learn, the better. Within two years, he was the youngest caddie at Augusta National and one of the most promising. He had something special that went beyond reading greens and people.

Emerson Boozer, Augusta's most outstanding athlete when Carl was in elementary school, helped the New York Jets win Super Bowl III.

A chain link fence separates Augusta Country Club from Augusta National and, like Augusta CC and the Sand Hill, they, too, are indeed two different worlds. Augusta's elite society belong to Augusta CC; America's elite powerbrokers – a few were from Augusta – are members at Augusta National.

Bobby Jones and Clifford Roberts wanted everything to be a cut above at Augusta National – and it was. From the service to the decorum to the private members' cabins to the names on the roster, the Club exuded the best.

Augusta National's 40 or so Club caddies were toward the top of the pay scale and weren't relegated to a field or a pen. They had earned a bit of privilege in a world that slapped so many of them around from the time they were born. Yes, there were still lines, but inside those gates that fronted Washington Road, everyone was family.

The Club caddies had a house – well, they called it that, but it was a couple of rooms, a pool table and nothing close to the house they built in 1994 or the one they have today – where they could have breakfast and lunch and, of course, kick back and gamble a little.

The games of choice? Checkers and cards. Dice took a back seat.

It wasn't anything new to 13-year-old Carl, but, every so often, someone would get a little paternal and chase him away from the game. "Get out of here little bull," they'd say.

Bull wasn't the kindest of terms because in caddie-speak it meant someone who was ignorant. Carl didn't mind. He knew it wouldn't apply much longer. He was soaking up every bit of knowledge he could from everyone he could – members and employees alike. His focus was on becoming one of the Club's best men on the bag, not on winning a $50 pot and spending it all that night. He had bills

to pay and he was looking toward the future.

A long line of caddies graduated from Augusta Country Club to Augusta National, but not everyone made a good living, let alone made it a career.

Caddies came and went, some working only when they needed the money. They had part-time jobs in the summer when the Club was closed, and some were happy to pull whatever bag on whatever day. They saw caddying as a way out of poverty or, at the very least, a way to make a little extra to spend down at Low Bow's or Tate's or to gamble or drink away.

Some became a member's regular caddie, which usually meant more money and a few more duties. Only Carl took that regular caddie job and transformed it into a full-time assistant's job for a future Augusta National Chairman.

Carl hadn't been there long when he was caddying for Gilbert Swanson of Swanson Foods one day and a member from Arkansas – Jack Stephens – joined them. Carl had no idea who Stephens was and he went quietly about his business, but he soon found out. Months later, Carl put in for Stephens' bag, only to find out Stephens had a regular caddie.

One day, Stephens' caddie didn't show up and Carl got the bag.

"The next day, the caddie showed up – we called him Harleman – and Mr. Stephens paid him off," Carl said. "He just handed him some money and said Carl is going to be my caddie from now on."

Five decades later, Carl looks back on his years as Stephens' caddie and right-hand man and smiles. He used words like blessed and fortunate and angel. At the time it was a great bag, a catch.

It grew into a right-hand-man job, a trusted friendship and a window into a world where wealth and power intersected with politics and economics and matters of state.

Carl was there for 18-hole rounds or social times with President Eisenhower, former Secretary of Defense (under LBJ) Clark

Jack Stephens was a mentor, employer and friend of Carl's for more than four decades.

Best Caddie Nicknames

All of the caddies had a nickname when Carl was working at Augusta Country Club and Augusta National. In fact, Carl admits to not even knowing some of their real names.

1. **Pappy**
2. **Ironman**
3. **Cemetery**
4. **Scoun**
5. **Long Distance**
6. **Monkey Man**
7. **Gipp**
8. **Stovepipe**
9. **Tweety** (Carl's brother)
10. **Little Tweet or Skillet** (Carl)
11. **Golf Ball**
12. **Daybreak**
13. **Cee Man**
14. **11**
15. **Snag**

Clifford, Arkansas Sen. J. William Fulbright, Jimmy Carter's budget director Bert Lance, and former Secretary of State (under Ronald Reagan) George Shultz, who was also Secretary of Labor and Secretary of the Treasury under Richard Nixon. And, he took care of Stephens' friends like Walmart founder Sam Walton, Darrell Royal, Alabama coach Bear Bryant and Arkansas' Frank Broyles.

> Some of the Augusta National caddies are almost as recognizable as their players, and the best ones became synonymous with them – Carl and Ben, Willie and Jack, Stovepipe and Gene Sarazen, Arnie and Iron Man.

"I didn't know it at the time, but meeting Jack Stephens changed my life," Carl said. "I venture to say I got a better education than I would have in the classroom just by the exposure of being around a billionaire like Mr. Jack."

He got a different sort of education on the bag.

There might not have been a lot of money in the Augusta National caddie house – not shack – but it was rich in outrageous characters and their stories. Most of them lived from paycheck to paycheck and could spin tall tales that paled in comparison to the reality of their own lives.

Some died young, most lived hard. So many of the old guard could drink all night, then stumble in mostly on time and caddie 18. Some wound up as happy drunks or just sad shells of men. Some chased women their entire lives and spent their last $5 on a bottle of whiskey or moonshine.

Others, like Carl, Buck Moore, who went on to caddy on Tour, LeRoy Schulz and Freddie Bennett wanted a different life. They turned a job into a career, changed the perception of men on the bag and made a comfortable-enough living to put their children through college.

*Big Charlie loved to put on his houndstooth hat, pose with his former Alabama fraternity brother **Bear Bryant** and watch people do a double-take. The resemblance is uncanny. That's **Big Charlie** on the right; **Bryant** on the left.*

Regardless of which path they took, almost every caddie had a nickname, and if Bennett didn't bestow it, the name still needed his blessing. All of them had a lifetime of stories.

Some of the Augusta National caddies are almost as recognizable as their players, and the best ones became synonymous with them – Carl and Ben, Willie and Jack, Stovepipe and Gene Sarazen, Arnie and Iron Man. Others, you simply know by those nicknames.

Carl had a couple of nicknames. To some, he was Little Tweet, to others, Skillet. But those fell by the wayside and today – in fact, for most of the last four decades – he's been just Carl.

Stovepipe – Thor Nordwall – got his name from the black silk stovepipe hat and white shirt he wore, even when he caddied. He got his notoriety from being the man on Sarazen's bag for the double eagle at the 15th hole in 1935 – the shot heard 'round the world.

Cemetery – Willie Perteet – started caddying in the mid-1930s, but back then he was known as Dead Man. It seems a girlfriend stabbed him 18 times one night and he was pronounced dead. Later that night, he woke up in a morgue and, the tale goes, the doctor who found him was never seen again.

Perteet, a wiry 5-6, maybe 130 pounds, never won a Masters, but started caddying for Eisenhower in the late 1940s. It was Ike who changed his nickname to Cemetery because "all dead men belong in cemeteries" and it was easier to say.

"Cemetery" Willie Perteet was President Eisenhower's regular caddie at Augusta National.

One of the best pairings ever was Iron Man and Palmer. Nathaniel Avery had lost a few fingertips and, depending on which tale you believe, he either sliced them off opening a golf ball with an axe and under the influence or lost them in a firecracker mishap. Hence, Iron Man. Nothing stopped him. He may have been a better player than he was a caddie, but he knew Palmer so well, which is why they won four times.

Iron Man was the gambler in the Avery family. Henry was at Augusta CC, Horace was assistant caddie master at Augusta National and Willie caddied at the Club. All were hard working family men. But not Iron Man. He lived large when he could. He made $1,400 for the first win in 1958 and spent it on a new yellow Pontiac, which he promptly wrecked the same day.

Nathaniel Avery, aka "Iron Man," was on the bag for all four of Arnold Palmer's Masters wins.

Matthew Palmer was Shorty Mac, the man who helped Billy Casper to the 1970 Masters title. Willie Peterson won five Masters with Nicklaus, who had his son Jackie on the bag for the sixth, while Ernest Nipper – Snipes – won in 1961 with Gary Player.

But the godfather of the caddie house was Pappy and he just happened to be the next in that series of angels that helped steer Carl's journey.

Pappy was patient, teaching Carl – as well as Iron Man, Peterson and Nipper – about the course, the greens and the people.

Back then, caddies didn't have yardage books. They had feel. They read their player's shots by eye, matched their knowledge with the player's skill and style and told them what club to hit, not how far. Pappy taught himself by putting his hands on the greens and learning the contours through feel and imagination.

> Back then, caddies didn't have yardage books. They had feel. They read their player's shots by eye, matched their knowledge with the player's skill and style and told them what club to hit, not how far.

He had a double head start. Not only did he grow up on the property when it was Fruitland Nurseries – it was an indigo plantation before that – but he also worked on the crew when they built the course. He was the water boy when crews were clearing trees for the course and he studied the land as mule teams moved and leveled the dirt and watched the rain drain across the course as it was being routed.

He started caddying at 12 – yes, he, too, skipped school – when the Club opened and won his first Masters in 1938 with Picard. He was 17. Pappy took a war-time break, serving in the Pacific during World War II, but he eventually settled down and married Iron Man and Henry's oldest sister, Odella.

How good was he? So good that Hogan watched him win with Claude Harmon in 1948 and heard Harmon rave about him. So, he hired him away from Harmon in 1951, sealing the deal with a then-huge $20 tip, which, the story goes, Pappy promptly spent at the liquor store.

Pappy saw something in Carl and became a mentor. He taught him where to be aggressive, where to back off. Where the wind comes into play even when you can't feel it. How the course plays – in every condition. How a good caddie can get a read on his player – and everyone else playing in the group – in just a few holes.

And, he made certain Carl understood feel and imagination were the two key components when he taught Carl to spot-putt – a technique Carl and Ben have used for the last 36 years.

"Pappy would know where things were that tricked you or if something was an optical illusion on a green," Carl said. "He'd take you there and put balls down. When you're putting on No. 11 green, you realize no way everything breaks to No. 12.

"We'd learn a lot playing with the members and their guests.

*An Augusta stalwart in the caddie yard, **Willie "Pappy" Stokes** was **Claude Harmon's** caddie in his Masters win in 1948.*

*When **Jack Nicklaus** played in his first Masters in 1959, **Willie Peterson** was his caddie. He is shown here celebrating as Jack made a dramatic 40-foot putt for a birdie on the par-3 16th hole in the fourth round of the 1975 Masters.*

He'd show us things as we went around."

Today, all Carl has to do is point. He knows Ben's stroke, he knows his speed. He knows that if he finds the spot, Ben can do the rest.

And if he's spotting the same putt for, say, Tiger Woods? He knows Tiger tends to drive ball into the hole, so Carl would find the perfect spot to suit his style.

Some putts on the course are mind-boggling. You've seen players aim at what look like crazy spots only to watch the putt curl across the green, ride a ridge and either drop in or cozy up to tap-in range.

"The lines and the aspects of putts change more there than anywhere you could play," Ben said, "because the greens are so keen and slopey."

Pappy taught Carl and the others to walk the course, make notes and learn it. This, after all, was a year-round job. They were Club caddies first, Masters caddies second. Yes, a win or a good finish could set them up financially for the year. There was always a party on the Sand Hill on Masters Sunday night when a caddie from there was on the winning bag. But it was the Club members and the Club tournaments, like the annual Jamboree held each spring, that kept them employed.

Freddie Bennett, meanwhile, kept an eye on everyone. He was the gatekeeper, the man who made Masters matches and kept the caddie shack humming. He put Peterson with Nicklaus in 1959 for Nicklaus' first Masters, and thought Jariah Beard might be a good match for Masters rookie Fuzzy Zoeller. He was so right. Beard guided Zoeller to a Green Jacket his rookie year – 1979.

And when Tiger Woods played in his first Masters in 1995, Tiger asked for a Club caddie and Bennett chose his cousin Tommy Bennett - better known as Burnt Biscuits – to show him the course. The nickname? Seems one day Tommy was on his way out a window after stealing fresh-out-of-the-oven biscuits from his grandmother's wood stove when he tipped over a pot of boiling water and burned his legs.

Burnt Biscuits may be the all-time best nickname. The pairing? Not so much. It produced a T-41 and lasted one Masters.

Jay Brunza, a sports psychologist, caddied in 1996 when Tiger played two practice rounds and the first Tournament round with Ben. Then Tiger went to his regular Tour caddies – Mike "Fluff" Cowan (won in 1997) and Steve Williams (won in 2001, 2002 and 2005). Now, Tiger has Joe LaCava, who won with Fred Couples in 1992, on the bag.

Carl got to Augusta National in October 1960 and worked hard enough toting for members that got his first Masters bag – 1931 U.S. Open champ Billy Burke – in April 1961. He was only 14.

"I had made a good enough impression on Freddie that he issued me a bag at Masters time," Carl said. "He thought Billy Burke, who was a ceremonial player, would be good for me. At least I could handle the job. He was an older guy and I didn't even know what a ceremonial player was then.

"He was just a player in the Masters and we were going to try to win. Those were my thoughts. I remember when I first saw him, he had on a starched white shirt, a necktie and wore the knickerbockers. That's how he dressed every day."

Carl went to the range to meet Burke, who won the '31 U.S. Open in a marathon, 72-hole playoff – the longest playoff in U.S. Open history. Burke decided not to warm up on the range because he thought the Tournament practice tee was far too dangerous for his young caddie.

Mike "Fluff" Cowan caddied for Tiger Woods in his epic 1997 victory.

"He said, 'I'm not going to send you out there,' " Carl said. "It was like a war zone out there. So he never hit practice balls, but he was like another angel."

Burke knew Carl was inexperienced so he told him flat out he was going to teach him how to get around the golf course during Masters week.

"He didn't play a lot of practice-round golf," Carl said. "Then Thursday and Friday, he told me where to go stand or what to do in the group and how to handle situations on the greens."

Burke was long past his prime. He finished T-3 in the first Masters in 1934 and T-3 again in 1939, but he hadn't been competitive there in years. The 59-year-old shot 81-79 and missed the cut, but there was one important positive that came out of it – Burke got Carl comfortable on the course.

The next year was Burke's final Masters, but when it came to making bag assignments Freddie Bennett moved Carl to another bag. Carl was something special and everyone from Pappy to Shorty Mac to Snipes and Mutt Boyd saw it.

"They see you got the knack for catching on," Carl said, "then they'd show you things."

*Carl caddied for **Billy Burke** in 1961. Burke is pictured here practice putting prior to his match in the 1931 Ryder Cup.*

Subtle things. Things that set even a young caddie like Carl apart.

"They'd try to make you understand," he said, "why you didn't see what you should have."

The amazing part? With Carl, they never had to repeat themselves.

*   *   *   *

The metallic green Grand Sport 455 kicked up a dust cloud as it blew into the parking lot at Morris Williams Golf Course, tires squealing from the combination of speed and turning radius.

Texas sophomore Brent Buckman turned around to see what the heck was happening. When he did, he saw a kid with floppy blond hair jump out of the car, grab his golf shoes and clubs and fly toward the first tee.

Ben Crenshaw was late again. This time, it was for an Austin High match and he was on the tee. Ben – shoe laces untied – whapped his drive off the first tee then tied laces as he walked down the fairway.

Made it. And didn't even blow up the car in the process.

It was an achievement. The first car Big Charlie had bought for Ben and Charlie to share was an ice blue two-door 1965 Cutlass hardtop, and it met a rather unceremonious end during what Ben will tell you was the worst day and a half of his young life.

He must have been 15 when he and Jake White, whose dad was former Democratic National Chairman John White, decided it would be a great idea to drink a 12-pack of Schlitz Malt Liquor and hang out. Of course, someone else had to buy it for them, and that was Jake's older brother Richard. They had it iced down and ready when a policeman pulled up. They shoved it in the trunk and Jake wanted to run, but didn't.

When they popped the trunk, the policeman asked them what they were going to do with it. Jake mumbled something about just finding it and before they knew it, they were following the officer to the police station.

Big Charlie and John picked the boys up around midnight and an uncomfortable silence lingered all the way home in the Crenshaw's car. Ben got in bed – he and Charlie shared a room – and Big Charlie walked by to close the door.

"Son, it was just like someone sticking a knife in my back," Big Charlie said. Ben cried for a few minutes before Charlie even asked what had happened.

Ben was supposed to pick up his high school team at 6:30 a.m. the next morning for a match and he was late. They flew into the clubhouse parking lot five minutes before their tee time – and with the Cutlass engine smoking. A player from Johnston High School noticed it, understood cars and yelled for Ben to keep it running.

"Don't shut it off!!!"

But Ben didn't heed the advice, shut it off and there was a

boom. On the way home, he found out he had melted the engine. They put four quarts of oil in the car and drove 35 miles an hour all the way home.

A few years earlier, Harvey had a little visit with Big Charlie about Ben's future. Ben was tearing up amateur tournaments in the city and around the state. He had a gift and Harvey had known it since that first day Ben put his hands on a club.

> While Carl had angels guiding his journey, Ben has had a series of visit-ers. Not just people who popped in and out of your life, but people who changed your life by simply sitting down and visiting for a while.

Big Charlie knew it too, but he wanted Ben to follow his heart. Charlie was always going to have golf in his life, but he, like his dad, was a baseball player. Ben had spent so long on the fence between the two sports and when Harvey mentioned it, Big Charlie knew it was time.

When Ben put down that bat, he knew his prayers had been answered.

"He didn't reveal it to me, but dad was really relieved," Ben said. "We talked about it certain nights and it wasn't crystal clear. He was going to suggest it."

He didn't have to. That night on the baseball field was merely the exclamation point. To be honest, Ben had been drifting – and, at times, even sprinting – toward golf. The Price book had piqued his interest; the Brookline trip had opened up not just a new avenue for competition, but kindled a passion for the game.

The summer before his senior year, Ben just missed qualifying for the 1969 U.S. Open, but Terry Jastrow, who was three years older and had won the 1966 Texas State Junior, was working the Open for ABC and he told Ben to c'mon over to Champions. He'd give him a job.

It was, in many ways, Ben's first job. The Crenshaw boys didn't have to work – they didn't even have to mow the lawn.

When he was 15, Charlie did work on the Tarrytown Baptist Church construction site, doing this and that. His first day, it was about 106 and no wind – a normal central Texas summer day – the foreman asked him to fill up the water cooler. Charlie did it, but used a garden hose that left the rubber taste in the water. Lord, did he get chewed out.

He went back, unhooked the hose and filled it from the faucet. Everything was fine until he got tired of carrying and stacking 16-foot long 2 x 4s and leaned up against a truck tailgate. Got chewed out again. That night at dinner, Charlie told his dad he wasn't going back. Big Charlie said, oh, yes he was.

While Ben was playing golf everyday that summer, Charlie was putting on 15 pounds of muscle that earned him a starting linebacker spot at Austin High that fall. The team went 9-1.

Ben came close to having a job at 14 – the same age Carl was when he caddied in his first Masters – when he thought he might cut the greens at Muny or work behind the counter, but that didn't work out.

Since the '69 Open was just two and a half hours away at Champions, some of his friends had driven over to caddie that week. Ben took Jastrow up on his offer and sat in the 15th tower, where he spotted for Bud Palmer. He knew Palmer a bit because the broadcaster would come over and take lessons from Harvey from time to time, but this was a lot to take in.

"I had a ringside seat," Ben said. "I remember watching a lot of the players come through. Bob Murphy hit it close – about eight feet – there and he made a beautiful stroke with his Arnold Palmer putter. Bobby Cole was a player who everyone admired his swing, played well for three days, then faded at the end.

"I remember Miller Barber – everybody called him Mr. X – was leading after the third day. In the final round, he started out pretty well, made a couple of boo-boos. At the 12th, he was very upset with himself and he walked around the lake and tomahawked his iron into the ground. His caddie had a hard time getting it out."

Relatively unknown Orville Moody won that Open and got a call from President Richard Nixon. Ironically, Barber would become one of Ben's practice round playing partners years later. When they were all at the same event, Barber and Don January would take on Ben and Bruce Lietzke in Texans-only Tuesday practice round money games. Bill Rogers would jump in sometimes, too.

*Ben's good friend and practice-day companion **Miller Barber,** the infamous "Mr. X."*

While Carl had angels guiding his journey, Ben has had a series of visit-ers. Not just people who popped in and out of your life, but people who changed your life by simply sitting down and visiting for a while. Mostly it was about golf or life, always with a message that was woven through the fabric of a rich story, a funny moment or a lesson learned.

The underlying message? Always compassion and integrity.

Big Charlie was a visit-er. Harvey was a visit-er. Burke and Demaret? Visit-ers. Heck, Ben is a visit-er. And his longtime friend Bill Munn is *the* visit-er.

Munn, who is in the oil and gas business in Midland, was one of Harvey's players at Texas back in the '60s and one Sunday he went out to play Austin Country Club. He laughed that he could get a good tee time because he was Catholic and went to church on Saturday. All the Protestants were in church that Sunday morning.

Harvey wasn't much for anyone playing solo. Golf was a social game, plus, you always learned from watching your partners. Harvey asked if Munn minded playing with Big Charlie and his son. Of course, Munn had no idea Ben was only 11.

Ben didn't hit many shots that day – maybe 20 or so – but the first time Munn saw Ben grip the club, he shook his head. "I see that grip and it's as pretty a grip as I've seen and he's only 11," Munn said.

Today, Ben and Munn talk and text, and every – yes every – conversation they have always leads to something about Harvey.

After nine holes, Munn stopped by Harvey's little shop and asked if he had seen Ben play. "Harvey said, 'He's special. He's special,' " Munn said. ". . . No, I mean special.

"I knew enough about Harvey that I knew that was someone I wanted to be around."

Munn and teammate Randy Geiselman used to pick Ben up at the house and bring him to the range to shag balls. He became a team tag-along. He would hang out with the guys and even caddied every so often for future Tour player Rik Massengale, who would pay him in gloves.

Ben wasn't doing it for the gloves. He was watching and learning.

"By the time Ben was 14, there wasn't anybody on the Texas team who could beat him," Munn said. "He was that good, that quick. He was remarkable. He's that gifted."

Although Munn is almost a decade older than Ben, the two have remained extremely close. And Munn teases Ben that he really was a bit in awe when he met him.

"I'll never forget the first time I watched you," Munn told him. "When you put your hands on the club, I just said that's not fair."

Munn introduced Ben to someone who would become another close friend over a quail dinner in Midland one night – then-oil man George W. Bush. They hit it off and had a lot of mutual friends, including Bill Hooten from Dallas. "The circle of friends," Ben said, "just melded together."

A number of years later, Bush was a part-owner of the Texas Rangers, when the Bills – Munn and Hooten – got Ben, Julie and his manager Scotty Sayers together with the Bushes at a Rangers game. Munn just knew Julie Crenshaw and Laura Bush would hit it off too, and they did.

About the same time, Ben and Julie got an invitation to George H.W. Bush's State Dinner for Jordan's King Hussein and Queen Noor at the White House in 1989. They found themselves there with Chicago Bears coach Mike Ditka.

"I just remember looking at him and both of us saying: 'What are *we* doing here?' " Ben said. "And how did we get here?"

Today, Ben and Munn talk and text, and every – yes every – conversation they have always leads to something about Harvey. The same goes for everyone Harvey touched.

"He made deep, deep impressions on people," Ben said.

Munn played Arkansas' R.H. Sikes one day in an 18-hole match at Austin Country Club and shot 67. Sikes hit about nine greens and shot 66.

Afterward, Harvey told Munn he was proud of the way he played, but added "Billy, don't ever think what you saw out there today was luck." It was Harvey's way of reminding him how important the short game really was.

Harvey's lessons were always short and to the point. And he never gave a group lesson. Didn't believe in them. In fact, when ABC offered him three or more times his Austin CC salary to do a lesson on tournament broadcasts each week, he turned them down. He wasn't going to compromise his integrity for a big check. He said thanks, but they might want to call someone else.

Harvey knew everyone was unique. Take Tom. He loved to hit balls and still does. He used to close down the ranges on Tour before Vijay Singh came along. He was something special, too, but Harvey knew Tom needed something completely different than Ben.

Tom and Harvey worked on the range. Ben and Harvey – just like Munn and Harvey – more often than not, visited in the golf shop. Harvey talked about a lot about two great Texas players – All-American Ed White and the late Morris Williams Jr., a Korean-war pilot who was killed at 23 when his F-86 Sabre crashed at Eglin Air Force Base in Florida. It was Harvey who delivered the news to Williams' father and comforted him when he collapsed.

Williams was one of the best amateurs in the state and even though Crenshaw never met him, there was more than just the Harvey connection. Legendary sportswriter Dan Jenkins was playing for Texas Christian University when he faced Williams in a match. It was all-square after 16 and Jenkins hit an incredible approach out of nowhere to gimme range. Williams hit a 7-iron into the hole for an eagle-2 and an eventual 2-and-1 win.

A few decades later, it was Jenkins who would give Ben his first national media lesson.

"We loved to talk about players and what I need to observe," Ben said. "Harvey was wanting me to watch players and how they got it done.

"I knew I was under somebody special at a really young age but to talk to these people who remind me every week that I talk to someone Harvey touched, I could not have been luckier in my life.

"The stories are way richer than the golf. The people I met in the game form who I am."

Where Tom would seek out a lesson, Ben tended just to drop by to chat on his way to or from the course. Harvey would keep an eye on both of them in high school and college, but it was Tom who called him out to the range most every day.

"He would always watch me, whether it was a city tournament or a college tournament," Ben said. "When I would come back out to the club, he would make maybe one suggestion every once and awhile."

Texas won two NCAA team titles in Ben's three years at Texas, while Ben won all three individual NCAA championships, sharing the second one with Tom Kite. Ben did more than play golf at Texas. He was a star just walking across campus.

"My relationship with Harvey was ongoing, but it was totally the opposite of what he was doing with Tom. He would say something every once in a while to me like, 'Get that ball up in your stance to where it's on your left instep and point that handle to your zipper.'

"I always remember him saying, 'That's your swing.' "

That swing sometimes got him in trouble, but his putting stroke was piling up wins. When it came time for college, everyone wanted the blond kid known as Gentle Ben.

Big Charlie mentioned playing at his alma mater Baylor, but that wasn't going to happen. Ben briefly considered going to Southern Methodist University because his then-girlfriend Nancy Hager lived in Dallas. Powerhouse Houston recruited him too. Who wouldn't? He won 18 of the 19 total tournaments he played during his senior year at Austin High.

But when signing date rolled around, he didn't waver. He was a Longhorn.

For the next three years the story on the golf course was Ben and Tom. Not so much a rivalry as a one-two punch.

"We were always competing against each other," Ben said. "This was our chance to play together and we had fun."

The Houston Cougars and legendary golf coach Dave Williams were an NCAA championship machine. George Hannon, who took over for Penick in the early 1960s, was building a championship program too.

Hannon didn't have as many scholarships as Williams early on, but when Darrell Royal realized the problem, he made sure the Longhorns weren't battling swords with pencils. And there was room for two Austin kids who would, along with Harvey, be inducted into the World Golf Hall of Fame a few decades later.

Texas won two NCAA team titles in Ben's three years at Texas, while Ben won all three individual NCAA championships, sharing the second one with Tom Kite.

Ben did more than play golf at Texas. He was a star just walking across campus. He pledged to Kappa Alpha as a freshman, but didn't have to go through the hazing most pledges did. One, he was an athlete and, two, Charlie was an active member of the fraternity and was a starter on the Longhorns baseball team.

But Ben declined an extended invitation from the Texas Cowboys, an elite service group that shoots off Smokey the Cannon at football games and lists pioneering heart surgeon Denton Cooley, former Secretary of the Treasury Lloyd Bentsen, Texas governors Dolph Briscoe and Allan Shivers, and Tom Landry, Earl Campbell and Colt McCoy as alums.

"My brother ran interference for me (with KA)," Ben said. "He also dissuaded me from being a Texas Cowboy. When I saw what they did to him . . . he couldn't sit down for three weeks."

By that point, at least, the Cowboys had stopped the practice of branding their members on the chest.

Ben was going to football games and meeting Charlie's friends like former quarterback and pitcher James Street and pitcher Burt Hooton. Street threw a few no-hitters, but became a Texas legend at quarterback when he engineered a 15-14 comeback win against Arkansas in 1969. And, of course, there were the parties.

"Needless to say I was having a great time," Ben said.

He lived at home his freshman year and his monthly scholarship check was a whopping $160. It covered books, laundry and not a whole lot more.

For his first two years, he and Tom anchored a team that included, among others, Brent Buckman, another visit-er who became a lifelong friend. Hannon had his two closers and had four other players who were pretty strong on the collegiate level, too.

Four of the best golfers who attended the University of Texas. From left, **Mark Brooks** *(PGA),* **Ben** *(Masters),* **Justin Leonard** *(U.S. Amateur and British Open) and* **Tom Kite** *(U.S. Open). In Austin it is referred to as the "Longhorn Slam."*

They were focused on college events, yet their eyes drifted toward the Tour, too. Tom, who finished his degree in 1972, had played in the Masters in both 1971 and 1972 and made the '72 Open field, where he tied for 19th as an amateur. The following week, he turned pro.

Ben stayed in school, winning 11 of 15 tournaments his junior year, including his third NCAA individual title in the spring of '73.

Ben signs with the University of Texas. From left, **Coach George Hannon,** *Ben,* **Dad** *and* **Coach Darrell Royal.**

"He had absolutely no fear," Brent said. "In my eyes, Ben was the greatest player I've ever seen. When he left college, no one could beat him."

Ben will tell you he played some of his best golf when he was 17 or 18. He won that City Amateur at 15, but the Firecracker Open win at 17 was the best.

"I felt like I had the ability to hit it," he said. "I was much more athletic then. I was good at 15, but I wasn't the player when I was 17 and 18.

"I don't know. I think I matured a little earlier. I hit some good shots back then, before I was unaffected in the brain or, let's say, afflicted in the brain."

Ben and Tom spent their summers traveling to play against the best. The Eastern Amateur, the Western Am, the Porter Cup, the Sunnehanna. You name a young player back then – Lanny Wadkins, Eddie Pearce, Lietzke, Bill Rogers, Jerry Pate – they were there. No one dominated, but any of them could have.

Ben's first attempt to get to the national stage came at age 15, when he played in the National Junior qualifier at Houston Country Club. It was August in steamy Texas and he was soaked by the second hole. He looked up and saw Harvey there watching.

All he had to do was two-putt the last hole to make the field. "I missed it because I kicked my ball at the 18th hole and missed by a stroke," he said. "I remember marking my ball and walking out to see the line and I accidentally kicked it and moved it this far (three feet). I was heartbroken."

Lanny Wadkins, an amateur competitor of Ben's, went on to win the 1977 PGA Championship.

He walked off the green and Harvey said simply, "I'm mighty sorry about that."

Two years later, there was no sorry. Ben qualified for the 1970 U.S. Open at Hazeltine and his dad flew up there with him. They stayed at a Ramada Inn near the ballpark, of course. One night they took in a game and watched Minnesota's Harmon Killebrew hit a 440-foot home run.

"It was a blast," Ben said.

And the Open? A whirlwind and quite an education.

First, then-ABC broadcasters Byron Nelson and Chris Schenkel stopped by to chat and get a good look at this Crenshaw kid. Ben, of course, was in awe of Nelson, who he had seen so many times on newsreels.

"We knew each other a bit because we had mutual friends in Dallas," Ben said. "He just offered a lot of encouragement, which meant a lot to me. It was a nice little pep talk."

Over the years, they got to know each other well. Ben won Byron's tournament in 1983, but he also won two Colonials in nearby Fort Worth in 1977 and 1990. They, too, visited every chance they got. Tiger remembers being in awe sitting beside Ben and Byron at the 1998 Masters Champions Dinner – the first he hosted as a champion – while they chatted about the grip and used their dinner knives to demonstrate.

> Tiger remembers being in awe sitting beside Ben and Byron at the 1998 Masters Champions Dinner – the first he hosted as a champion – while they chatted about the grip and used their dinner knives to demonstrate.

"That was a very special night for a lot of reasons," Tiger said. "We were talking about the full-swing grip, about grip pressure. I had Byron to my left and Ben to my right and the two of them were talking grip philosophy.

"They were nice enough to ask me my opinion, and I told them, 'I didn't have one. I just want to sit here and listen to both of you.'"

Ben and Byron did play together in the Masters Par 3 Contest a few times, but the measure of Byron's respect for Ben came when he was nearing 90 and stepped aside as the host of the Champions Dinner. His first and only call was to Ben asking him to take over for him.

"It's such a sentimental honor because – let's face it – everyone who knew Byron Nelson thought so highly of him," Ben said. "I remember him saying, 'Ben, I've admired you greatly all through your career. As you know, I've been coming to the Masters since 1935 and I just can't get around now. I want you to take over as host of the Masters Champions Dinner.'"

Byron Nelson, a member of the World Golf Hall of Fame, was a close friend of Ben's and tapped him to be host of the Champions Dinner prior to the Masters each year.

Ben dropped the phone. Byron heard the clatter.

"Ben, what happened?" Byron said.

Ben admitted he dropped the phone. Byron chuckled. "Just keep it light," he said. I know you'll do a great job."

Ben hung up, still stunned.

"It just floored me," he said. "What a deep honor."

Lee Trevino had already won twice in 1970 and had five other top 10s by the time he got to Hazeltine. He and Chi Chi Rodriguez grabbed Ben for a practice round that week and Trevino couldn't resist a little mischief.

"Lee said, 'Ben, watch this,' " Ben said. "He pulled out a jar of jalapenos, picked out a nice older lady in the crowd and asked if she wanted a piece of candy. She ate it and went straight to the water fountain."

The crowd doubled over, laughing. So did Ben and Rodriguez. It was a rough start to the week – and we're not just talking the weather and the golf. Winds kicked up in the opening round and the scores soared. Trevino shot 77, Raymond Floyd shot 78, Johnny Miller and Arnold Palmer shot 79s and Nicklaus shot 81. All rebounded to make the cut, but they were never in contention.

Ben opened with a 75. "The weather was so vile," Ben said. "It was a wild and wooly week. It was a test of golf."

Eventual champion Tony Jacklin – he beat Dave Hill by seven shots – led going into the weekend at 141. Ben was in at 148 after rounds of 75-73 and would go on to beat both Nicklaus and Palmer.

Hill had been none too kind to Hazeltine, which had just been completed. He said the course "really did lack only 80 acres of corn and a few cows. They ruined a good farm when they built this course."

Ben shook his head. "He did say some terrible things about the course and the press jumped on him. Everybody jumped on him."

On the other hand, Ben's first Open press conference drew some chuckles. Especially from Dan Jenkins, then with *Sports Illustrated.*

"I happened to play well and they brought me into the press tent," Ben said. "The USGA guy (moderating the interview) said, 'Ben would you go over your card and facts and figures about your round?'

"I picked up the card and went 'four, three . . .' "

Dan started laughing in the back of the room. "No Ben. That's not what they want. Ben, they want you to describe something."

"He just made light of it," Ben said. "It just showed you how green I was."

The great sportswriter **Dan Jenkins**.

At the end of the tournament, Ben and former Houston All-American John Mahaffey tied for low-amateur and were part of the presentation ceremony. So were Hill and Jacklin, who, a year earlier had been on the receiving end of one of the most gracious moments of sportsmanship in Ryder Cup history.

Jacklin eagled the 17th hole at the 1969 Ryder Cup at Royal Birkdale to even his match with Nicklaus, then Nicklaus conceded Jacklin's 2-foot putt at the final hole to halve the match. Earlier that year, Jacklin had won the British Open at Royal Lytham & St. Annes. The crowds loved him and the amateurs. They booed Hill.

"John and I are punk amateurs," Ben said. "The USGA official had to introduce Dave before Jacklin. People in the crowd started mooing and booing.

"Dave starts yelling at the people. I remember he yelled, 'If I couldn't moo better than that, I'd send you all back to the slaughter house.' "

Mahaffey shook his head. "Is this what we have to look forward to?"

The following summer, Ben found himself at another of those magical courses Price talked about – Merion. Ben roomed with his amateur buddy Danny Yates, while Big Charlie and Dan Yates, an Augusta National member whose brother had played in the first Masters, shared a room. Over dinners, the dads would talk about Augusta National.

"Danny's father and his uncle were so prominent at Augusta," Ben said. "He and dad just reminisced. Dan had that beautiful Southern drawl. They'd talk about Jones and the Masters.

Lee Trevino was one of golf's great players and personalities. He is pictured here before the 18-hole playoff with *Jack Nicklaus* for the 1971 U.S. Open at famed Merion.

"The IV was starting to kick in somehow. But I did know this, all the players who got to the Masters had the same feelings. Their eyes got a little wider when they talked about it. They were all nervous. They all said, 'Wait until you see it.' "

That was the Open of the amateur, Trevino and the rubber snake. After leading by two strokes after the third round, Jim Simons came within a double bogey on the 72nd hole of joining Trevino and Nicklaus in a playoff. Three amateurs finished in the top 30 – Simons (third), Lanny Wadkins (T-13) and Ben tied for 27th.

But it was Trevino, wearing an African safari-style pith helmet, who stole the show. When he stepped to the first tee in the playoff, he pulled a rubber snake out of his golf bag. Nicklaus laughed and asked him to toss it over. Jack tossed it back, birdied the first hole and promptly lost the 18-hole playoff to Trevino by three shots.

In February of that year, commander Alan Shepard hit two 6-iron shots on the surface of the moon during the Apollo 14 flight. They were replayed almost as often as Apollo 11 commander Neil Armstrong's first step on the moon in 1969.

In September 1971, Ben hit some game-changing shots of his own. He finished fifth at the U.S. Amateur at Wilmington Country Club behind Canadian Gary Cowan and that opened up *the* door – the door to the locker room at Augusta National.

"I was trying to travel and play golf on courses I couldn't imagine," Ben said of those amateur days. "I had to adapt. You can play well around your state, but you have to learn how to apply your game in other places, and it's hard to embrace sometimes."

> (Clifford Roberts) was *the* voice when it came to Club membership and Club matters. He set the rules, he called the shots – even down to making sure those attending the Masters were called patrons, not ticket holders or fans or members of the gallery.

Other times, everything just falls into place.

At the time, the top eight finishers in the Amateur were invited to the Masters. They knew they were in. The only suspense was waiting a few months for the invitation to arrive in the mail.

It came one day in a simple envelope with a formal card inside.

Mr. Ben Crenshaw was invited to play in the 1972 Masters.

"Before I got there, I had an inkling of what was so unique," Ben said, "but when you receive your first invitation, it hits you.

"Oh my god, I'm going over there."

*   *   *   *

Clifford Roberts ruled Augusta National with an iron fist.

People didn't just admire what he and Jones had done with the property and the Tournament, they actually feared the Chairman. He was a no-nonsense Northerner. He demanded, folks delivered. He had seen the Club through tough financial times. The partnership Roberts formed with CBS put the Masters on the cutting edge of televised network sports back in 1956.

He was *the* voice when it came to Club membership and Club matters. He set the rules, he called the shots – even down to making sure those attending the Masters were called patrons, not ticket holders or fans or members of the gallery. Roberts' friendship with Ike put a powerful spotlight on the Club; his inveterate tinkering with the course was always with an eye to the future. And his obsession to detail was flawless – to the point of being over the top.

Roberts had a habit of walking parts of the course from time to time, just to make sure everyone was in line with his attention to detail. Just, he said, checking things out.

Carl used to trail him – not too close, not too far away. He had always helped out with the carts for a little extra money, but when Bob Kletcke and Dave Spencer took over as co-professionals in 1966, Carl added cart man to his caddie duties.

"He would walk around and I would make myself available on the golf cart," Carl said. "I didn't follow him, but I wouldn't ever be too far away. He was checking the tree limbs. He hated to see a dead limb.

"He knew all these people would be on the course and he

wanted it perfect. Any time he found something wrong – it was usually a tree – he would wave me over and yell for me 'to go get that goddamned (superintendent) John Graves. I want to see him out there this very second.' "

Carl didn't get up in their business, but he knew Graves was getting worn out. It got to the point that Graves would see Carl on his cart and not even say hi. Instead, he asked what was wrong.

"Mr. Roberts was a no-nonsense guy," Carl said. "He didn't respect you if you feared him. He didn't disrespect them, but he loved strong people that would stand up to him. He was a person of deep thought.

"It could be a normal Monday morning, I'm going from golf shop to the kitchen to get a cup of coffee. I'd walk past him, count to 15 and he'd stop and say, 'Well, top of the morning to you too!' "

Roberts had been opposed to Carl working there full-time at 14, but Stephens' word that he would take care of Carl's education was all Roberts needed. By 15, Carl was working for Stephens down at one of the cabins – he mostly used the Lupton Suites/Firestone or California cabins until his was built between them in 1969 – mixing drinks for whoever dropped by in the afternoon.

He had no idea what he was doing, but he learned fast. "They would tell me how to do it," he said. "Obviously they would have to tell me sometimes to get off the pedal a little bit, but I figured things out."

Clifford Roberts served as Augusta National Chairman from 1934-76.

Carl caddied during the day, laid out Stephens' clothes and helped entertain at night. Each time Stephens arrived, Carl got his itinerary.

"I would make sure I took care of his guests and anything they needed and he could just entertain," he said. "They would always go up to the Clubhouse for dinner. There was always something someone forgot or they needed something from the drugstore. Or someone needed to go back to the airport at a different time.

"I always made sure that was covered. Some of them even wanted golf lessons. Mr. Stephens was evidently bragging about me. He told them I knew what I was talking about."

Stephens was a high single-digit handicapper when he joined the Club in 1962, and that didn't always sit well with Roberts. He was known for giving members a hard time if they played poorly when they were playing with him. In fact, he'd warn them that he'd leave them off at the Clubhouse after nine holes if they didn't pick it up.

> Stephens kept an eye on Carl when it came to Masters bags, too. He had Bennett's ear and, if something wasn't right, Stephens would speak up.

One day nothing much was going right for Stephens, prompting Roberts to give him the warning at the seventh hole. Stephens parred the next hole and, just as everyone finished the ninth, he told Carl to stay put. They were heading for the practice tee.

"He turned to Mr. Roberts and said, 'Cliff, I quit. I think me and Carl are going to go over and work something out on the practice tee,' " Carl said. "It shocked Mr. Roberts. He was just standing there with his hands in his pockets looking at Jack Stephens walk away. Mr. Roberts hadn't had anyone treat him like that."

Carl paused. "From my perspective, it was that day when Mr. Jack walked off and didn't play the back nine that made Mr. Roberts' respect grow for him."

Not long after, Augusta National installed gas lights at the Club after Stephens told Roberts about a gas company in Little Rock that could handle the installation. Roberts agreed, installed them and sent Stephens the bill.

Another time, they were playing the Par 3 course and Stephens suggested the sixth hole – it's now the fourth in the annual Par 3 Contest – would benefit from a bunker. Again, Roberts agreed.

"That summer, Mr. Roberts had the trap put in and sent Mr. Stephens a letter that the trap was a heck of an idea, and here's the bill."

Carl was sitting in on Stephens' parties and business meetings with Roberts and Stephens' associates by the time he was 17. By then, Roberts and Stephens had grown closer. In fact, when Roberts' health was failing in 1977, he called Stephens after doctors in Houston, where he had undergone a battery of tests, couldn't give him a clear picture of what was wrong.

It was late September, and Stephens sent his plane to bring Roberts back to Augusta for the last time. Stephens' crew told him Roberts didn't look good and even Roberts declared, on the way back from the airport, that he wasn't sure he would make it home.

When he was found dead on the property of a gunshot wound that was ruled a suicide, Roberts had his medical chart from the Houston doctors in his pocket.

Carl doesn't believe it was suicide.

"He had been talking to Jack Stephens seriously about putting another nine holes going that direction (where he was found)," Carl said. "He was serious about it. That was his last project that I knew of. He felt that would be good for the Club to have 18 holes over there. Some people didn't feel that way."

Today, Carl shrugs when asked to go into detail. He says simply it's best left alone.

Stephens remained a major voice at Augusta National. Houstonian Bill Lane, Mr. Roberts' hand-picked successor, was named Chairman after Roberts died in 1977, but Lane fell ill in 1979 and Hord Hardin became the acting Chairman. Hardin became the Chairman after Lane's death in 1980 and passed the Chairmanship to Stephens, who served from 1991-98. Augusta welcomed its first African-American member – Ron Townsend – in 1990 and, a year later, Stephens started to build the Club's philanthropic efforts toward junior golf.

*Carl caddied for **Downing Gray** in 1963, 1966 and 1967. Gray is pictured at the far right of the back row along with **Gary Player**, far left, **Jack Nicklaus** and **Arnold Palmer**. **Bobby Jones**, left, and **Clifford Roberts** are seated.*

"Mr. Roberts really talked to Mr. Stephens about the ideas he had for the Club, where Chairmen should be in their careers and other things," Carl said. "They talked about things I'll never talk about to anyone."

Stephens kept an eye on Carl when it came to Masters bags, too. He had Bennett's ear and, if something wasn't right, Stephens would speak up.

Billy Burke played his last Masters in 1962, but Carl wasn't on the bag. Instead, Carl drew amateur Deane Beman, the future PGA Tour commissioner, who shot 80-75 and missed the cut.

"He was very straight off the tee, but he couldn't hit it that far," Carl said. "He was really good at chipping, getting it up and down. He was a good player and a good bag to have."

The next year, he took the first of three different turns – 1963, 1966 and 1967 – with amateur Downing Gray. They finished tied for 36th twice and tied for 54th in 1966.

*Carl caddied for Australia's **Bruce Devlin** in 1964.*

"I was really skinny then and he was a little guy too – wasn't nothing big about him but his feet," Carl said. "He wore a size 13 and his feet looked big. I remember we were playing the 16th hole and the crowd was getting all beered up and yelling, 'Hey, what size shoes you wear?' "

Big enough that his nickname in the locker room was Footsie. To this day, his contemporaries still call him Footsie.

In 1964, Carl worked for Australian Bruce Devlin and, at one point, they were leading the Masters. Carl was 17 then and working hard for whichever player he had.

Devlin's mind was elsewhere – a wife, two children and two not-so-great years on Tour. The talk was, if Devlin didn't have a good week, he would go back to Australia and go to work as a plumber.

They got along, but not once during the week did Devlin call Carl by name.

"He reached into the lower pocket of his golf bag and said 'Hello, my man,'" Carl said. "He never called me by my name. When he'd get to his shot, he'd say, 'Whatcha think my man?' We was going off the eyesight."

> Carl was getting a little itchy in 1969 when he drew [Tony] Jacklin and [Gary] Player in back-to-back years. He was ready to settle in with one player since he had caddied for 11 different players in his first 15 years.

Ironically, they played the final round with South African Gary Player, who would have Carl on the bag in 1970. Palmer ran away with the Tournament, beating Dave Marr and Nicklaus by six shots. Devlin finished fourth, two shots out of second and two shots ahead of Player.

"Come Sunday morning, we were a stroke or two out of the lead and he got off to a good start on the first three holes," Carl said. "We get to fourth hole and Devlin said, 'Whatcha think my man?' I said a 4-iron and he said he liked the 5.

"We're sort of going back and forth and, in the meantime, Player is trying to give him a signal that wasn't enough club. Player walked out onto the tee just looking at the hole and tried to give me time to talk him into the 4."

The flagstick was just over the bunker and Devlin went with the 5, buried it under the lip, took a triple-bogey 7 and never got his momentum back.

Souchak was a powerful-looking man and was playing in his next-to-last Masters in 1965 when Carl picked up his bag. They made the cut and finished middle of the pack, but the chemistry wasn't there. Just a couple of amusing stories.

On the third day, they faced a front-right hole location at No. 14 and Souchak asked what Carl thought. Carl said 7-iron. "He was thinking a 5-iron, at worst a 6," Carl said. "He snapped at me. 'A 7-iron?' He was questioning me and I had been doing a good job for him."

He went with the 7-iron, but added, "If it don't get up top, you better beat me down through those woods. He hit the 7-iron and, sure enough, it almost went in the hole, but I already knew that if that ball didn't get up, I was going to throw that bag down at his feet and run."

It happened again at 18 when Carl called a 7-iron again. Souchak birdied it, but Carl had the throw-and-run in the back of his mind again, just in case.

Bob Goalby was in the final group on Sunday in 1968 and was hitting on the left side of the range. Goalby had gotten to his woods, when a guy walks onto the range with a flag and starts waving cars onto the range to park. Goalby, who went on to win when Roberto De Vicenzo signed an incorrect scorecard, just teed

Carl caddied for Gary Player in 1970, the year he finished third, missing the playoff by one stroke.

up his ball and hit it toward the Par 3 course.

Carl's player – R.H. Sikes – didn't even practice. Didn't make the cut, either.

"He was so overwhelmed by being in the Masters, he would sit there and watch everyone tee off," Carl said. "He went out and played his two days and went about his business. He was a really nice guy, but I guess for some reason, he didn't think his game was ready and he didn't put in whole lot of effort."

Players came and went, and caddies moved from bag to bag. Carl was getting a little itchy in 1969 when he drew Jacklin and Player in back-to-back years. He was ready to settle in with one player since he had caddied for 11 different players in his first 15 years.

Instead, he got two memorable bags.

It was seriously windy when Jacklin got to the 12th hole during a 1969 practice round and the flagstick was front-left. He asked Carl what club and Carl said a 3-iron. He went with a 5-iron.

"The wind was howling," Carl said. "He looked at me like I was stupid. He pulled out that 5-iron, hit it straight at the flagstick and it went in the water."

Jacklin opened with a 73 and missed the cut.

The 1970 Masters was, for lack of a better term, an interesting year for Carl. South Africa's apartheid policies had started a firestorm and the National Association for the Advancement of Colored People protested that movement – and Player's appearance in the Tournament – outside Augusta National's gates.

Carl had been offered a not-so-great bag and declined. Then Player's regular caddie – Ernest Nipper – got a death threat and refused to caddie. Carl took the bag.

"I was doing some work as they were roping the course and Dave Spencer left the golf shop and drove onto the course and caught me on the 18th fairway and asked if I want to caddie for Gary Player," Carl said. "Before I could say anything, he explained that Nipper had gotten some death threats and that he had quit and wasn't going to caddie at all.

"My answer was yes. Gary Player was a world-class player and a guy who could win the Tournament, and I had to pay my bills. And I didn't care if the NAACP was out there or not. They weren't going to pay my bills come Monday morning."

It wasn't a bad pay day, just an education. They finished third and Carl got his cut of the $14,000 check, but it was what happened the rest of the week that left a really bad taste in Carl's mouth.

They played their first practice round with Jacklin. Player, who felt lost without Nipper, introduced himself and Carl felt the chill. If that wasn't enough, their group was surrounded by a security detail because of the threats. Carl was never threatened and never felt scared, but he did have an agent attached to him who was with him on property and checked in with him during the round.

*Carl also caddied for **Charlie Coe** in 1971. Coe won the U.S. Amateur in 1958, shown here.*

Going down the second fairway, Player told Carl he was going to make his job very easy that week. "All I want you to do is just keep up with me, keep my balls and clubs clean and we'll be OK," Player said.

Carl was a bit insulted. He was one of the better caddies at the Club and this was his 10th Masters.

Player and Jacklin talked about strategy every hole and Carl kept quiet until the 13th hole. When Jacklin and Player were wondering about a 3-wood or 4-wood, Carl said if they hit the 4, the ball would land in a tributary of Rae's Creek. Player snatched the 4-wood and the shot went into the water. At 15, they went back and forth again. They thought 3-wood, Carl said 4. Player went with the 3 and hit it over the green.

When Player got to his approach shot into the first hole Thursday, Carl was standing there with the bag, ready for Player to pick a club. Player sized up the shot and then asked Carl what he thought. Carl said 7-iron. Player apparently learned from the practice round and went with the 7.

"He had me on every club until the 72nd hole," Carl said. "He didn't put me into the green reading until the 27th hole. He had three- putted several times. Then, after 27 holes, he asked me to help him read greens. On Saturday afternoon, he knocked in a curling putt on the ninth hole off my read. And by then he was calling me Laddie.

"He went with every club I suggested until we got to the last hole Sunday. Gene Littler had parred the hole to finish and Player and Billy Casper were the final group playing together, tied with Littler. He asked me what club and I said 5-iron. He said he was pumped and he was going to hit a 6 and, playing to that Sunday flagstick, he hit the 6-iron and it fell in the bunker."

Player didn't get the ball up and down and Casper beat Littler in the last 18-hole playoff at the 1970 Masters. A sudden-death playoff was put into effect in 1976. The first Masters decided by this new procedure was 1979, when Fuzzy Zoeller prevailed on the 11th hole, the second playoff hole.

> Ironically, that was Ben's first Masters [in 1972]. He tied for 19th, three shots behind [Steve] Melnyk, and was low amateur. The next year, Ben was low amateur again and beat Melynk by two shots.

Carl was upset when he got to the caddie area because Player hadn't taken his advice and Player was upset, period.

"He said something in the presence of Jack Stephens and I didn't know it at the time, but it was in motion that I wasn't going to caddie for him the next year," Carl said.

At the closing party that year, Stephens told Carl he'd like him to caddie for former U.S. Amateur champion Charlie Coe in 1971. Carl protested because Coe was an amateur and not as lucrative a bag. The classy guys, as Carl put it, took care of their caddies. They paid better. If you made $500 and your man made the cut, that was good.

*Carl had the bag for professional **Steve Melnyk** in 1972 and 1973. Melnyk won the U.S. and British Amateur titles.*

"If Gary Player wins the Tournament," Stephens told him, "I'll pay you what Gary Player pays his caddie."

Player didn't win, but Carl got the additional check nonetheless.

Coe won the 1958 U.S. Amateur at age 34, then lost to a 19-year-old Nicklaus 1-up in an epic final match at the 1959 Amateur at The Broadmoor. But in '71, he was well past his prime. His game was not sharp, he missed the cut that year and Carl switched bags again, spending the next two years working for former U.S. and British Amateur champ Steve Melnyk, who was a good friend of Dave Spencer's. Melnyk, now a broadcaster, would partner with Nicklaus in practice round money games.

Carl asked for Melnyk, who played in his first Masters in 1970 and was low amateur in 1971. "Melnyk was at the height of his amateur days," Carl said. "Nicklaus would cover his bets in practice rounds and Melnyk would go out and make five or six birdies and they were playing some serious bets."

> "My title was Get the Job Done ... So I was a good ol' country caddie from Georgia working for a good ol' country boy – who was a billionaire." – Carl Jackson

They tied for 12th in 1972, but Carl said Melnyk could have won had he been able to get a good speed with his putter. Instead, Melnyk shot 282 and finished six shots back.

Ironically, that was Ben's first Masters. He tied for 19th, three shots behind Melnyk, and was low amateur. The next year, Ben was low amateur again and beat Melynk by two shots.

The Melnyk years were pivotal for Carl. He had parted company with Augusta National as a full-time employee in June 1972 and went to work for a bit with his mother's brother Romeo and other relatives in Portland. He came back to Augusta in the fall when his grandfather Lewis – that first angel – passed away.

Carl's grandmother passed away when Romeo was born and he was 15, when he, his oldest sister Lilly and brother Albert moved to Portland. The family had been fractured years before over who knows what and they stayed away. They didn't stay in touch, they didn't help financially.

But as he lay dying, Lewis looked up at Carl standing over his bed and thought he was Romeo.

"That really hurt my granddaddy," Carl said. "If I attempted to leave the side of his bed he would say, 'Romeo come back, don't leave me.' He thought I was Romeo and he was missing all his loved ones that had left him a long time ago.

"I wish he knew that I have never let him go . . . that he is in my heart."

Life took another turn in December, when Stephens called and offered Carl a full-time job as his right-hand man in Little Rock.

He had been working for Stephens during the past few summers, but this was so much more. Carl spent much of the next 10 years living in Little Rock with Stephens, traveling with the Arkansas billionaire and working for him full-time until 1990.

Carl managed the staff, worked on menus, kept Stephens' schedule and attended to any guests. In other words, he pretty much ran the household. And he learned more about business and people than he ever thought possible.

"My title was Get the Job Done," Carl said. "He was not a married man (he was divorced) at this time and he would call me up at the last minute and say, 'Carl I've got 40 people coming out to the house. So I have to figure out if I'm going to have a buffet and is it good enough weather to put it outside? I can't sit down 40 people inside the house. I've got to get the florist, I've got to get the food.'

"I was smart enough to go around and befriend these people and befriend the people at the hotel so when I needed help, I could call them. I always got it done.

"It led me to books and the meaning of things and how to do things. I had to learn how to do special sit-down dinners and six-course meals. So I had to learn how to be a butler.

"I knew you could go to school for this, but Mr. Stephens was a big old country boy and as long as you served the ladies first and you fixed the proper drinks and poured the wine, that was good enough for him. So I was a good ol' country caddie from Georgia working for a good ol' country boy – who was a billionaire."

Carl always wore black pants and a tie. And he was on-call from the time Stephens woke up until he fell asleep.

"When he got business calls at night, I would answer the phone," Carl said. "He would tell me to stay on the line. I would be listening to the conversations. I'd listen to how they solved situations or what not. My job was to play the main points back to him in a conversation the next morning. I was like his assistant too."

Carl never knew who was coming through the door or who would be joining them on the plane before they took off. Stephens was at the center of Arkansas business and politics and was influential in everything from Bill Clinton's runs for governor and president to companies like Federal Express, Dillard's and Walmart going public.

One year, Roberts was on his way back from Europe and made a stop in Little Rock so he could fly to Augusta with Stephens. Carl loaded the luggage and clubs and walked onto the Falcon jet. Roberts and Stephens were seated, so Carl started back to the couch so they could have some privacy.

"Before I could get past them, Mr. Stephens said, 'Cliff, you're sitting in Carl's seat,' " Carl said. "Mr. Roberts just looked at him and he looked back."

Roberts shot back: "The hell, you say."

Stephens wasn't budging. Roberts took the seat facing Stephens. Carl chuckled remembering it.

"As we're doing our approach to Augusta, Mr. Stephens said, 'Cliff, how does it feel to fly backwards?' "

Augusta National member Gerald Achenbach, the retired president of Piggly Wiggly, played with Ben in 1972 and, during a visit, told a few people about how he played with this blond headed kid, a college player, and how high and long he hit the ball. Carl was there that day and made a mental note. This player sounded like someone who might some day win at Augusta.

Augusta caddies prided themselves on going by eyesight. They'd find out a yardage if they needed to, but mostly they just clubbed their players. Some of them couldn't have read a map if they'd tried, but they had the feel. But as technology ramped up, players started relying on yardage books on Tour and wanted them at the Masters.

Nicklaus had been using his own yardage book at the Masters since the early 1960s, and a few others started making notes too. Clubbing the way they did back in Jones' day was charming, but the financial stakes

> "The invitation reflects a lot about the Tournament," Ben said. "The invitation is simple and elegant. It's like a wedding invitation, a handsomely done party. There's a touch of formality in it and it's elegant. And that's the way the Club is."

were growing as fast as ball flight and club heads, and players wanted hard numbers. It was the way they learned the game.

In 1973, Masters players and caddies were using yardage books. Even Carl had one tucked in his pocket. The change, Carl said, was coming.

That year, Ben opened with a 73 and followed it with a 72 and was four shots off the lead after 36 holes. He was playing well and had Luke Collins, one of Carl's buddies, on the bag.

"I remember Ben birdied nine and I went to the 10th tee to watch them tee off," Carl said. "Luke told me how good he thought Ben was and I wanted to see."

He was impressed. When 1974 rolled around, Luke was back on Ben's bag and Carl had Lou Graham. Graham hit it straight, but, in two years together, they never got anything going.

Carl was getting a little frustrated. He had the knowledge. He had the touch. What he didn't have was a player who had that same feel and same vision on the course.

In some ways, Carl was out of sight, out of mind in Little Rock and a little frustrated that Freddie wasn't warming to his hints about a new bag.

Little did he know Stephens and member John Griffith had a plan.

Right after the 1976 Jamboree – the Augusta National Golf Club's big members event each year – Stephens turned to Carl and said simply, "Go see Freddie. You got a bag."

The bag, it turned out, of a lifetime.

* * * *

Ben turned the invitation over in his hands.

It was really happening. He was going to Augusta. The course he had read so much about, the Tournament he was dying to compete in. . . . He knew he was in the field, but holding that card made it real.

The invitation hasn't changed in decades. It's a simple off-white card with the Augusta National logo at the top and the following engraved below it in rich black lettering.

The Board of Governors
of the
Augusta National Golf Club
cordially invite you to participate in the
Nineteen Hundred and Seventy-Two
Masters Tournament
to be held at
Augusta, Georgia
the sixth, seventh, eighth and ninth of April
Clifford Roberts
Chairman

R.S.V.P.

Today, players tweet pictures of their invitations or post them on Facebook. Back in '72, you showed it to your friends and your family. You put it aside in a safe place, not knowing if you'd ever get another one.

Ben hasn't stopped getting them. The 2013 invitation will be his 42nd. Each year it arrives in the mail and each year, he hand-writes a letter to the Club and says, yes, he will attend.

It's a tradition that never gets old.

"The invitation reflects a lot about the Tournament," Ben said. "The invitation is simple and elegant. It's like a wedding invitation, a handsomely done party. There's a touch of formality in it and it's elegant. And that's the way the Club is.

"Everything is tasteful. Not over the top, but it's a bit proper. Believe me, I've spent my whole lifetime studying this and almost everything over there is tied to Jones' personality and Cliff Roberts."

And the RSVP isn't just there to be polite.

"You know what it means," Ben said. "They want to know if you're coming. It is special. It is a special invitation."

He doesn't remember that first drive down Magnolia Lane, but he had other things on his mind. He wanted to see the course, meet the players and compete – not just play – in his first Masters.

He had studied everything he could about the Tournament and Jones and Roberts. He found a map of Augusta National in one of Herb Wind's books and devoured it, detail by detail. Ben was taken with Jones' writings that painted vivid pictures of the course and the game.

"They're still the best words about golf from any player that I've ever read," Ben said. "By far."

And then there was his career. A Grand Slam in 1930 – all four majors – that captured the hearts of the world and stunned them all at once. The feat prompted O.B. Keeler to write that "others may attack – in vain – forever."

The one thing Ben never got to do was shake Jones' hand. The consummate gentleman and the heart and soul of the Club had passed away just before Christmas. It was one of those cruel ironies that a man who had such a profound impact on another – Ben

*In 1930 **Bobby Jones** became the only man to win golf's Grand Slam.*

has a Jones area in his study – would never get to meet.

He did meet Roberts that first year, though. Ben stuck out his hand and introduced himself. Roberts mentioned how fond they were of Texans at the Club and hoped Ben played well. He paused for a moment and added in his autocratic style that Ben might want to know there was a barbershop on the grounds. In fact, it was right up there off the porch.

It was the 1970s and Ben's hair was trailing down his collar just like every other college kid. But when Roberts said something . . . well, he went in and got it trimmed.

Ben was really only semi-intimidated. "People had told me the fear of Roberts, but at the same time spoke of him searching for the very, very best ideas and way to run a Club," Ben said.

There was so much to take in that week, not the least of which was the course. No matter how much he'd read, no matter how much all his buddies told him, he wasn't prepared to walk onto the lawn and see the course for the first time.

"I was in awe," Ben said. "You're just not prepared to see what you see when you first lay eyes on it because it is so different. Scale-wise, you just don't know how vast it is when you step out in back of the Clubhouse.

"God bless, I can't believe it's this big. It's a huge expanse and latitude and when you see your first couple of greens, you go, good Lord, this is completely different."

Fifty years later, he's still amazed by the course and what he doesn't know.

"That first time, you're like any of the television audience that comes to the Tournament and wonders why it looks so different," he said. "Today, they're coming up with a million different camera angles to show you what you can't see, to show you the differences.

Ben spent the week in the Crow's Nest atop the Clubhouse with most of the other amateurs. It's a functional, rather than comfortable room. Nothing but beds and dressers and a seating area. Kind of like a camp cabin, but this one is above one of the most famous clubhouses on earth.

"No privacy at all in those places," Ben said. But there was camaraderie. And one of his nest-mates Richard Bendall, now a doctor in Virginia, was old enough to buy the beer for everyone.

The other amateurs that year included Tom, Marvin "Vinny" Giles, Marty West and Jim Simons. Tom finished two shots behind Ben that year, tying for 27th.

"We sat around and talked," Ben said. "We went downstairs and looked around, too."

They didn't sneak into the Champions Locker Room as some amateurs have, however, and try on a jacket or two. And they ran through all the stories they'd heard from amateurs who had played in the past.

"Collectively, they all said they'd never been so nervous in their lives," Ben said. "They were choking their guts out getting to the first tee."

Ben has been in two car wrecks in his life and both have been in Augusta. The first one happened when he and Danny Yates were with their fathers and someone rear-ended the car. The second, he was in a car with his then-girlfriend Nancy Hager and they were on their way to Luigi's downtown. They were following someone and a guy turned right in front of them. Boom.

When the week was over, Ben got his first bill from the Club.

He stayed there seven nights, ate three meals a day and got a bill for $7! You can't even buy a turkey sandwich in the men's grill for $7 today.

Sometime that week, Ben went over to the parking lot and bought a driver and 3-wood from non-competing Masters invitee Toney Penna – right out of his trunk. Ben liked the way the clubs looked and thought he'd try them. "He had an established equipment company, but he carried extra clubs," Ben said. "He wasn't going to give you a club; you had to buy it."

Vinny Giles, who won the U.S. Amateur in 1973 and was runner-up three times, was one of the players who bunked in the Crows Nest with **Ben** in 1972.

Ben couldn't take things in fast enough that week. He was stunned by the scale, mesmerized by the powder-white bunkers and the lush, sparkling green course that didn't have a speck of rough. And, of course, the greens.

"Honestly, you're in shock when you see the fifth green for the first time. You go – *what?*," Ben said. "And when you see 14, they give you an oxygen tank. It is so completely different.

"I'd heard everything in the world about St. Andrews before I got there, too. There aren't many who don't like Augusta, but there are some who don't like St. Andrews. It takes you years to study both of them, but there is a kinship there."

Ben couldn't take things in fast enough that week. He was stunned by the scale, mesmerized by the powder-white bunkers and the lush, sparkling green course that didn't have a speck of rough. And, of course, the greens.

Freddie Bennett looked around his caddie yard that year and matched Ben with Luke Collins, a thin 40-something caddie with an easy gait.

"Luke was jolly," Ben said. "He had a funny laugh. He kind of chuckled."

The funniest thing about Luke? Every time he got to the fifth hole, he'd part company with Ben and head way over to the bamboo on the right side. It was less steep, he said. Easier to walk."

Carl chuckled. His buddy, he said, "wasn't lazy, but almost."

Luke was also, hands down, the best gambler – pick a game – in the caddie house. That house was Luke's office. He played poker, whist and, of course, checkers. He'd all of a sudden make about three fast moves, then jump all of his opponents' checkers. Game over.

"He had a memory for cards that you wouldn't believe," Carl said. "On cold, slow days, the guys who gambled around the city would come down to try Luke. If we were breaking, someone was gambling.

"Checkers was the most fun because they'd be talking to each other. One guy would be studying the board, the other one would yell, 'move, fool.' Amos Washington was one of those who, when you stuttered for a minute, he'd say, 'you done quit.' "

Ben had no idea about Luke's gambling side. What he did know was the guy could read greens and make him laugh.

One day, they were on the fifth hole when Ben was sizing up his approach. He thought it was a 5-iron, but told Luke he wasn't sure he could get it there. Ben was looking for feedback. Instead, he just got blowback.

Luke's voice went up an octave. "Well, hit the 4 then!!"

Ben laughed. Luke didn't mean to be flippant. Neither did Ben. He was just a young player who was trying to learn the course.

"I was listening very hard to Luke," Ben said. "He's been around this course so many times, he knows things. I was in my

Players Carl Caddied for at the Masters

1961 – Billy Burke

1962 – Deane Beman

1963 – Downing Gray

1964 – Bruce Devlin

1965 – Mike Souchak

1966 – Downing Gray

1967 – Downing Gray

1968 – R.H. Sikes

1969 – Tony Jacklin

1970 – Gary Player

1971 – Charlie Coe

1972 – Steve Melnyk

1973 – Steve Melnyk

1974 – Lou Graham

1975 – Lou Graham

*1976-present –
Ben Crenshaw

*Carl underwent surgery in spring 2000 and did not caddie that year. Linn Strickler, Ben's PGA Tour caddie for 13 years, stepped in that year only.

total incubation period. I was trusting of his decisions."

The greens in Ben's first year were Bermuda over-seeded with rye, which made Augusta's difficult greens even harder to putt. Especially for a rookie. Even one who could putt the way Ben could.

Jackie Burke calls Augusta the most tempting course in the world. Play it safe, or use your imagination and feel and pull off the shot of a lifetime. Or two. It just takes time to get there – to learn, then understand, then just feel.

Ben knew it even before he stepped onto the course. He had read so much, listened to everyone – from Harvey, to Burke and Demaret – talk about the place that he just wanted to get going.

"I was in full panic because I was so excited to play, God bless," Ben said. "At the same time, I was bewildered and trying to learn. Never had I seen such wide breaks or speed or putts that required such imagination.

"I hadn't played Oakmont yet, but these were the most challenging greens I'd seen. Everyone talks so much about reading the green you have a fear factor before you get there. When you start imagining these putts and where the flags are the first time . . . It's a lot to take in."

Nothing stirs a soul like Ben's more like Amen Corner. He uses words like magnificent, untouchable and indescribable when he talks about those three holes that never fail to give almost as often as they take away. It's where the Tournament unfolds every Masters Sunday and where cheers seem to have a different decibel level as the sounds reverberate through the tall pines, seemingly shaking them, as they swell and make their way toward the Clubhouse perched on a knob above the course.

Ben was low amateur at the Masters in 1972 and again in 1973.

Luke was a pleasant enough guy filled with some good stories about the shots or the members or even the other caddies. And he didn't do a bad job of getting Ben around the course and teaching him some things. They finished low amateur two years in a row.

That tie for 19th in his first Masters caught some eyes. It seemed as though it wouldn't be long until he won one or two. He was too good and had too much feel for this place after one week not to win here some day.

There was even more scrutiny in 1973. Giles had won the 1972 U.S. Amateur after three runner-up finishes from 1967-69. Ben and Mark Hayes were the runners-up in 1972, at Charlotte Country Club. It was a few months before he would win his third NCAA title, but the eyes, without question, were on Ben.

He shot the same score – 295 – and tied for 24th that year, but he gave it a run for 36 holes.

> Nothing stirs a soul like Ben's more like Amen Corner. … It's where the Tournament unfolds every Masters Sunday and where cheers seem to have a different decibel level as the sounds reverberate through the tall pines, seemingly shaking them …

He was paired with Palmer in the first round and opened with a 73 to Palmer's 77. He drew defending champ Nicklaus in the second round and shot 72 to Jack's 77. Nicklaus was in the midst of one of those runs of his – in 10 years he won twice ('72, '75) and didn't finish out of the top 8 – and finished T-3 behind winner Tommy Aaron. Palmer joined Ben and a few others in that tie for 24th.

Ben had met Palmer at a tournament in Wichita Falls, Texas, one year. And Jack? Well, that's a pretty good story.

Bill Sansing was a friend of the Crenshaw family and just happened to be Nicklaus' marketing guy at the time. Ben mentioned one day that it would be great to meet Nicklaus and Sansing said when you see him, just go up and say hello.

Nicklaus was changing his shoes in front of his locker at the 1971 U.S. Open at Merion when Ben saw him. Nicklaus finished and went into the bathroom. Ben followed him – all the way to the urinals.

"I'm so nervous I can't see straight," Ben said. "I walk up to him, hold my hand out and say, 'Hi Jack. I'm Ben Crenshaw from Austin. Bill Sansing told me to say hello.'

"Jack just looked at me and said, 'Uh, I'll be with you in a moment.' "

Ben has laughed about that moment for the past four decades. He was so in awe, so young. So star struck. So embarrassed.

"I made quite a first impression," he said.

He wasn't alone. More than a few players, reporters and tournament officials were tongue-tied when they met Nicklaus. After all, the man was the best player of his generation and one of the best ever to play the game. Eighteen majors – 20 if you count his two Amateurs, and he does – was just the tip. For decades, he contended in almost every major he played and finished second or third at one of those four events an incredible 28 times.

And Arnold? Who didn't love Arnie? He'd won four Green Jackets in his first 10 Masters and finished out of the top 10 just once in his first 13 Tournaments at Augusta National.

When Ben stepped to the tee with them, he was playing in just his eighth professional tournament.

"I just thought I could play with them," he said. "And I caught them both on off days. I was happy to perform decently with them. But at the time, I was starting to feel more comfortable playing with two of the biggest names in the game. I felt like I wasn't going

Jack Nicklaus in *the 1971 U.S. Open at Merion, where* **Ben** *first introduced himself to* **Jack** *in the men's bathroom.*

to expire out there."

His mind was racing, though. So much to learn, so few rounds to learn it in. He was puzzled, but determined.

"I was thinking, where can I cut down on mistakes? What am I going to have to do to learn the shots into the greens and the putts?" he said. "There is no possible way you can learn all that the first time. There are lots of courses I've played around the world that you can pretty well get the gist of them the first time you play them.

"Not Augusta. Not only because the undulations in the greens, but the change of elevation and how it affects club selection. There are a million things involved in picking a club there. If it's cool, the ball goes nowhere there. If it's warmer, it goes really great. I still don't know why that is."

He points to the sixth hole where the green is 40 feet below the tee box. That means a half club to a club shorter. The 18th plays longer because it's all uphill. At 15, the approach plays shorter than you might think.

"You've got to learn where to play, where to miss," he said. "What the chances are of a recovery shot. And the little shots are amazing. You have to have some skill and touch to play them. And with not one speck of rough, you can play the ball however you want. There is nothing in the way of a person using their imagination."

Ben was in his element. All those visits with Harvey, all those little shots he had created at Muny or Morris Williams or Austin Country Club and practiced so many times had been preparing him to take on this course he didn't just love, he revered.

A few months after the '73 Masters, Ben made the decision to turn pro. He'll admit he never was the best student. He floated around the University of Texas, drifting from business classes to arts and sciences, but the only thing that made sense and held his interest was golf.

Not many players left college after three years back then, but Ben did. It wasn't that easy. The Crenshaw house debated the decision for a bit. Big Charlie really wanted Ben to get a diploma, but left it up to Ben. Pearl just saw the positives.

Ben thought the time was right and jumped. His degree – his Ph.D. – would come in golf course architecture, golf history and those two iconic Masters.

The sponsor's exemptions rolled in and Ben jumped into professional golf at the 1973 USI Classic at Pleasant Valley Country Club, where he tied for 35th and won a whopping $903. He finished 12th at an event in Raleigh, then tied for eighth at the Sea Pines Heritage Classic. That check was for $4,238.

A few weeks later, he went from just making the cut at a local qualifier for the PGA Tour Q-school to winning the final stage at Perdido Bay by a dozen shots. He made his official PGA Tour debut at the Texas Open at Woodlake Country Club, where he beat Orville Moody by two shots.

The media took note. Ben graced the cover of *Sports Illustrated* and Jenkins, who coached him in the press room in 1971, wrote the story. He used words like charm, charisma and appeal. He mentioned that this 22-year-old could pass for 17. Some people had to work to be this charismatic. Ben walked out of the locker room door with it.

Suddenly, everyone was talking about Gentle Ben – both the man and that Wilson 8802 putter. But he was learning this Tour game too and that wasn't easy.

"My first year," he said, "I didn't know what end was up."

Like Augusta, the Tour was a series of adjustments. There was a learning curve, whether it was the course, the city or just finding the right place to stay every week. Ben was learning how to react to different grasses and different conditions. He was finding where to hit high shots and where to keep it low. You have to learn focus, how to fix what's wrong on any given day and how not to listen to everyone who offers a solution on the range.

If that wasn't enough, life tossed Ben a curve that same year when Pearl was diagnosed with heart problems. She had kept the symptoms quiet and later said that she even had to stop under a tree on the 18th hole at

*Amateur **Ben** played in the Masters for the second time in 1973.*

Augusta when she felt pressure on her chest. There had been other symptoms, too, that she hadn't mentioned.

Austin didn't have a heart institute at the time, so Pearl was in Baylor Hospital in Dallas, where Big Charlie's brother Allen was a gastroenterologist, awaiting a triple bypass. Since this was before cell phones and e-mail, Charlie and Big Charlie kept Ben, who was playing on Tour, informed with daily calls. The night before the surgery, Pearl died of a heart attack.

She was the one who always kept Ben and Charlie grounded. She was their anchor, their confidante, the one he and Charlie both turned to when they needed life advice.

Mention Pearl and the reaction is always the same. Sweet, sweet lady. So dear. So caring. So kind. She was everyone's big hug, especially her boys. She could keep a secret better than anyone and while Big Charlie was playing golf – if the day ended in a "Y" he was playing – Pearl was making sure the boys were on track.

> The night before the surgery, Pearl died of a heart attack. She was the one who always kept Ben and Charlie grounded. She was their anchor, their confidante, the one he and Charlie both turned to when they needed life advice.

Pearl was the first visit-er in Ben's life – the one who set the tone for those who followed.

"Mom . . . Harvey . . . Carl," Ben said, pausing on each word. "There's something that just draws you to them. They're . . . I don't know. Sometimes I think it's their smiles and their countenance. You can see the kindness in them."

Pearl's death affected Ben more than even he wanted to admit. Even with Big Charlie, Little Charlie and everyone surrounding him, there was still a huge void.

"She was the glue," Charlie said. "I think we all spun out of control a little after that. There was a huge hole there for a long while."

Almost 10 years later when life hit Ben again, he was reflecting on the problem when he brushed away a tear. "I wish Mom were here," he said. "She'd know what to do."

She always did.

By the end of 1974, Ben was wobbling. His game was a bit ragged and things weren't feeling quite right. He had tied for 22nd at the 1974 Masters, then tied for 30th in 1975.

He could see that major, but . . .

Ben will tell you that in 1975, he unequivocally blew his best chance to win a U.S. Open. He had a few top-5s earlier that year, but nothing great. Then he found something at Medinah. He's still not sure how. He was getting married to his first wife – Polly Speno – the following week and everything was a jumble.

He opened with a 70 and followed with a 68. Despite a third-round 76, he and final-round playing partner Peter Oosterhuis were right there with Nicklaus, Frank Beard, Tom Watson, Hale Irwin, John Mahaffey and Lou Graham down the stretch.

Ben parred 16, then stepped to the 17th hole – it's No. 13 today – a tough, long par 3 over water.

"I thought if I could par the last two holes, then I would win," Ben said. "And I hit this 2-iron. I hit the ball on the toe of the club straight into the water. Double bogey. I parred 18 and missed the playoff by one."

Graham beat Mahaffey in the playoff and Ben tied for third with Beard, Irwin and Bob Murphy. Oosterhuis and Nicklaus were another shot back.

"That was my best chance to win the Open, but I didn't feel I played that well," he said. "I hit some miraculous shots out of the rough, but I was not consistent."

> The 20-year-old superstar, the man so many predicted would be the next Nicklaus, instead became a player whose career would be defined by incredible highs ... and serious lows.

Bob Toski had taken a look at Ben's swing down at the Doral tournament that year and everyone else was weighing in too. Nothing felt right.

It had been a while since Ben had spent time with Harvey. The Tour, the travel, a wedding. Life was moving fast and Ben needed a re-set.

He's not sure who called Harvey. It might have been him, it might have been Big Charlie. The message was the same – can you please look at Ben?

Harvey said surely and Ben headed out to his tiny shop and sat for a while.

"I kinda quickly started wobbling off the track," Ben said. "Harvey knew I was sort of listening to everybody and filled with different theories. I was uncertain. I was kinda lost.

"I knew that Harvey knew I was fouled up. He could tell by the first few swings what was wrong. My confidence was the problem. I was hitting the ball all over the place. Harvey pointed out a couple of things and said, 'Go try that out and see how it feels.' "

Harvey added one final thing. "Don't wait so long to come see me again."

No matter how many changes a player makes, no matter how many shots he or she practices to perfection on the range, it's all about how a player adapts to those shots on the course. Ben was still learning where to play and how to break down courses. Those were relatively easy compared to hitch in your swing.

Ben promised Harvey he wouldn't wait that long again, yet he did. More often than he'd like to admit.

His mind would get cluttered. He would try to work through things or find a quick fix. He would listen to everyone but the people he knew best. Then he'd come get fixed and the cycle would start again.

The 20-year-old superstar, the man so many predicted would be the next Nicklaus, instead became a player whose career would be defined by incredible highs – two Masters and a Ryder Cup win as captain in 1999 – and serious lows. The instinct, the confidence that was there during those teenage years – through Firecracker Opens and Austin High matches and NCAA Championships – would ebb and flow.

A few decades after Ben went back to Harvey that first time,

Dave Marr summed up Ben's career: "Ben, you're on your 21st comeback."

"He was very prophetic," Ben said, chuckling. "I was a very up-and-down player by nature anyway. I suffered some real lows and some highs. It always bothered me."

Big Charlie – and later Brent – would always be there, offering a Harvey-type hand. "He would see things," Ben said. "He knew what made me tick and I always thought his information was like Harvey's."

That visit with Harvey and those couple of things Ben went to work on were all Ben needed for that first comeback.

There would be so many more.

Ben tied for ninth in his second event in 1976 – the Phoenix Open – then won the Bing Crosby National Pro-Am and the Hawaiian Open back to back. By the time the Masters rolled around, Ben had added top-7 finishes at the Doral-Eastern Open and Greensboro to those wins and was one of three multiple winners on Tour that year. The others? Hale Irwin and Hubert Green had won twice too. Nicklaus and Floyd had won one each.

Ben was slowly beginning to realize just how special Augusta National was and how it honestly felt a bit like Austin Country Club. Harvey's kindness rubbed off on everyone, from Charlie and George in the locker room to assistant pro Julian Ramos to WC, the club dishwasher. Everyone had his own little fiefdom and controlled it with a firm, but caring hand.

Ben won the 1976 Bing Crosby National Pro-Am at Pebble Beach.

Ben saw the same thing at Augusta. There was Council Dandridge who ran the locker room. Arthur Williams was in the men's grill, Freddie Bennett in the caddie shack.

"It was one big family in Austin and when I got to Augusta, it was more of a family too," Ben said. "The clubs obviously depended on these long-tenured guys who control the action.

"There was a happy parallel to the atmosphere where I grew up."

Fort Worth businessman John Griffith had known Ben for a while and wasn't sure Luke was the man Ben needed on the bag. He'd observed Carl when he played with Jack Stephens and had been with him in Stephens' cabin socially too. Around Jamboree time, Griffith and Stephens had a chat.

Just before the Masters, Griffith called Ben and said he'd talked to Stephens and they wanted to make a caddie change. Ben didn't see too much reason for it – "Luke wasn't debilitating," Ben said – but he agreed to change.

Carl was soft-spoken, but got his points across. No one knew the course better. It seemed the perfect fit. Bennett signed off on it.

"I've been around Carl a lot," Griffith told Ben. "He's really smart, I think he'd be good for you."

No one could have imagined just how good.

CHAPTER 3

FINALLY, A JACKET

"It was a relief. I thought that I could win a major, but obviously there were doubts."
– Ben Crenshaw, after winning his first Masters in 1984

It was just a feeling really. Nothing more, nothing less.

Ben was in awe of Augusta National before he ever saw it. Those books by Charlie Price had opened up a window into an almost magical and certainly mystical golf course that captured his imagination. No other course in the world could be so perfect, so endlessly fascinating. So complex, so intriguing. So tantalizing. So frustrating.

He remembers watching Arnie charging. Gay Brewer with that cigarette hanging out of his mouth. Jack. De Vicenzo. Hogan shooting a third-round 66 in his final Masters in '67 to give himself a chance before the magic disappeared in a closing 77 and tie for 10th.

But when he got there? He was simply mesmerized. This wasn't just another course to figure out. This was like nothing he'd ever seen before. He was blown away because there was no way you just played 18 holes here. You experienced them. You felt them. You saw that not even a 3-foot putt took a simple route.

This vast piece of property was gorgeous. It drew Ben in with the enormity of the trees and the greens and the vibrant colors everywhere you look. A tangerine azalea. A perfect dogwood. Delicate cherry blossoms. The rich deep color of the greens.

It wasn't a course you played for a few years and then moved on. It was a course that, quite simply, grabbed you for forever and a day.

*Some of **Ben's** fondest memories of Masters he watched as a boy were **Ben Hogan's** second-nine 30 in the third round in 1967 (left); **Arnie's** charges (top); and **Jack Nicklaus** and **Gay Brewer** (bottom).*

Ben was doing fine at Augusta National. Every year he learned a little bit more about the greens; every year he felt just a little more confident, a little smarter about the way he was playing the first major of every year.

Luke was teaching him some things on the greens and had helped him to four top-30 finishes – and those two low amateur honors – in his first four years. But, the gentlemen decided, it could be better.

*Left: 1983 Masters champion **Seve Ballesteros** places the Green Jacket on '84 winner **Ben Crenshaw**.*

They liked Ben. They liked who he was and what they saw. They could feel – even back then – that he was forming a bond with the course. He needed a caddie that was a step up, maybe two, from

Luke. Someone with the same feel for Augusta National. Someone with a deep soul, a keen eye and, most of all, someone who would share his knowledge, not guard it.

Just who brought it up first, who had the idea and who agreed? It just doesn't matter. Griffith and Stephens thought Ben and Carl might be a nice fit. Both were inspired by the course Jones and Roberts had built; both

To start the year, Ben had won at Pebble Beach and Hawaii, and recently finished fourth at Doral and seventh at Jacksonville …

saw shots and putts that most people didn't. They'd never seen Ben and Carl together and, in fact, didn't even know if they had ever seen – let alone met – each other.

But, as with so many things at Augusta National, the merger was wrapped up at the annual Jamboree and the partnership would debut in a few weeks at the 1976 Masters.

Stephens told Freddie Bennett, who told Carl. Griffith told Ben.

Today, Griffith will tell you it just seemed to be a good change for Ben and a stabilizing move for Carl. Something that just seemed to fit together like springtime and azaleas and the Masters.

Jack Stephens, top, and John Griffith, right, were instrumental in being the "marriage broker" in bringing Ben and Carl together in 1976.

Carl had gotten the word from Freddie that he would be moving to Ben's bag and when he showed up that Monday morning, Luke – his buddy – was standing at the gate.

Carl looked at him with those huge eyes and shook his head. "Luke, man, I'm sorry. I had nothing to do with this."

Luke shrugged his shoulders. "Hey buddy. Hell, I'm not mad at you. If I were Ben, I'd pick you too."

It broke the tension.

Of course, there was no picking involved. No questions. No discussion. It was by request of two members, one who would eventually become Chairman.

Ben didn't know what to think other than two men who he respected thought this would be a good thing. Big Charlie agreed.

"I'm trying to think of the words John Griffith used to describe Carl," Ben said. "He said, 'He's smart in a different way of thinking about the course. He is studious about it."

And Freddie? "Listen, Freddie Bennett? I knew him pretty darn well and he said something like,

'You've got a really good man there,' Ben said. "And I could tell he meant it."

Yes, Carl had been through a lot of bags over the past 15 years, but that was part of the game. It wasn't an issue. Some players went through three caddies in a week. The bottom line was Carl had grown up on Augusta National and he knew the course like only a handful of caddies did.

They said hello and went to work. They were both curious – Ben wanted to know the course better: Carl wanted to learn how to handle Ben and teach him at the same time.

"He was pleasant," Carl said of their first meeting. "He was just Ben. And I was just Carl in return."

Ben didn't know until decades later that Carl had stepped out to watch him play in 1974. Carl saw just a hint back then. But when they went out for their first practice round, well, he almost jumped out of his regulation caddie shoes.

"I got excited," Carl said. "After we played the second hole, I was like, 'Oh my gosh, look at this guy putt the ball. I've got to get ready, get focused cause this guy can hit it where he's looking.'

"His stroke was just beautiful. Putting those greens and just laying that ball up by the hole if it didn't go in. So I knew right away if I could be of any help, it would be on the greens."

So Carl started figuring out drills. With Ben's talent and his keen eye . . . this could be fun. He'd point, Ben would putt.

"Ben had to think I was being silly or crazy," Carl said. "I'd put something down and ask him to go there. It might have felt like I was overdoing my job, but Ben knows something no one else knows about putting.

"I don't know in my lifetime if I'll see another putter who can hit putts with such great speed. We were unlucky or he'd have won four Masters or more. His ball was tracking like... I can't explain it."

Ben was shaking his head. Jones and Alister MacKenzie had set out to build something different and they succeeded. The greens were incomparable and maddening and Ben had never seen anyone read greens better than Carl.

"We played well and we just got along so well together," Ben said. "And the caddie-player relationship, getting along is more than half of it. I was elated. He did the very best job. He was very much in tune with my emotions. He was learning about me too

*As a student at the University of Texas, **Ben** played in the 1973 Masters as an amateur. He eagled the eighth hole on Friday to take the lead.*

and what he thought I could do. So it was enthusiasm on both parts."

To start the year, Ben had won at Pebble Beach and Hawaii, and recently finished fourth at Doral and seventh in Jacksonville, while Nicklaus, who would eventually edge Crenshaw for the money title that year, had won the 1976 Tournament Players Championship. Nicklaus was also the defending Masters champion as he headed into Augusta.

All eyes were on Crenshaw and Nicklaus, but Floyd was working on a comeback of his own at that point and simply dominated. He came in without a win that year, opened 65-66 and set a then-tournament record with a 271, thanks to a magical 5-wood. Ben was second, eight shots back at 279 – a total that would have won or gotten into a playoff at 37 of the first 39 Masters. Nicklaus tied for third, three shots behind Ben.

"Raymond Floyd was shooting up the course," Carl said. "I was jumping around, just waiting for him to make a mistake and Ben was going to go catch him.

"I was looking forward to every day. And when the Tournament was over, I was looking forward to next year."

There never really was any formal discussion about who would be on Ben's bag in 1977. It was just accepted – by both sides – that this was working, so why change?

Ben tied for eighth at both the U.S. Open and PGA Championship in 1976, and finished second to Nicklaus on the money list. When the Masters rolled around the next spring, he had a lot of eyes on him again.

It was hard not to pay attention to the thoughtful, soft-spoken Texan. He wasn't just an incredible putter and he wasn't just one of the best players at the time. He was a man who couldn't learn enough about Augusta National and its history.

He was only 25 and was already on that same short list of players whose knowledge and passion for the history of the game and infatuation with architecture made them go-to interviews on so many subjects. Heck, he had read Price's *The World of Golf* so many times he knew it by heart.

Ben finished second in the 1976 Masters, eight strokes back of the winner Raymond Floyd. Ben's final score of 279 would have either won or played off in 37 of the first 39 Masters.

Brent Buckman quizzed him on it one night. He would describe a picture and Ben would tell him who was in it. He would read a passage and Ben would direct him to the right chapter and sometimes page.

Ben had grown up listening to Harvey and Hogan and Jimmy Demaret and Jackie Burke tell so many stories. They told him about the wild exploits of Titanic Thompson and Lee Trevino's journey from a kid who grew up in the

Lee Trevino hits balls on the driving range.

cotton fields hustling his way around a par-3 course with a taped-up Dr. Pepper bottle as a club.

Harvey and Jimmy and Jackie were visit-ers too. They didn't just tell the stories. They brought them alive. They gave them con-text and made certain they were wrapped in a lesson of some sort. And it all started with Harvey.

If you knew Harvey, you knew his amazing depth and love for the game – not just the shots – had rubbed off on Ben. If you didn't, you just saw the handsome, charismatic kid who everyone figured was good enough to win a major one day.

Ben had played three good rounds in 1977 – an opening 71 fol-lowed by a pair of 69s – and led the Masters going into the final round by a shot over Rik Massengale, who had paid him in gloves to caddie for him at the college level years before. He played with Watson on Saturday and drew Nicklaus on Sunday. Watson played a few groups behind.

By now, Ben was used to playing with Nicklaus. Now, that didn't mean he – or anyone else for that matter – wasn't still in awe of the best player in game and arguably the best ever, but it wasn't as scary as those first few rounds. Now, Ben could learn from Nicklaus rather than fear him.

*Few have studied Augusta National in such detail or played it as well as **Ben** and **Jack**, who have played a lot of practice rounds together over the years.*

Ben calls that final round a learning day. As in a closing 76 and his third con-secutive T-8 in as many majors. As in the day he learned a lot about himself and a lot more about Nicklaus.

Nicklaus was trying to win a record fifth Green Jacket – he and Palmer had both won four – and 15th professional major that day. He birdied the 17th and came to the final hole needing a birdie to tie Watson. He drove into the fairway and hit a fat 6-iron to the green. The rest wasn't pretty.

He bogeyed to close with a 66 and finish second for the third time at the

Masters and 14th time in a major, period.

"Jack played a flawless round of golf until 18," Ben said. "I remember him walking off the green and saying to (caddie) Willie Peterson, 'Geez, that was too bad Willie.'

"I would think he would have been more upset, but it was his maturity. What he said to Willie was a gentlemanly way to put it. He just walked off and handed him the putter.

Caddies like Carl had more than just yardages and breaks on their minds. They had the sense of the situation. … What's the wind speed and humidity? And no one was better at Augusta National than Carl.

"I tried to put myself in that position. It was such a mature statement and 90 percent of the rest of us wouldn't have taken it that well. I don't know what the heck we'd have done. It told me this guy is treating this as a game, not as a life. It was just a really mature statement. . . . I would have shot myself."

Ben was feeling like it, anyway. He'd been so inconsistent that day. Everyone knew you only had so many chances at majors and he was none too happy he had just given one of his away.

Jack knew it too. And, he knew what had gone wrong with Ben's game.

"I remember in the scorer's tent, Jack said, 'Would you mind if I say something?' " Ben recalled.

"I said, 'No sir go ahead.' He said, 'Your right knee is floating and you need to stabilize that knee.' "

Ben was stunned.

"I think it was very nice of him to say that," Ben said. "If he'd have parred the last hole, who knows what would have happened. I always thought very highly of him. He didn't have to do that for me. He did it in such a nice way, I'll never forget it."

Bobby Kay Ben's college roommate, later attended many major championships with him.

Jack was just . . . Jack. The best golfer in the world, the best at offering advice and the most adept at handling the media. And there wasn't a better example anywhere this side of Palmer of how important a local caddie was at Augusta National.

"Both of the giants of the game had relied on these people," Ben said. "There is no other course on Tour like Augusta National where a professional would say 'Look, I need some local help.' It takes a lifetime to learn those greens."

The same could be said about St. Andrews and the rest of the British Open rotation. Two years before Ben got together with Carl, he went to his first British Open without a caddie and found one for life.

Ironically, neither one was really looking.

Ben took old friend Bobby Kay with him to Royal Lytham & St. Annes, while Scot Bobbie Millen drove down from Glasgow to help a friend. Willie Hilton was supposed to caddie for Ben, but couldn't, so he rang up Millen, a friend and good amateur player at the time, and asked him to take the bag. Millen wanted to see how the pros worked and he had heard about Ben, so he said yes.

They met for the first time at St. Annes Old Links the morning of

Peter Thomson, Prince Andrew, BenBobbie Millen

the qualifying round and, after a couple of pars, the story of the first par 5 they played pretty much says it all.

It was a typical links course – rock hard – and Ben's second shot to the hole ran through the green and up a bank. Suddenly, he's looking at a shot off a bare bank with a downhill lie onto a downhill green.

Millen knew Ben was a feel player and a magician on and around greens. What he didn't know was the nudge Ben needed was a description of the shot.

"He had a wee look," Millen said. "In those days, he had long golden hair – it was shoulder length those days and he said, 'Bobby, what would you do?' I said if it were me, I'd bumble it down.

"He went bumble? He looked at me. He was so talented, so skilled and he did exactly what I said. He bumbled it down. He kept it close to the surface went over the wee humps and hollows and rolled up almost stiff to the flagstick."

Ben just stood there looking at Millen. "Bumble. God, what a great description."

It only got better. They finished second in the qualifier and headed a quarter mile down the road to Lytham and their first Open Championship.

They would be together for 19 more Open Championships and, in fact, every tournament Ben played in the United Kingdom, which also included, the 1981 Ryder Cup, several Scottish Opens, two Irish Opens and the World Match Play. They tied for second twice at the Open – in 1978 and 1979 – and had four other top-8 finishes there. They also won the 1976 Irish Open and nearly won another in 1977, but Hubert Green edged them by a shot.

Like Carl, Bobbie was more partner than caddie and, like so many others, he was a visit-er. "I knew that when I met those guys and got to know them, there never was a reason to change," Ben said. "Never an instance when I thought about it."

Where Carl caddied by sight and club, Bobbie would give precise yardages – he did his own yardage books – and a detailed picture of the shot.

"Bobbie's a good player and he telegraphs really well," Ben said. "Carl is much different in that it's feel and imagination but in a different way than Bobbie. Bobbie loved to chart golf courses, so I had tremendous information."

> Caddies like Carl and Millen had more than just yardages and breaks on their minds ... And no one was better at Augusta National than Carl.

Both methods worked. Both settled in without much – if any – discussion.

"You feel like you've known that person for a long time," Ben said. "You're similar in your observations. You get along, but, more to it, you see things in the same way."

Added Millen, "We became such great friends. Ben's such a lovely person. He could probably have done with being a little meaner. He was too nice sometimes."

Both could read Ben so well, so fast. When he was pressing, when things were getting tight down the stretch, Millen would remind him to "dig in." He'd have a cigarette ready, too.

Millen never smoked a day in his life, but he carried Ben's pack in his shirt pocket. "I could pull them out like Frank Sinatra in one of those movies and flick my wrist and a cigarette would pop out of the carton. A number of times I would just have one ready and Ben would say, "God, Bobbie, you know me better than I know myself."

Carl would get him focused in a quiet way too. When things were spinning, he'd just lean over and say, "It's time to get to this next shot. It's the most important one."

Ben would nod to them and always say simply, "OK."

Caddies like Carl and Millen had more than just yardages and breaks on their minds. They had the sense of the situation. What's the temperature? What's the wind speed and humidity?

And no one was better at Augusta National than Carl.

"There are a million things that go into a club decision, which is really an art," Ben said. "Couple that with the fact that he's seen a million shots go out at Augusta, knowing the way certain holes play . . . we have enjoyed working out a situation by feel, by instinct. It's very, very, very instinctive with Carl."

Two other things that stand out about that 1977 Tournament? Well, Carl's big old foot landed in Nicklaus' line on the 15th green – just barely. He had warned Carl when he saw him get close to the line, but his foot was on the way down.

"We putted out and prayed that Nicklaus' ball would go in," Carl said. "I was just excited."

The other footnote to '77 was Mr. Roberts. Not Clifford Roberts, but Mr. Roberts, the legendary great horned owl who lived in a tree at the sixth hole. Roberts committed suicide on Sept. 29, 1977, and the owl took off the day after. The caddies swore they never saw the owl again.

Ben was on a roll. Six top-10 finishes in his last six majors. He was on the short list at every major now, especially the Masters … that was the one everyone thought he would win.

But it didn't take long for people to start wondering if the British Open wasn't a magical place for Ben, too. After finishing tied for 28th in 1974, he and Millen went on a five-year run when their worst finish was a share of eighth in 1981. He tied for second in both 1978 and '79 and was T-15 in 1982.

Ben was right there at Turnberry in 1977, but got off to a bad start on Sunday and, like the rest of us, watched Watson beat Nicklaus in the "Duel in the Sun."

But of all the close calls, it was 1979 that both Ben and Millen felt slipped away. If only Ben had parred the 71st hole at Royal Lytham. . . . If only Seve Ballesteros had opened the door just a sliver. . . . But he didn't.

*Seve Ballesteros won the 1979 British Open at Royal Lytham & St. Annes. **Ben** finished second, tied with **Jack Nicklaus**.*

Ben missed the fairway on the 17th and his approach landed in the bunker. Instead of a 3, he took a 6. Ballesteros hit it wildly offline too, but got his 3.

Ben and Nicklaus – the runners up – and their caddies watched from under the stands, just in case, as Ballesteros finished off

a three-stroke win, his first major and his first Claret Jug.

"I didn't realize Jack Nicklaus smoked at the time, but he was standing, having a cigarette, and Ben was smoking as well," Millen said. "We watched Seve coming down, zig-zagging all over the place and he still managed to make par. It was fantastic.

"I remember Jack Nicklaus looking into Ben's eyes and saying, 'Well, the story continues.' "

The story? It was that no American had won at Lytham since Bobby Jones in 1926. The streak continued until 1996 when Tom Lehman won there.

Ben had tied for second in the 1978 Open at St. Andrews but had a fast finish to finish two shots behind, tied with Tom Kite, Floyd and Simon Owen. And his third-place in 1980? Watson beat Trevino by four shots, Ben by six, at Muirfield.

There was nothing pretty about the 1979 Masters for Ben and

Carl. After opening with a 73, Ben followed with an 80 and missed the cut. He jumped back on track in 1980, closing with 68-69 to finish tied for sixth and followed that with a T-8 in '81 and a T-24 in '82, despite a second-round 80.

Seve came into the 1983 Masters with two majors and a world full of charisma. The dashing Spaniard and swashbuckling Australian Greg Norman, playing in just his third Masters, were drawing headlines. Seve had won two majors and Norman had finished fourth in his first Masters in 1981.

The weather was so much of the story in 1983. The field played Friday's round on Saturday, Saturday's round on Sunday and finished up on Monday for the first time in a decade. Ben and Tom went into the final round chasing Seve and finished in a tie for second, four shots back. Norman had a chance to finish top 5, but closed with a 79 to finish in a tie for 30th.

"Seve got off to such a great start," Ben said. "He eagled two and birdied No. 4, so he was 3-under after 4 and everybody was kind of reeling from that. It seemed like the whole day Tom and I couldn't get any closer."

Carl had already taken off his overalls and was standing next to the scoreboard when Seve came up 18. "He hit his approach through the green, left his next shot short and I saw a little hope," Carl said, thinking for a split second he might have to jump back into his uniform. "Then he chipped the next one in."

If the ball hadn't hit the hole, it might have run off the front of the green and . . . bottom line, it didn't.

Carl and Ben were both frustrated. They had two runner-up finishes at Augusta and Ben had four other close calls at other majors. What everyone – including them – thought would happen, hadn't.

"When '84 came around, I felt realistically I'd had six or seven

Ben closed with two strong rounds in the 1980 Masters, 68-69, finishing tied for sixth.

> Carl and Ben were both frustrated. They had two runner-up finishes at Augusta ... "When '84 came around, I felt realistically I'd had six or seven pretty close calls at majors," Ben said. "I told myself I'm capable of doing this if things go right. When that did happen, it was such a relief."

pretty close calls at majors," Ben said. "I told myself I'm capable of doing this if things go right. When that did happen, it was such a relief."

* * * *

Jack Stephens grew up plowing fields and picking cotton in Prattsville, Ark., during the Depression. He was the youngest of six kids and was just six when Wall Street crumbled in 1929 and the country settled in for hard times. By the time he was 15, he was a bellhop, a shoeshine boy and the kid who delivered telegrams at the Barlow Hotel in Hope.

Jack Stephens

He graduated from the Naval Academy in 1946, and remained in school another year after that, but could not go on active duty because of his poor eyesight. So, he went to work with his brother Witt and, by the time the good old country boy was 40, he was a multi-millionaire, a power player in Arkansas politics and a member at Augusta National.

His daddy, a farmer-turned-politician, once told him it wasn't a disgrace to be poor, it was a disgrace to stay poor. Stephens applauded hard work, initiative and imagination and never forgot that giving back was something that came from the heart.

Stephens and his brother didn't always see eye-to-eye – Jack was a Republican, Witt a Democrat – but when it came to making decisions and moving Arkansas forward, they always found political common ground. Nothing much happened in the state that wasn't blessed by one or both of them.

"They knew," Carl said, "how to take care of their politics."

Stephens was as much a professor and parent as he was employer. He made sure Carl got his GED and kept an eye on him when he was younger. By the time he moved to Little Rock in 1973, Carl was divorced from his first wife and had a daughter and a son – Carretha and Carl Romeo. Stephens was divorced, too, so they were two bachelors, which allowed Carl time to learn about Stephens' business and his role as Stephens' right-hand man.

Carl wasn't afraid of hard work and, even as a teenager, was mature enough to realize that details and punctuality and learning what you didn't know were more important than any test he'd ever take. Whether it was mixing drinks or sitting in on late-night power calls, Carl made himself indispensable for Stephens when he was at the Club. The effort translated to a $500-a-week paycheck – a fortune for a 14-year-old whose mother was making $5 a day to clean a house.

But each year when the Club closed for the summer, the checks stopped. Stephens always told Carl to call if he needed anything, and there were times Carl did.

"I tried not to have to call him," he said. "But sometimes things would go the other way. But when I did call him, there was an immediate response to the situation.

Carl wasn't afraid of hard work and, even as a teenager, was mature enough to realize that details and punctuality and learning what you didn't know were more important than any test he'd ever take.

"It was a fearful thing to do. That's what made you scared. The Club frowned on that, but at the same time some members were encouraging that. They left that door open. If you get out of work and you need money, you're probably going to take that chance."

Carl had been working at Augusta full-time for seven years – long enough to move up to cart man and bring four more of his brothers into the fold. Tweety, of course, was there before Carl, and caddied a few times for Palmer. Melvin worked in the bag room until his back gave out. He was just getting his life together when he passed away in 2011.

When he was about 10, Justin, better known as Bud, helped Carl with carts at Augusta. Bill was on Ed Sneed's bag when he lost a playoff to Fuzzy Zoeller in 1979. All eight Jackson boys worked there at one time or another. Like the Avery boys – there were four of them – it was that first step out of the Sand Hill.

Carl laughs about his job being get-it-done, but it was. Stephens never hesitated when he invited 40 people for a last-minute dinner. He'd simply call Carl and it would get done. It could be as easy as calling a driver on the 18th hole at Augusta or as complicated as deciding on a club at the 12th tee on a nasty, blustery day.

"So I have to figure out if I'm going to have a buffet and is it good enough weather to put it outside?" Carl said. "I can't sit down 40 people inside the house. I got to get the florist, I've got to get the food sense. I was smart enough to go around and befriend these people and befriend the people at the hotel so when I needed help, I could call them. I always got it done."

Carl had a room in the house that overlooked the

*Jariah Beard was on the bag for **Fuzzy Zoeller's** playoff win in 1979. **Carl's** younger brother **Bill**, far right, caddied for runner-up **Ed Sneed**.*

Arkansas River. It wasn't far from Stephens' room – just in case and especially after Stephens had a back operation. Carl lived there full-time when he was single and, even after he was married to his third wife, Carl was still at Stephens' house early in the morning and late into the night. He could always catch a nap in the middle of day or find family time when he needed.

Part of Carl's job was to answer those late-night business or political calls and stay on the line. His job was to play back the main points of the conversation to Stephens the next morning.

He listened to a lot of deals and decisions and he learned from the way those politicians and businessmen handled themselves.

"I learned to be patient and think things through," Carl said. "I adopted (Stephens') thing that you always work around people who are smarter than you. All of my best friends are well educated."

Carl was almost always with Stephens when he zipped around in the Falcon business jet. They'd play backgammon and gin rummy to pass the time. "I could hold my own," Carl said. "That's the only time I could see myself getting under Mr. Jack's skin."

There were times when things got under Carl's skin, too. President Jimmy Carter was a friend and classmate of Stephens' at the Naval Academy and stopped by the house when he was running for the Oval Office. The Secret Service was with him, of course, and, after looking at the house and the choice of bedrooms – there were two guest bedrooms upstairs and a guest apartment on the street level – they wanted Carl to move out of his room so Carter could sleep there.

Logistically, it might have been the best decision, but the Secret Service men were pretty rough on Carl. When they asked about giving Carter the room, Stephens told them they'd have to ask Carl.

"I knew what they were doing and I didn't want to deal with it," Carl said, "so I took off to see my girlfriend."

On Saturday afternoons, Stephens liked to sit around the house and be a little lazy. He'd have a baseball game on television or some type of sports event and he'd just chill out.

The cook was fixing Stephens' lunch one Saturday in the late 1980s and Carl was in the kitchen visiting when he saw someone walk up the driveway. He looked like one of the kids from the neighborhood, so Carl answered the door and let him into the foyer. He wanted to see Mr. Stephens.

Carl told Mr. Stephens the boy was waiting and went back through the dining room and into the kitchen.

"I could hear Mr. Stephens talking loud and I said, 'What the world?' And I went back," Carl said. "He was saying to this guy – 'You don't deliver papers to me at my home on the weekend. You deliver to my office.' And the guy got really ornery.

"I'm the one who let him in the house without checking him and all of a sudden I'm in his face – 'Didn't you hear what Mr. Stephens said?' And he got ornery with me and, next thing you know, I just helped him out the door."

Carl laughed. "So come Monday morning, they have a picture of me in the paper at the main door and the caption said, 'Butler throws out assistant.' It turned out he was an assistant to some long-sitting federal judge up in Washington, D.C. and I done threw this guy out of the house."

> "You could hear the whispers, 'Who is that tall black man walking with Mr. Sam Walton? He must be someone.' " – Carl Jackson

He paused, "I really did the Fred Sanford – oh my god, what have I done? What have I done?"

Stephens had to hire a lawyer to keep Carl out of trouble, and for at least eight months Stephens didn't let up. He was constantly teasing Carl.

"He would come home at different times and he'd come on over and say, 'Carl did you have a good day?' I'd say yes and he'd look right at me and say, 'Well, Carl, I talked to the lawyers in Washington, D.C. and we may have to go to jail.' He'd look at me and walk off.

"He didn't crack a smile, but walking away he was having a good time with it. I know who *we* is."

Carl never did go to jail, of course, but Stephens never stopped teasing him about it, either.

One of Stephens' good friends was Sam Walton, founder of Walmart. The Stephens brothers had helped Walton finance the venture and take Walmart public, so it was never a surprise to see him as a guest.

Stephens was at his hunting club in south Georgia one day in the late '80s when he told Carl to go pickup Walton at the airport in Moultrie. It wasn't difficult – turn left on the highway and go three miles, then take a right. There was a huge oak tree 50 yards off the road.

"My internal compass never steered me wrong," Carl said. "But when I drove up to that airport road and got close enough to where the fields started to open up, there was only one building and it looked like a barn.

"Was I in the wrong place? But I retraced my steps, and rationalized that this was the correct airstrip and I had to be at the right airport. But how was Sam Walton's plane going to land on such a short airstrip? All of those demons of doubt were playing in my mind and again I wondered, 'Am I in the wrong place?' "

By the time he smoked a cigarette and replayed the directions in his mind again, he heard a single-engine plane in the distance and thought he was at a crop dusting hangar. He had to be at the wrong place. There had to be another landing strip. He was wrong. The plane growled down and landed on the short strip.

"Sure enough, the door opens and two bird dogs, both labs,

bound down the ramp and off to parts unknown," Carl said. "I remember thinking those are the fastest dogs I've ever seen. There wasn't enough room for anyone else to be on that plane – so that meant Sam Walton was flying his own plane."

It took Walton 15 minutes to corral one of the dogs – his name was Duke and he was hard-headed. That done, Carl loaded the car and they left for the gun club. Or so Carl thought.

He was slowing to make a left to the club, when Walton told him to turn right. Carl patiently explained that Stephens was waiting for him.

"Young man, turn to the right and go that way," Walton demanded.

Carl wound up driving 15 miles to the Walmart in Thomasville and was preparing to wait when Walton asked him to come in with him. Walton went up and down each aisle, inspecting the store. He talked to all the employees – not just the manager – and checked the merchandise.

"At that same time, he was making me a hero in Thomasville," Carl said. "You could hear the whispers, 'Who is that tall black man walking with Mr. Sam Walton? He must be someone.' "

It was a fleeting moment. Stephens was waiting. This was long before cell phones or pagers and Carl had no way to tell him what was happening.

Sam Walton, founder of Walmart, was a frequent guest of Jack Stephens at Augusta.

"When we did arrive at the lodge two and a half hours later, I directed Mr. Walton to the entrance," Carl said. "It was as if they planned it to see what my reaction would be. I had a few encounters with Mr. Walton after that and he knew that I was someone he could trust."

It was yet another in that long line of lessons Carl learned from Stephens and Stephens Inc. Everyone who worked for Stephens had a professionalism about his/her job and everyone worked hard under pressure.

Stephens even came to rely on Carl for a once-over when he gave a speech. It's another piece of knowledge that Carl draws on today when he has to speak in front of a group.

"After his best people had put the speech together, Mr. Jack wanted me to make sure there was nothing critical to minorities," Carl said. "And he used my suggestions."

Carl will talk about that "who's who" of characters he met during those 17 years with Stephens, but never about specific details of meetings or phone calls or conversations. Those stay with him.

By the time the 1982 Masters rolled around, Augusta's caddie policy was under fire. Of the four majors, only the Masters still required players to use a Club caddie during Tournament week, and that hadn't been sitting well with a lot of top players. The PGA Championship and British Open had changed the rule in 1975, and the U.S. Open in 1976.

In 1975, Raymond Floyd saw Roberts in the pro shop and asked if players could start using their year-round PGA Tour caddies at the Masters. They were part of a player's team on the Tour and Floyd wanted his caddie. Roberts wasn't amused.

By the time the 1982 Masters rolled around, Augusta's caddie policy was under fire. Of the four majors, only the Masters still required players to use a Club caddie during Tournament week, and that hadn't been sitting well with a lot of top players.

Ironically, Floyd won the Masters in 1976 with Fred "Hop" Harrison on the bag. Hop was a mill worker for most of the year, but he took Masters week off to caddie. Watson won two Masters with Leon McCladdie, a full-time Augusta National caddie, on the bag.

But so many of the old caddies – the guys who taught Carl – had retired and, honestly, there weren't many Carl Jacksons out there. Old-school caddies, no matter how hard they lived during the year, stepped up during Tournament week. The newer group just wasn't following their lead.

Champions like Palmer and Watson and Floyd were extremely vocal about it. Some, like Palmer, admitted the newer caddies weren't as conscientious as the group used to be. The caddies worked other jobs during the year and needed to work only a couple weeks at the Club to qualify for a caddie job at the Masters.

There were stories of caddies napping, showing up late – or not at all. Even Lee Elder, the Masters' first African-American player, criticized the Augusta caddies. He had cab driver Henry Brown, who caddied for De Vicenzo in 1968, on the bag and he didn't like that Brown clubbed him rather than give him yardages, the way Tour caddies did. Of course, Tour players were becoming more yardage-centric around that time, too.

It all blew up in 1982, when an all-day rain and cold temperatures – it was in the 40s – halted first-round play at 4:23 p.m. Fuzzy Zoeller was leading with a 72 and everyone scrambled to get back to their rooms to get warm and dry. Some caddies assumed the round was washed out and they would use Thursday's tee times for Friday.

Actually, there were 36 players left on the course and they were to resume the first round at 7:30

Ben and Carl in the 1982 Masters. The next year the Club permitted players to bring their own caddie.

a.m. Friday. It was in the newspaper, which also noted the field would be re-paired and the second round would start at approximately 11:30 a.m. off both tees.

Some of the caddies never got the word, partied too hard

Thursday night and were late Friday morning, forcing players to find other caddies. Heck, Patsy Graham even jumped in to shag balls on the range for her husband.

"It was a disaster to the caddies over there," Carl said. "There came talk of racism and everything, but the truth of the matter is everything was handled badly."

Ben was among the 36 and when Carl went to put his clubs up, there were wet bags piled up on top of each other. Carl took Ben's bag into the back, cleaned the clubs and turned the bag upside down to dry.

"Freddie had told guys to put the clubs down and go home," Carl said. "I had enough sense to go override Freddie. I can see the bags now.

"The next morning, everybody else was playing with wet, sloppy clubs."

Carl was on time and Ben's clubs were dry.

Roberts died in 1977 and by 1982, Hord Hardin was the Chairman. He admitted the Club didn't have 80-plus caddies who were Tour-level. In fact, many clubs didn't even have caddies anymore. All that, coupled with the complaints and the debacle in '82, forced a change.

When the membership met in October 1982, they voted to allow players to use their own caddies beginning in 1983.

*Under **Chairman Hord Hardin**, Augusta National modified its caddie policy in 1983.*

"If I were a player under today's conditions, and I think Bobby Jones would agree," Hardin said before the Tournament, "I would want to bring my own caddie."

But there was no breaking up Ben and Carl. "Ben became the caddies' great hope," Carl said. "Ben needs to be commended for what he did. It took a special man not to go with the crowd.

"That's courage when 99 percent of your peers are doing one thing and you do another."

Ben shook his head and grinned: "Pretty easy decision for me."

Ben finished second that year to Seve and, Carl said, made a statement that using an Augusta caddie could make a difference. Players knew that, but what was happening was they would sign up an Augusta caddie for a day or two to learn something, then use their regular caddie in the Tournament.

"I could see what was happening," Ben said. "It was a golf course where you needed people with more local knowledge."

Even then, players didn't always listen. Or ask.

In 1979, when Carl's brother Bill was on Sneed's bag, Carl swears that if Sneed had relied on Bill's knowledge down the stretch, he might have been wearing the jacket that year instead of Zoeller, who beat him and Tom Watson in a two-hole playoff.

Sneed had a five-shot lead at the start of the day, but was up by just three with three holes to play. He never asked Bill for a read those last three holes and he missed par putts on each of them. All he had to do was ask if Bill saw what he did.

"He might have been the Masters champion," Carl said, "if he had only put his caddie in the game."

To this day, both Ben and Carl look back at 1984 and, as well as they played, wonder what if.

That year, Watson chose to use his regular Tour caddie Bruce Edwards again. Bruce, who passed away from Lou Gehrig's disease in 2004, was a Hall of Fame caddie and one of the best ever on the bag. But at Augusta, he was just a year removed from being a rookie.

Ben and Carl were paired with them in the third round in 1984 and Carl was still wondering why Watson had let McCladdie go. They'd won twice together and finished second another time.

"Even Ben said, 'What's going on?' " Carl said. "To me, Watson was trying to get out of Bruce what Leon was doing. Bruce was an excellent caddie, but he couldn't match Leon on his own course.

"Watson could have put the Tournament away that day – that's how close he hit the ball – but they kept missing those short putts. And that left the door open for Ben."

* * * *

When Ben walked away from Southern Hills in 1983, he was disgusted. He didn't understand how everything had gone sideways. Why shots that were so simple had become daily adventures, why everything in his life was so uncertain.

Ben

A decade earlier he was hailed as the next Nicklaus. He was swinging free and winning everything in sight. Now, the career everyone expected would be filled with majors and wins was filled with peaks and valleys. That major that was supposed to come so easily had become a series of close calls and questions of whether he could indeed close out a major.

The early 1980s had been difficult. He had a strong 1980 season, finishing in the top 10 six times – including a joint sixth at the Masters and a solo third at the British Open – before winning the Anheuser-Busch Golf Classic in the fall. He finished fifth on the money list, but then another period of malaise started to settle in.

Ben lost two playoffs in '81 – at the Crosby and the Texas Open – but still finished 20th on the money list on the strength of nine top 10s. But in 1982, he slid to 85th on the money list and had just two top 10s. The following year, he finished second to Seve at the Masters, won the Byron Nelson a few weeks later and almost won the Memorial.

> (Ben) didn't understand how everything had gone sideways ... why everything in his life was so uncertain. ... That major that was supposed to come so easily had become a series of close calls and questions of whether he could indeed close out a major.

As a member of the American Ryder Cup team in 1983, Ben went 2-1-1 as the United States won a close match. Even that win didn't obscure the fact that he was struggling. A good finish somehow still felt like he was pulling it off with smoke and mirrors.

"I'd pick up the paper if I wasn't playing and look at the scores," he said. "It's like I'd play well and finish well, or I'd go to the bottom. I wasn't consistent."

Eight years before, he had promised Harvey he wouldn't stay away so long again, but yet he did. Life got in the way. Golf got in the way. There just never seemed to be enough time.

He looked around and, once again, that phenomenally talented kid who won Q-School by 12 shots and won his first start on the PGA Tour, the one whose potential seemed limitless, had disappeared.

Back then, he said, "I didn't think. I just did."

It felt like a lifetime ago. The person who did that? He was buried under the weight of his own expectations and circumstances he needed to change.

Ben calls it a period of uncertainty – one of so many that dotted his career. He woke up in the morning and his head was already spinning, wondering how he was going to figure this out.

"I fluctuated about so many things," Ben said. "Equipment, not seeing Harvey enough. I had only a few successful tournaments during those years and I had lots of valleys. It was so typical of me."

He was listening to every little tip offered to him on the driving range again and trying so many different things. His equipment didn't feel right. Neither did his swing.

"I was so bound up," he said.

*Ben felt his shot-making had to be perfect to compete at the highest level until **Dave Marr** reminded him even **Ben Hogan** occasionally hit bad shots.*

So, he sat down with Dave Marr and asked him if he'd ever seen Ben Hogan hit a bad shot. Ben had visited a bit with Hogan recently and had even tested out some Hogan clubs. It was a little like getting caught up watching Seve. Ben was mesmerized.

Hogan was the epitome of consistency – who didn't put him on a pedestal – and somehow, Ben had gotten it into his mind that the best players in the game didn't miss shots.

> Brent knew his old friend was lost and reminded him that he was the same person he always had been. He'd simply forgotten how to play like Ben.

"I was that far gone into the idea that if I missed a shot, I wasn't worthy," Ben said. "It was just one of those deals. Dave looked at me and said 'I've seen him hit some horrible shots.'

"That relieved me from a psychological standpoint. That was poignant to me. I was so bound up if I started out and missed a shot, I got frustrated. It's kind of funny. Where he said it, how he said it, took a little pressure off it."

What it didn't relieve was the pressure at home. He wasn't sure of his future with Polly and that, too, took a toll.

Ben visited with Harvey a bit, but he also turned to Brent. His former college roommate had taken over the head professional job at Onion Creek Country Club, the site of the original Legends of Golf Tournament and, by extension, the cradle of the Champions Tour, which meant he was just a short drive from west Austin. And he knew Ben inside and out.

Brent got his first look at Ben the day he whipped into the Morris Williams parking lot. The first time he played with him, he was stunned.

Ben had pulled his right shoulder playing tennis not long before the 1970 U.S. Amateur. He struggled through it, then wound up sitting out most of the fall semester of his freshman year. His first competitive round back, he was paired with Brent in a team qualifier.

"He hadn't played in so long, he shot 40 on the front nine," Brent said. "He was hitting it all over the place. Then on the back nine, he shoots 30.

"I thought . . . you know, this guy is pretty good."

Something clicked and they became fast friends. Ben was living in an apartment with Bobby Kay and Brent knocked on their door. When Ben opened it, he saw Kay down the hall and noticed that he was – in relation – about four feet taller than Kay. Now, Brent is a few inches taller than Kay, so he said something to them. It turned out the building was sinking and they hadn't noticed. They got out of there fast .

Moments like that led to lasting close friendship between the three of them and Scotty Sayers, who took over as Ben's agent in 1985. Scotty didn't play on the team, but he was also a part of what became an incredible bond.

When Brent left Austin, Kay and Ben saw him off in the parking lot. "Boys, gotta go. I love ya," Brent said. They all started crying.

"I was bawling when I left and I think I was still crying when I got to Temple," Brent said. "A week later, Ben wrote me the coolest letter. It was four pages long and my mother saved it. There were tears on the letter. That's the kind of friendship I have with Ben, Scotty and Bobby."

Brent didn't fish when he came to Texas and Ben fixed that. He got him out in a boat, and in Ben's junior year and Brent's senior year they spent more time fishing than going to their Monday-Wednesday-Friday classes.

Big Charlie's friends would always let them fish on a private lake or at a ranch, and something crazy always happened. The propeller would fall off the trolling motor. They'd forget a battery. Or the motor. And one day in Smithville, they decided to go out in a boat that someone had shot holes in with a shotgun.

They'd been sitting and fishing for a while when Brent, who was at least 40 pounds heavier than Ben, noticed he was sitting in four inches of water. He mentioned there might be a problem and they might want to head back. The boat was sinking.

"I'm perfectly dry back here," Ben grinned.

Brent was a visit-er too. He could tell tales like Harvey and give Ben a shot of confidence personally, but that's the only place their styles intersected.

"Brent was a little more mechanical," Ben said. "He certainly pointed out some good things. He always knew I liked to draw the ball so he was always trying to get the ball a little further back in the stance because it's hard to hit a draw off your front foot."

They didn't stand on the range. They played a lot of golf and spent a lot of time just talking about the game and life.

"Brent's always been like a coach to me as well as a great friend," Ben said. "He's always had a great way of buoying my confidence."

Ben needed that. He also needed a new driver and found that – thanks to a tip from former University of Houston and Tour player Keith Fergus – in a small shop in Humble, Texas.

It was a blond M85, oil-hardened MacGregor driver. The old Tommy Armours had dark heads – this was, after all, still the age of persimmon – but this blond look was special. Fergus, who shared Ben's taste in clubs, had two of them.

"I think it cost me $200 or $300," Ben said. "I showed it to Jackie (Burke) and he thought it was a pretty good club."

It was better than good. That driver was in the bag for the 1984 Masters.

That week at Southern Hills in 1983 proved to be a turning point. He opened with a 68 and followed it with a 66. He closed

71-77 and shared ninth.

It was, as he said, the worst golf imaginable.

Ben went home and put his clubs away. He didn't touch one or play for three weeks. His game and his life were one knotted up – one huge kerfuffle – and he had to figure this out.

> "I played my best golf when I'd hit it, chased it and hit it again … I hit my best shots when I didn't have anything to think about," Ben said. "I always liked the way Bobby Jones put it. If I wasn't thinking about anything, I'd play well."

Brent knew his old friend was lost and reminded him that he was the same person he always had been. He'd simply forgotten how to play like Ben.

"I love the guy and I tried to help him as best I could, but what I learned was Harvey was so simple," Brent said. "It was always just a thought. I tried to get him to do a few things and it was a struggle for me too because Ben had never really talked to anybody about golf other than Harvey.

"Harvey could tell Tom Kite all kind of mechanical things, but Ben wasn't a mechanical guy. Ben was such a feel guy. To this day, he has a hard time with anything mechanical. That's just the way he's built."

Harvey understood that and knew exactly what to say to get Ben to respond and understand. Sometimes all he'd do was move his hands a touch. It was imperceptible to most, the simplest fix for Ben and Harvey. It was an extraordinary relationship.

"I remember one time going over to Austin Country Club with Ben when Harvey watched him hit putts," Brent said. "Harvey just told him his thumb was over to the side a little. It was always something so simple."

When Ben struggled, everyone around – from Harvey to Brent to Big and Little Charlie – felt it. They knew the talent was there. They'd seen it for so many years and they'd seen the bad times too. They set out to help Ben find himself again.

"I had these stretches where I was disgusted," Ben said. "I was striving way too much for something I was incapable of, really. It's certainly not the way I played my best golf.

"I played my best golf when I'd hit it, chased it and hit it again … I hit my best shots when I didn't have anything to think about. An

Bob Jones emphasized the value of playing golf with a clear mind. Ben emulated this philosophy.

uninhibited mind is a dangerous thing, I think, for a golfer, meaning that player will do well.

"I always liked the way Bobby Jones put it. If I wasn't thinking about anything, I'd play well. If I was thinking about one, two or three things, then it would get a little worse."

Ben also talked himself off the Hogan ledge. He knew he wasn't ever going to repeat shots the way Hogan could. "It was so silly, so immature to think that way," he said.

The break did him good. He went to the '83 Ryder Cup in Palm Beach Gardens, Fla., and went 2-1-1, beating Sandy Lyle in singles. By the time the 1984 season rolled around, he was close. Piece by piece, things began to resolve themselves.

In the spring of '84 he signed with the Wilson company to play Haig ultra irons and the company's new ProStaff ball. He tied for 10th at the Hawaiian Open and shared sixth at Doral, where he knew good things were close.

"I remember hitting a lot of good iron shots at Doral," he said. "It wasn't long, but it was a very consistent ball. And a good wind ball. I was excited about that piece coming together."

Two weeks later, he tied for ninth in New Orleans and another piece had fallen together. He and Polly had made the decision to divorce.

Then, he closed out the Greater Greensboro Open with a 67 and a tie for third. He walked into the Clubhouse at Augusta ready to go.

"I felt like I was going to freewheel it," he said.

After an opening 67, it was hard to argue.

"That first round was really a good round of golf," he said. "It got me to thinking more positive."

He paused.

"That's still my lowest score over there."

*Ben and his "caddie" daughter **Anna Riley** at the Par 3 Contest.*

* * * *

Maybe it was the baseball player in Big Charlie. Or maybe it was the Masters historians and sportswriters who kept reminding him of what hadn't been done. Or the fact his son had come so close to winning the Masters so often that the whole family was itching for a win. Crossed fingers and superstitions became the norm for Team Crenshaw at Augusta National.

Everyone knows that no one has ever won the Par 3 Contest and the Masters in the same year. No one knows why. It's just one of those traditions like no other. And no matter how hard a player huffs and puffs and threatens to end that curse for good, it still hasn't happened.

That said, Big Charlie was one heck of a force at every Par 3 Contest. He wanted Ben to play well, just not well enough to win.

So every time Ben got close, there was Charlie leaning over the ropes, begging his son to stop it. In fact, in 1987 when Ben took dead aim and let another good shot fly into a green, Big Charlie was fit to be tied.

[In 1984] Ben opened with his lowest round at Augusta National – a 67. "I didn't make any mistakes," he said. "I missed only one green. What helped too was I only missed two fairways – the first and 17th."

"Son, what the hell are you doing? Hit it in the water."

Ben didn't. He won the Par 3 Contest and tied for fourth at that year's Masters, missing that chip-and-run miracle of a playoff – eventual winner Larry Mize, Greg Norman and Seve Ballesteros – by a shot.

Enough said.

Carl used to work Ben hard on the greens. He'd be ready to walk away and Carl would find another line, another over-the-ridge-around-contour-into-the-hole putt to work on. C'mon over. See what you think of this one.

"I might have been at the point of overdoing my job, but I felt I was showing him something," Carl said. "He obliged every time. I don't know that he might have said, 'Carl's getting a little ridiculous,' but he didn't. We always worked at the toughest putts, the toughest speeds."

Ben knew from the start of their partnership that Carl was special. He certainly stood out in a crowd, but he stood out in the caddie house too, and not because he was tall and lanky. He just had a manner – a way about him – and a knowledge that commanded respect.

"Carl has helped me do everything over there," Ben said. "I have benefitted from his advice so many times, I've leaned on his judgment and golfing instincts, and at the same time believing we can get the job done."

Even though they had been together nine years, they went into the 1984 Masters still learning each other. The were friends, but the relationship wasn't as close personally as it eventually would be by 1995. But that didn't matter.

Big Charlie had the superstitions and cheerleading covered. Carl had the knowledge. Ben had the talent. And finally, that crushing weight at home – that kerfuffle that tied him in knots – was gone.

It was time to do. Not to think.

They were walking off the first tee for a Monday morning practice round when Ben told Carl about the divorce. Carl had been through two of them, so he knew what Ben was feeling – and it wasn't a good feeling, no matter how amicable the split. He listened to Ben as they walked down the fairway and it was cathartic.

"Divorce had been on my mind for a long time," Ben said. "I was elated and felt free."

So, what started off as "I've got something sad to tell you" ended in an exclamation point when they got to the bottom and to the ball.

"We'll just win this damn thing this week," Ben said.

Fred Couples,

Now, he's not the first player to utter something like that at a major. He was, however, one of the few who ever backed it up.

Big Charlie whispered the decision into a few ears during the early part of the week, but it was off the record or something to keep to yourself. He didn't want anything distracting Ben. His boy had closed with a 67 at the Greater Greensboro Open and, well, it just somehow felt like it might be a good year.

Brad Faxon thought so too. He didn't make the field, but he was there as a patron and he passed on the man so many were talking about – THE PLAYERS Championship winner Fred Couples. That closing 67 and a tie for third at Greensboro did it. He picked Ben.

Early that week, Ben ducked out of the rain and stopped for a moment on the Clubhouse porch to talk about the elusive major.

"I've tried too hard. I haven't controlled myself like I needed to," he said. "I think that goes back to me putting so much emphasis on winning a major and trying too hard.

Ben and his blonde M85, oil-hardened persimmon MacGregor driver.

"I really don't need to be reminded of it. But everyone reminding me doesn't bother me because, in my own thoughts, those questions are valid.

"I can't hide my feelings about the way I feel about the major – about this Tournament. There's no way I can treat this like another week. It's special for what it means to the game."

Ben's driver – that blonde MacGregor – was the talk once the Tournament began. The Club was probably older than Ben, but it felt right. And it was keeping him in the fairway – a novel approach for the Texan.

He got a little word of advice, too, from Jackie Burke, who reminded him, "You don't see Vladimir Horowitz looking around and wondering what's going on. He is always concentrating on those ivories."

Ben was concentrating on fairways and greens.

It worked. Sam Snead joined Gene Sarazen for a ceremonial nine holes to begin play Thursday and Ben opened with his lowest round at Augusta National – a 67.

Ben holed a bunker shot on the ninth hole in the third round of the 1984 Masters.

"I didn't make many mistakes," he said. "I missed only one green. What helped too was I only missed two fairways – the first and 17th."

That old driver – with 10 degrees of loft – gave him about 15 yards less off the tee, but it was indeed straighter.

"It was, by far, my best opening round," Ben said. "I've had some terrible ones, you know."

His previous best was a 70 in 1976 when he finished runner-up, but most of them had been 73 or above. Including 1983, when he opened with a 76 and tied for second behind Ballesteros.

His putting wasn't as strong the next day and he followed with a 72, which left him four shots behind leader Mark Lye, who shot a 66 and tied a Masters rookie record of 135 for the first 36 holes. Kite chimed in with 68 and was three behind Lye.

"We've had those days when it just didn't go," Carl said. "Ben was displeased with it. We had five birdies and five bogeys and he three-putted the 18th."

The weather took over, as it often does sometime during most every Masters week, on Saturday. Rain and hail pelted the course, and play was suspended for 55 minutes earlier in the day, then called at 5:35 p.m. with 19 players still on the course.

The key, Carl said, was at the ninth hole, where Ben holed a bunker shot for birdie. "I loved that birdie because we really didn't have a tough shot into the green, but here we were in the bunker," he said. "And here we made it. I was sky high. He was going at the flagstick and he just pulled it. That changed the momentum, that was a momentum swinger right there."

So, in a way, was the suspension. Ben faced an 80-footer for eagle at the 13th – "I think it ran from here to Macon," Ben said – when the siren went off. He and playing partner Tom Watson had the option to finish the hole and did. Ben tapped in a 2-foot birdie to get to 7-under, two shots behind Lye and one behind Kite.

Watson marked his 15-footer to finish the following morning.

"If he had waited, we would have come back to a different feel on the green, different feel on the putt," Carl said. "Ben had three-putted 12 and wanted to go in with a better feeling."

Sunday began with Bobby Kay and Griffith searching everywhere for Ben. The Clubhouse. The parking lot. The locker room. The range. He had a way of cutting it close for tee times and the restart was at 8 a.m., so when they got there and didn't see him they split up. They just knew he'd overslept.

Ben and Carl line up a putt on Sunday at the '84 Masters.

He hadn't. He was already down near the 14th hole, just waiting for the day – the day that would erase all doubts – to unfold.

Carl had a dream Saturday night, the same one he'd had several times prior to the Masters.

"It was a tough time in my life," Carl said. "I had been with my pastor for a while and I had been at a Bible study camp. I'd been having this dream. I saw Ben at the 18th hole. I saw the clothes he had on and I saw where his approach would go on the 18th hole."

When Ben came out of the clubhouse Sunday morning for the restart, he wasn't wearing the clothes Carl saw in the dream, so Carl didn't say a word. In fact, he dismissed it.

Ben missed a 12-foot birdie on the 18th, so they finished up with five straight fours, leaving them two shots behind Kite and one behind Lye after three rounds. Kite and Lye were in the final group, Ben was paired with Nick Faldo in the next-to-last group.

Ben and friend Larry Gatlin in 1984.

He didn't want to let another chance slip away. "I really wanted to win Augusta," Ben said. "I needed to stay in there and see the right things happen, then hold together."

Ben had rented a house near the course that year and buddies Larry and Steve Gatlin arrived early that week – fresh from a concert – and parked their tour bus across the street. Rudy would have been there too, but, as Larry said, he was off "courting a starlet."

Somehow – no one is sure why – the brothers always paired off at pro-ams in the same twosomes. Larry played with Ben, Rudy played with Tom Kite and Steve played with Curtis Strange. Afterward, they were all buddies and hung out together.

Larry watched a practice round or two before heading off to a quick holiday in the Caymans with his wife Janis and their children, while Steve stayed in the house with Ben. Larry didn't realize it at the time, but he was battling alcoholism – "Back then, I thought of it as sometimes being just a little too festive," he said – and the trip was to help work out some of the strain and problems of marriage and family.

> No one goes for the flagstick at the 12th. It's a capricious hole – too tempting and too cruel. Yet Ben's 6-iron somehow went right at it, settled 12 feet away and he made the putt.

There was one tiny beer joint in the town and they peeked in daily to see what was happening in Augusta. By Saturday, Larry and Janis were sitting in the bar, glued to the only TV around.

"It was 1984," Gatlin said. "It wasn't like today where you get 1,000 channels on your iPhone . . . We watched the third round, which was rained out. Ben was only one off the lead and our friend Tom Kite was there too.

"Janis looks at me and says, 'Go home. He's (Ben) going to win it. Go home. You need to be there.' "

Gatlin kissed her. "That's a pretty good wife right there," he said.

He called Ben, made sure he could get a ticket, then found a flight from George Town, Cayman Islands, to John F. Kennedy Airport in New York. From there, he took a 3:50 a.m. plane to Atlanta, then a regional jet – we called them puddle jumpers back then – to Augusta.

After finishing the third round, Ben and Steve picked Larry up at the airport and went back to the house. Ben took a nap, Steve and Larry went to brunch, then came back to wake Ben up.

The brothers were amazed at how calm Ben was – and how nervous they were.

"I could have threaded a sewing machine with the damn thing running," Larry said at the time. "I've never in my life wanted something so much for someone as I wanted Ben to win this golf tournament."

Ben showered and put on fresh clothes before he headed back for his 1:58 p.m. tee time. This time, when Ben walked out of the locker room, he was wearing the blue and white striped shirt and blue pants Carl had seen in the dream.

Carl did a double take. Could this be happening?

On the ninth hole Friday, Carl saw an opening to remind Ben it was time to, for lack of a better term, man up. He was looking at a birdie putt and if there was ever a time . . . it fell in the hole. Game on. He added birdies at 10 and 11, too, before the rain delay.

"He said 'I know you can do it, buddy,' " Ben said. "It calmed me down. He didn't dwell on the fact that not enough good things hadn't happened. Whatever he said, in the way he said it, is what you want to hear to get your confidence bolstered.

"He's effective when he speaks. He says it silently and softly and says it with that smile of his."

Kite didn't start off well Sunday afternoon and Crenshaw took control with birdies at the eighth and the ninth holes. His approach to the 10th green landed 60 feet from the flagstick and, on that green, all he was hoping for was a safe two-putt.

Then . . . boom.

The putt was long and difficult. Carl and Ben didn't say one word to each other. They didn't need to. Carl headed to tend the flagstick, while Ben searched for the right pace on such a wide-breaking putt.

The putt broke about eight feet to the left and was flying toward the hole. If it was hit too hard, the ball would run well past the hole, and Ben was worried. Then, with 10 feet to go, it slowed as it crested a slight rise and curled into the hole.

"It was a preposterous putt," Ben said.

The roar shook the ground. Ben had a two-shot lead.

Ben bogeyed the 11th hole, but let it go. He'd stolen one at 10 and he was just trying to stay calm.

No one goes for the flagstick at the 12th. It's a capricious hole – too tempting and too cruel. Yet Ben's 6-iron somehow went right at it, settled 12 feet away and he made the putt. He was up by three shots with six holes to play.

Afterward, Griffith wondered why Ben had gone for it. He hadn't. He pushed the shot.

Griffith smiled at him: "I knew you were smarter than that."

Ben's tee shot at 13 found the fairway and, as he and Carl were sizing up the approach, two things happened that have always seemed a bit mystical. They're also so Ben.

First, Ben turned and glanced back at the 12th – the site of an old Indian burial ground – where both Kite and Lye's tee shots dove into the water. What were the odds? Kite eventually took a triple, Lye a double.

Ben wanted to go for the 13th green in the worst way. He figured he could get there with a 4-wood, but when he looked over toward the patrons, he had a Ben moment. He thought he saw Billy Joe Patton standing outside the ropes, which caused Ben, the historian, to lay up.

Patton had a chance to win the 1954 Masters as an amateur, but he went for both the 13th and 15th greens and both approaches landed in the water, ending his bid. Ben couldn't shake the image and played it safe on those holes.

As it turned out, Ben hadn't seen him. Patton, who was serving as an on-course rules official in 1984, wasn't working on that hole.

The magic – and that preparation he and Carl put in all those years – came into play again at the 14th, where Ben effectively put the Tournament away. After pulling his tee shot and overdrawing his approach, Ben had a 40-foot putt from the shelf on the left. He tried to putt it down and let it release toward the hole, but it never got that far. It stopped on top of the ridge. Six inches more and the ball would have rolled down the hill.

Instead, he had a really nasty 15-footer to save par.

> "Carl is the whole ball of wax. Experience, patience, not the cheerleading type. Someone you listen to and gain confidence with." – Ben Crenshaw

There was a subtle – almost innocuous – hump on the right side of the green that affects everything like a magnet. Ben and Carl saw it, found their spot and . . . the ball crested the slope and ran straight into the hole.

"That desperate putt meant more than the one at number 10," Ben said, "because it held things together."

A birdie at 15. Another tee shot down the middle at 18, a 5-iron to the center of the green and a two-putt par.

Twelve years after his first Masters, Ben Crenshaw had finally won a major – and not just any major. It was, in a delightful coincidence, the 50-year anniversary of the inaugural Masters in 1934.

"It was a relief," Ben said. "I must confess, I thought that I could win a major, but obviously there were doubts. Until you prove it to yourself . . . you just don't know."

Watson played in the group ahead and waited for Ben to finish. Ben and Carl walked arm-in-arm off the green toward Watson, who was standing near the scoring house. "Welcome to the majors club," Watson said. "You deserve it."

*Runner-up **Tom Watson** congratulated **Ben** on his first Masters victory by saying "Welcome to the majors club."*

Big Charlie and his second wife Bobbie went every stitch of the way that day – with a lot of company. The Gatlins, Bobby Kay, Griffith, Bob Hughes . . . the list was endless.

But the most important thing to Ben was that his dad was there with him.

"It was such a relief and joy," Ben said. "It was something my father and I could share together. His little boy had just won the Masters, the finest tournament we knew.

"I won Bobby Jones' tournament. He knew that I could do it. He told me I could do it and that meant so much."

This one, Ben would say over and over again, was for his friends. No one ever meant it so much.

Herb Wind took it a step farther. He walked up to Ben after the winner's press conference and said, "Ben, it's a great victory for golf."

Reflecting on it decades later, Ben said it came at just the right time in his career. He had seen Darrell Royal win national titles at Texas. He would eventually watch his friend Mack Brown win the 2006 national title game against Southern Cal with Vince Young and, a few years later, lose one to Alabama when he lost quarterback Colt McCoy on the fifth play from scrimmage.

Seve Ballesteros, the 1983 champion, shakes **Ben's** hand after his two-stroke win in 1984.

Winning a major wasn't a whole lot different than an elusive national title.

"I think about what Coach Royal said – it's hard to win one of these things," Ben said. "These things boil down to a lot of these factors together. It is why it makes it difficult and how you have someone by your side who understands it."

There had been so many days at Augusta National when things just didn't go right. Putts didn't fall. Perfect shots took mysterious turns. An inch became a mile.

"Those three or four shots that happen during that last day were proof to me that, yes, to win one of these things you have to have the right things happen to you," Ben said.

"Then it's a matter of holding on somehow. Only seldom does somebody play demonstratively better than the field. We've seen that, but I'd say that doesn't happen five or 10 percent of the time at majors. Usually it's a free-for-all."

Ben handled it all down the stretch. The putts. The pressure. Those incredible temptations that only Augusta lays in front of a player. He also drove the heck out of the ball and hit crisp irons.

"His golf swing was just beautiful," Carl said. "The years before you could feel the stress of his driver. I think his rhythm was better in '84 than it was in '95. He drove the ball well both Tournaments and, being the caddie, when that driver's not straight, I feel the stress too."

No one understood that better than Ben. He made sure everyone knew he didn't win the Masters by himself.

"I know this, I have always felt like over there, I've had the benefit of having *the* best set of eyes and experience and someone you could play for," Ben said. "Carl is the whole ball of wax. Experience, patience, not the cheerleading type. Someone you listen to and gain confidence with.

"Even in the first two or three years we were together, there was never an instance where I would want to change anything about our relationship. I was trying to learn from him as hard as I could. And play for him. And after all these years, I really do consider myself really lucky."

After the jacket ceremony, Ben was whisked to the press building for interviews. By the time he was finished, the sun had gone down, the grounds crew was hard at work and Steve, still in shorts, and Larry were on the lawn waiting for Ben. "He had the car keys, but we weren't leaving him," Larry said. "Not that day."

> A surprise waited for Ben when he stepped off the plane in Austin the next morning – Harvey. He was frail even then, steadying himself with a cane. "It was very meaningful," Ben said. "It was very deep and very emotional and such a proud moment for both of us."

Charlie Yates brought Ben up to the Clubhouse – they heard a chug, chug, chug as Yates' cart eased up the hill with Ben on the passenger side – and the Gatlins joined them in the locker room.

"Aren't y'all gospel singers?" Yates asked. They said yes and he launched into "Just a Closer Walk With Thee" and they joined in with harmony.

When they were done, Yates invited them to join him in his annual Sunday night singing at Butler Cabin with Tennessee Ernie Ford and the Augusta National quartet, made up of Club employees. They accepted and have done it – since Yates passed away in 2005, his son Charlie now hosts it off-property – for 24 of the last 28 years. They also sang at Yates' funeral.

In years past, tradition held that the winning caddie threw a party in the Sand Hills Sunday night. He'd buy the food and gallons of adult refreshments and the legendary celebrations would last until the wee hours.

But now that only a few Augusta National and Sand Hills caddies were working the Masters, Carl didn't have a party to host. Instead, Augusta National steward Frank Carpenter delivered a steak dinner and a nice bottle of wine to Carl, who celebrated quietly with a few friends.

The next day, he was up early and driving back to Little Rock.

Ben headed to the house, where he was greeted by Steve and Larry – in their pajamas – standing on their heads. They ordered pizza, drank a little beer, played some gin rummy, watched a little television and finally they hit the wall. It was 1:30 a.m.

A surprise waited for Ben when he stepped off the plane in Austin the next morning – Harvey. He was frail even then, steadying himself with a cane.

"I knew I'd see him sometime," Ben said, "but didn't think I'd

Ben collapsed into Carl's arms at the conclusion of the 1984 event. It was a scene that would be repeated, although more dramatically, in 1995.

see him at the airport."

Harvey, as always, held out his hand and smiled: "I'm mighty proud of you."

He was like a second father to Ben, and memories of all those childhood days at Austin Country Club came flooding back.

*Harvey surprised **Ben** by meeting him at the Austin airport the morning after his 1984 Masters victory.*

"It was very meaningful," Ben said. "It was very deep and very emotional and such a proud moment for both of us. Seeing Harvey, who taught me the game and who was there every time I needed him … He was proud, too."

That night, Brent, Scotty, Bobby Kay and their wives joined Ben for a little Mexican food, but the big celebration came a few weeks later when Ben was honored at the March of Dimes' "Sports Stars Serve" dinner.

This wasn't a last-minute thing. The March of Dimes had planned to honor Ben months earlier. That he won the Masters only added to the night and allowed all of his friends to celebrate with him.

In accepting the honor, Ben read from Bobby Jones' book, *Golf is My Game.* He quoted portions of Jones' impromptu speech about friends, which he gave in accepting the Freedom of The City of St. Andrews at the 1958 Eisenhower Cup matches.

Ben has used those same words over the years at special times and with special people. He read them at close friend Alec Beck's funeral, he gave them to President George W. Bush and to Bill Munn.

"The words in Jones' speech give people an insight into Jones' character and stature," Ben said. "His command of the English language should be evident in the words he spoke that evening and the beautiful words he left behind in his writings."

As you might guess, Ben didn't make it through that March of Dimes speech. Not even close.

He thanked everyone, then moved to Jones' words:

"When I say, with due regard for the meaning of the word, that I am your friend, I have pledged to you the ultimate in loyalty and devotion. In some respects, friendship may even transcend love, for in true friendship, there is no place for jealousy. When, without more, I say that you are my friends, it is possible that I may be imposing upon you a greater burden than you are willing to assume. But when you have made me aware on many occasions that you have a kindly feeling toward me, and when you have honored me by every means at your command, then when I call you my friend, I am at once affirming my high regard and affection for you and declaring my complete faith in you and trust in the sincerity of your expressions. And so, my fellow citizens of St. Andrews, it is with this appreciation of the full sense of the word that I salute you as my friends."

As he finished the passage, the tears running down his cheeks underscored what he had been saying for days.

That Masters was for his friends.

Greatest Shots Carl
Has Witnessed at Augusta

1. Ben's 60-foot putt on #10 in final round in 1984

2. Ben's two-putt on #14 in the second round in 1995

3. Ben's second putt for par on #14 in the fourth round in 1984

4. Ben's 80-foot two-putt on #13 in third round in 1984

5. Ben's up-and-down from back bunker on #7 in 1995

6. Sandy Lyle's approach shot from fairway bunker on #18 when he won in 1988

7. Ben's final birdie on #17 in 1995 was just the sweetest putt ever, and that was all Ben; he knew that putt

8. Jack Nicklaus' famous 1-iron on #15 in final round to win his fifth Masters in 1975. I was in the gallery, on the left side of fairway. When I saw that he pulled iron out of bag, I thought he was laying up.

9. Ben's last birdie on #15 in final round of 1984 Masters – another very sweet putt

10. Jack Nicklaus' birdie at #17 in his 1986 Masters win

11. Jack Nicklaus' shank on #12 in 1964 and still makes bogey

12. Ben's hole-out from bunker on #9 in 1995

13. Sandy Lyle's long chip-in on #4 in final round in 1988

14. Practice round about the year 1974. On #2, Nicklaus' second from 18 yards short of bunker – 3-wood (all carry) to middle of green

15. Jack Nicklaus on #10 in 1971. He is on the downslope of the left side of fairway. Even with big pine trees close to the fairway, his 1-iron got as high as the top of the trees to the middle of green.

Ben finally breaks through

On Thursday morning of the '84 Masters I sat talking with my good friend Herb Wind in Augusta's press facility – then simply a World War II style Quonset Hut. Playfully, Herb asked who we should follow that day. Of course we knew we'd follow Ben, but Herb was just having some fun.

As Herb talked about Ben's playing career, the conversation took a somewhat serious turn, as it had been filled with many close calls in the majors – a playoff loss in the PGA to David Graham in 1979, a narrow loss in the U.S. Open at Medinah in 1975, a close one in the British in 1979 and some tantalizingly good rounds and finishes at Augusta, most notably in 1976 and 1983 – but not a victory. It seemed that most golf aficionados wanted to know if he would ever fulfill what appeared to be his destiny. He was perhaps the first person to be labeled "best player never to win a major."

I remarked that I hoped Herb didn't have to write an article as he had on Harry Cooper in his opus, *The Story of American Golf,* where he titled a chapter "The Tragedy of Harry Cooper," referring to his narrow losses in the U.S. Opens of 1927 and 1936 and the 1936 Masters, after he had seemingly won each event. Despite being one of the most consistent players on Tour and winning 31 times, the only blemish on Cooper's record was not having won a major.

So off we went following Ben. Ben opened with a 67 – his lowest round in 12 years at Augusta. We saw every shot. He shot an even-par 72 the next day. Again we saw every shot. A third-round 70 put Ben in prime position for his first Green Jacket. And once again we witnessed every single stroke.

Needless to say on Masters Sunday we followed Ben. We wanted to see if he could do it. He went out in 33, three under. The excitement was building to a crescendo. On the 10th – the gorgeous downhill par 4 that plays to almost 500 yards – he hit a good drive, but a somewhat light approach iron to some 60 or so feet from the flagstick.

As we worked our way down the hill, Herb turned to me and noted how difficult it was to get through the mass of people around the 10th green, as this area is near where people congregate to see the teeing ground for the 11th and 15th holes.

Then Herb said the ominous words that I would tease him about for the rest of his life: "Oh, Ben's a good putter, I'm sure he'll two putt. So let's go down to the drive area on 11 where we could see Ben's tee shot and his second."

As we stood about 200 yards from the 11th tee, we heard this incredible roar, one like I had never hear before, coming from the area of the 10th green.

Could it be?

Did he make it?

Word quickly spread that Ben had made the putt.

I looked at my friend and said, "Herb, I'm never going to forgive you for this."

And for the rest of his life, each time I saw him I teased Herb about how we would end up witnessing all 276 strokes out of the winning total of 277, but missed the big one – the defining moment in Ben's first Masters victory.

Herb loved the story. Almost as much as he loved Ben.

– Martin Davis

Two key shots in the final round:
Left: Ben's decision to layup on the par-5 13th hole proved pivotal. Wanting to go for the green with his second shot, Ben thought he saw Billy Joe Patton and recalled Patton's shot ending in a tributary of Rae's Creek fronting the green in 1954. Ben laid up, taking the risky shot out of the equation.

Photos right: Ben's monster 60-foot putt on the 10th hole was the most spectacular shot of the Tournament. It was his third birdie in a row and the most unexpected of the three.

1984 Masters

Top row:
Left: Larry Nelson, *with a third round 66, was in the hunt. His final round 70 left him in fifth place.*
Center: *With a disappointing 74 in the final round,* **Payne Stewart** *finished tied for 21st.*
Right: Nick Faldo, *Ben's playing partner in the final round, faded with a 76 to fall into a tie for 15th place.*

Middle row:
Right: *Two-time Masters champion* **Tom Watson** *finished in second place, two strokes behind Ben.*

Bottom row: Ben *at the formal presentation ceremony as 1983 Masters winner* **Seve Ballesteros** *looks on, awaiting to place the winner's Green Jacket on Ben.*

DISAPPOINTMENTS AND CLOSE CALLS

I t was a lazy Monday morning in the Stephens Cabin. Jack Stephens was perusing the newspaper. There wasn't anything on the agenda. Time was irrelevant.

Just outside the cabin, Augusta National was buzzing. Carts were zipping around the property, tending to the course and loading up merchandise from the small outside pro shops that used to dot the course.

A few dozen reporters and broadcasters were attempting to play the course as lay, which meant Sunday flagsticks and rock-hard putting surfaces. It also meant scrambling to get to the green and a lot of golf balls that got picked up when the stroke count got too high on a hole. After all, they had to be off the course by noon, so the members could play.

The Club employees were scurrying to clean up, sort out, box up leftover merchandise wrap up any post-Tournament details so the Club could get back to normal.

The day before, Fuzzy Zoeller had become the first Masters rookie to win a Green Jacket with Carl's buddy Jariah Beard on the bag. The win was bittersweet for Carl since his brother Bill had been on Ed Sneed's bag and Zoeller beat Sneed and Tom Watson in the playoff.

Stephens was the only member on the grounds and it was getting close to noon when he decided to play 18. He asked Carl to call over to the pro shop and tell Bob Kletcke and Dave Spencer, the pros, that he was going out.

"And," Stephens said, "that you and I want to play them today."

Carl was so excited, he didn't call. He pretty much ran over to the shop.

"I went over there and part of the reason was because I knew I was going to have to find some clubs and shoes to play in," he said.

Spencer was busy with inventory, but lent Carl his clubs and a pair of shoes. Assistant pro Mike Shannon, now a short-game guru at Sea Island, Ga., rounded out the foursome. Shannon was still pumped up from Sunday. Zoeller had been his roommate in junior college and he had helped Freddie Bennett settle on Beard for his bag.

Carl was about to become the first Augusta caddie to play as a member's guest and word spread fast. In fact, Carl said, the news flew through the property and, before he could get back to the cabin, the office called Chairman Hord Hardin.

Stephens never minded stirring things up a bit. And, this was stirring.

*1989 proved to be the third disappointing Masters in a row for **Ben** and **Carl**.*

"I told Mr. Stephens, they called Mr. Hardin," Carl said, "and he looked at me and said 'We're playing.' "

Before he knew it, he was teeing off with Stephens, Kletcke and Shannon. By the time Carl got to the first tee, there was a crowd gathered on the lawn.

> On April 13, 1997, Tiger Woods would change the face of the game. He was up by nine shots with 18 holes to play and there was no question. Everyone knew this wasn't just another Masters, another major. … This was history.

"Everyone from kitchen down to pro shop and administration was standing out there watching this happen," Carl said. "Everyone got up and hit it over the trap. I was the last one to hit and I hit it over the trap too and the caddies went wild.

"I was excited. I was too excited to play any kind of decent golf."

Carl and Shannon were hitting at the same time to see who was longer off the tee. At the 15th, the proof was in the approach. Kletcke hit a 5-iron, Shannon hit a 6-iron and Carl hit pitching wedge. He had 114 yards to the front.

Four years earlier, Clifford Roberts had been at the Clubhouse to welcome Lee Elder when he arrived to play in his first Masters. Roberts always made sure to greet players, but Elder was more than just that. He was the first African-American to qualify for the Masters field. Other African-American trailblazers like Bill Spiller, Ted Rhodes and Charlie Sifford had never met the qualifications for the elite field.

Carl understood the significance and was standing on the first tee that Thursday to be a part of history. "I wanted to see the expressions on the faces of the members and patrons when [Elder] teed off," Carl said. "There was a different energy."

Twenty-two years later, there was totally different energy on the grounds. It was a combination of excitement and anticipation, a moment everyone at Augusta National would remember in vivid detail, a day that would be etched on golf's timeline.

On April 13, 1997, Tiger Woods would change the face of the game.

He was up by nine shots with 18 holes to play and there was no question. Everyone knew this wasn't just another Masters, another major. In his first major as a professional, he was playing against a number in a record book, redefining the game as we knew it.

This was history.

Patrons gathered on the lawn to watch him walk from the practice green to practice tee and back again. African-American waiters and other staff gathered under the tree to watch him tee off and again when he

Tiger Woods changed the face of golf when he won his first Masters in 1997 by a record 12 shots. At 21, he was the youngest-ever champion at Augusta.

walked up the 18th hole. Elder stood on the lawn trying to put the day in perspective. "No one will turn their head when a black man walks to the first tee after this," he said.

Everyone studied his body language, his stare and ultimately marveled at his incredible focus. You didn't see it, you felt it. Something special was happening.

A year earlier, Tiger had asked to play a few practice rounds with Ben and they were paired together the first two rounds because Ben was defending champion and Tiger was the reigning U.S. Amateur champion. It was Tiger's second Masters as an amateur, and he was still like a kid in a classroom.

Pictured at Alotian, **Carl** *and* **Tiger** *formed a mutual respect.*

He knew how good a team Ben and Carl were and he paid attention. During the practice rounds, he hit every shot, every putt that Ben hit. He listened when they told him where the holes would be and how the putts would break.

"It was great playing with Ben; it was fun," Tiger said. "I remember outdriving him, but it didn't help. I couldn't hit a green with a wedge to save my life."

Even though he missed the cut in 1996 – the agonizing year Greg Norman took a six-shot lead into the final round and slowly imploded with a 78 while Nick Faldo closed with 67 for his third Green Jacket – Tiger stopped by the caddie house to thank Carl for helping him learn a bit more about the course. Ben and Carl didn't teach him every nuance in those few days, but what he did learn … well, it did make a difference in '97.

"I was very, very impressed when I just said hello to Tiger as we were walking up No. 1 fairway," Carl said. "They way he introduced himself was impressive. You could see he was a well-raised young man."

A year later, Tiger was the first African-American major champion.

"Oh man, I was elated," Carl said. " It meant so much to me as a black man. I saw the world opening up for golf at that time. I can remember seeing more black spectators at the course. More blacks were getting interested in the game."

What caught Carl's eye was his putter. After opening with a 40 on the front nine in '97, Tiger came back in 30. He didn't have a three-putt all week. Neither did Ben in 1995.

Augusta National only began keeping that stat in 1986, but there have been at least two other winners who didn't three-putt on the way to a Masters win – Jackie Burke in 1956 and Billy Casper in 1970. Both were, like Ben, incredible putters.

"Being an aggressive putter like Tiger is, it's a testament to how close he hit it," Carl said. "He hit the ball so well."

Everyone was caught up in the swirl of excitement and celebration of, not just an African-American winner, but a player who would change the face of the sport. The world was mesmerized by a dozen-shot win, a phenomenal talent and an unbelievable charisma.

Stephens was in Butler Cabin as Masters Chairman – only the fourth in history – and presided over the ceremony that Sunday afternoon. He was always pushing for change and never shy with his opinions. He directed the Club with a firm hand and was in full support of a more diverse membership, which started with Hardin welcoming Ron Townsend as the Club's first African-American member in 1990.

Stephens had presided over some pretty impressive Masters, including Ben's win for Harvey in 1995 and Faldo's come-from-behind win in '96. Tiger's first Green Jacket came in Stephens' next-to-last Masters as Chairman and it helped fuel his decision to support the fledgling First Tee.

That afternoon in 1997, Miles Stephens – Stephens' 9-year-old grandson – was beside the 18th green with member Joe Ford's grandson Jonathan Crawford. Crawford had been holding the seats and asked Miles to join him. As Tiger came off the green, his caddie Mike "Fluff" Cowan gave Miles the winning golf ball.

*Warren Stephens said **Tiger's** 1997 win solidified his dad's decision to donate $5 million to help launch The First Tee.*

"He stuck it in his hand," said Warren Stephens, Miles' dad and Jack's younger son. "It was pretty amazing."

He still has that little piece of history tucked away safely in a drawer.

Warren, an Augusta National member and current CEO of Stephens Inc., said Tiger's win solidified his dad's decision to donate $5 million to help launch The First Tee. The time was right. Golf had a bona fide star that was bringing younger people and minorities to the game.

That gift, the leadership of President George H.W. Bush (the first honorary chairman of The First Tee) and a lot of advice from the elder Stephens gave the PGA Tour a roadmap to follow with The First Tee and handed Augusta National a mandate to grow the game.

Stephens had taken over the Chairman's seat in 1991 from Hardin and handed the job off to Hootie Johnson in 1998. Johnson is best known for his verbal tussles with Martha Burk over an absence of female members, but he was responsible for moving the course layout into the modern era. Beginning in 2002, he oversaw a significant lengthening of the course – about 500 yards was added from 2002-06 – to keep up with technology.

> (Jack Stephens) directed the Club with a firm hand and was in full support of a more diverse membership, which started with [Hord] Hardin welcoming Ron Townsend as the Club's first African-American member in 1990.

Current Chairman Billy Payne took it a step further, adding structures on the Berckmans Road side of the course, a gorgeous driving range, a new caddie house and a TV house. The Club also bought up land on the other side of Berckmans, which has become a massive parking area.

In 2012, Payne announced the Club's first two female members – former Secretary of State Condoleezza Rice and South Carolina businesswoman Darla Moore. It's safe to say Stephens, who died in 2005, would have applauded that decision too.

Stephens' reach was always broader than just Augusta National. For all the advice and nudges he gave to Roberts over the years, he was at the forefront of civil rights issues in Arkansas. And, he was a member of the board of trustees of the University of Arkansas when the university integrated the law school in 1948.

"I can tell you personally he did many things that he doesn't want credit for," Carl said. "He was on boards of universities when he was breaking barriers for the black athletes. And he was saying it's not right, things need to change."

He could be tough, but he had a clever way of getting a point across, too. Back in the 1970s, the story goes, a new member joined Stephens' foursome one day. Stephens was happy to have him, but when the member started throwing out big numbers for some wagers, Stephens drew the line.

They played friendly games, Stephens said, for $2 at Augusta National. The new guy bragged that, back home, club members played for $100 Nassaus with automatic two-down presses. Stephens nodded and reminded him it was $2 at Augusta.

The guy grumbled for 18 holes and was griping about the low stakes at such a powerful Club when they got to the card room and suggested they play gin rummy. Stephens said fine, members played for a penny a point. Back home, the new member harrumphed, they played for an expensive $10 a point.

Stephens had finally had enough and asked the man to add up what he was worth – stocks, real estate, cash, etc. He said, said, oh, roughly a half million.

Stephens grabbed the deck of cards and said simply, "I'll cut you for it."

The guy didn't say another word.

Stephens would play with Eisenhower when the Club had had special member weekends. Carl and the other caddies never called him President Eisenhower or Mr. President. It was always General Eisenhower.

And, of course, they all had to hear about his tree.

Ben's Favorite Playing Partners

1. **Seve Ballesteros**

2. **Lee Trevino**

3. **Tom Watson**

4. **Bill Rogers**

5. **Bruce Lietzke**

The 65-foot tall Loblolly Pine stands guard along the left side of the 17th fairway, about 210 yards from the tee. Eisenhower hit it so often, the Club nicknamed it the Eisenhower tree. Ike hated it so much that during a member's meeting in 1956, he brought up the idea of cutting it down.

There was no discussion. Roberts ruled Eisenhower was out of order and ended the meeting – to much laughter – before anyone could say another word.

But that didn't quiet Ike down.

"He carried on a lot about that tree," Carl said. "He commented on that tree every time he went by. It was true, he hit it or rolled it up under every time he played. He had to aim that way because of his slice.

"He used say, 'I'll pay any of you caddies to cut this tree down.' "

One day Mutt Boyd, who was Ken Venturi's favorite caddie, said, "You give me $500 and that tree won't be there tomorrow. It won't be standing."

Of course, no money ever changed hands and the pine is still there. In fact, Tiger hurt his left knee and Achilles while hitting a shot out from underneath the sprawling pine in 2011.

It was Mike Turpak's job to deliver the carts to the cabins, but it was Carl who almost always delivered Ike's cart. Every so often, Ike would have to leave Mamie there when the took a quick side trip away from Augusta and the club staff – mostly the wait staff or housekeepers – would check in on her. Carl made sure there was a cart there if she needed it.

"The Eisenhower cabin, you could drive the cart up under that cabin," Carl said. "That's where the Secret Service would be. Well, the Secret Service didn't like Mike and that scared him.

*At the 2011 Masters, **Tiger Woods** hurt his left knee and Achilles while hitting a shot from beneath the Eisenhower Tree on the 17th hole.*

There wasn't a dangerous bone in his body, but he didn't like doing that.

"So when the Eisenhowers would leave, they always saw to it that I got a tip."

Stephens and Roberts played a lot of golf together, and Carl was almost as amazed as Roberts with the way Stephens could come up with solutions to even the smallest of problems. "The man," Carl said, "had a lot of wisdom."

And a lot of friends. Coaches and broadcasters always seemed to be around – everyone from Chris Schenkel and Pat Summerall to Bear Bryant, Darrell Royal and Frank Broyles.

> (Warren Stephens) played his first round of golf at Augusta when he was about 16 and his partner was Hootie Johnson. A year later, he played with Clifford Roberts. Talk about a bit of pressure.

"It was a lot of fun times," Carl said. "I remember Bear Bryant always wanted to be in the group with Mr. Stephens. He always seemed to want me to be his caddie too and read his putts. He was the high-stakes guy. He'd want to bet the high dollars."

Carl was 10 years older than Warren, but they became fast friends during the summers in Little Rock. Warren's parents divorced when he was 12, so he would come for extended visits, which meant getting to know Carl as more than just his dad's right-hand man.

While Jack Stephens was at work, Warren and Jackson hung out at the house, played a little basketball or headed to the golf course. The age difference didn't matter.

Today, Warren remains in awe of Carl's knowledge at Augusta and of golf. When he built The Alotian Club west of Little Rock, Warren snapped up Carl as his caddie master.

The club's name? It came from a series of trips Warren took with his friends. They played some of the best courses in the country and called it American Lights-Out Tour. They were, of course, "Alotians."

Those summers with Carl were relaxed and fun. He and Carl were, Warren said, friends first. At the time, little did Warren know that those golf lessons his father had gotten him and the subtleties Carl was showing him would help golf become the backdrop of his life.

They usually teed it up at a Rebsamen Golf Course, a nice little public course in Little Rock. Warren doesn't remember who won, just fun times.

But basketball? Those games came on the driveway and, since the goal was above the garage door, a lot of bumps and bruises.

"We kind of kept a running total on basketball and my recollection was it was about even," Warren said. "That's funny because Carl is about 6-5 and I'm 5-10 and there wasn't such a thing as a 3-point shot. I wish there had been because then I would have killed him.

"I kept having to go farther and farther out away from the basket just to get it over his damn long arms. It was unbelievable how long his arms were. I actually became a pretty good shot because of that."

He played his first round of golf at Augusta when he was about 16 and his partner was Hootie Johnson. A year later, he played with Clifford Roberts. Talk about a bit of pressure.

> "I think Carl brought out the best in Ben's game at the Masters," Tiger Woods said.

A lot of the rhythm of staying at Augusta, as Warren put it, was leisurely. At the cabin, you didn't really get up early. And when you did, you had a little breakfast, then went out to play the Par 3 course. A spot of lunch in the men's grill and then it was time to tee it up on the big course.

One day, Carl and Warren, who was about 18, were standing there on the first tee at the Par 3 course – the old first tee because two holes over the pond weren't built yet. It was a sunny day and the sky was dotted with just a few clouds.

"Warren, when Mr. Roberts comes through that hedge he's going to look up," Carl said, looking toward the sky, "and he's going to say, 'Ummmff. Looks like rain.' "

Warren shook his head. "Get out of here. He's not going to say that."

Oh, he did. Roberts came through the hedge – the one that once shielded the Par 3 course from the cabins and road, the one Jack Stephens cut down to improve a pretty view – and said exactly what Carl said he'd say.

"And I'm over there – thank goodness Carl is 6-5 – trying to get behind Carl because I'm about to break out laughing," Warren said. "I didn't obviously want to do that. Nobody knew it but Carl because I was back there shaking behind him."

Decades later, Warren and Carl found themselves back together, this time at Alotian and in the stands at Episcopal Collegiate football games where they were cheering on their sons – running back Jason Jackson and running back/linebacker John Stephens. Jason went to SMU and eventually earned a football scholarship as a walk-on; John went to Penn.

Jason Jackson, Carl's son, played football for SMU.

For a year in the '80s, Carl not only worked for Stephens, but he also ran his own concert promotion company – Gateway Promotions. He put together one big show – April in Arkansas: Red, White and Blues – starring Bobby Blue Bland and B.B. King. The event was successful, but, after that, Carl stuck with one job – working for Stephens.

Carl really was a right-hand man and found the job gave him a bit of influence When he and Stephens came around the minority communities in Little Rock, people called them Jack and Black Jack.

"It was out of respect that I carried a big stick in a certain part of town as far as getting things done," Carl said. "I got involved a little in politics. I gave a little insight to the black politicians in town."

At Augusta National, his other partnership was even more respected. But there they were, just Ben and Carl.

No matter what Carl's role with Jack Stephens or his company, every April, Carl headed to Augusta to caddie for Ben. They were a strong team for their first eight years together, Masters royalty after that first Green Jacket in 1984.

Sure, the players watched them and tried to pick things up, but the patrons were watching too. They spoke their own language when they were on the course – an informal shorthand that often didn't need more than a nod, a finger point or a headshake to explain more than their playing partners could in a five-minute conversation.

"I think Carl brought out the best in Ben's game at the Masters," Tiger Woods said. "He not only won twice, but he was in contention a lot. Ben really knew how to play the course and putt those greens.

"I saw Ben play for years, and I can't remember him ever asking another caddie for reads. Ben really trusted Carl's eyes."

And Carl trusted Ben's instincts.

Always.

Well, almost always.

* * * *

For about 20 years there – give or take a few – Ben knew he was going to make a handful of 15- to 20-foot putts every time he teed it up at Augusta National. The only real question for the week was how he was going to play the rest of the holes.

Those 20-footers were like free throws. Automatic. Took the pressure off him and put it on whoever else was on the leader board.

"I made lots and lots of putts every day," he said. "That's a comforting feeling. It was just like clockwork. I knew I could

*Augusta National's incomparable greens helped bring out the best in **Ben's** exquisite putting stroke.*

rely on that. And you have no idea what that does to your long game just to have enough belief in your putting . . ."

And who didn't believe in Ben's putting stroke? All you had to do was look at his hands and feel the tempo. It wasn't just good.

At Augusta, it was lyrical; his feel for the greens was all but spiritual.

Starting in 1976, Ben was a short-lister at every Masters for the next 20 years. A very few could play it as well or better when everything was clicking. Everyone on the planet knew he was going to be in contention.

> (On the broken putter shaft) … "It sounds crazy, but putting is all about feel," Ben said. "It's ridiculous, but I've never been able to get that feel back."

He didn't just know it, he believed it.

That first runner-up finish in 1976 had been just a hint of things to come. The tie for second in 1983 followed by the win in '84 made believers out of just about everyone.

Most folks just couldn't forget that eye-popping 60-footer at the 10th hole Sunday afternoon. It was too good of a story. Ben with his $15 putter, Little Ben, heading into Amen Corner with the lead.

Now Little Ben was already a legend. The old Wilson 8802 bore some serious scars from back in the day when you never knew what he'd take out or how high he'd fly into a tree. Ben had found hiding on a display rack at Muny one day and loved the feel.

Ben had his first taste of national competition behind him and he was looking to improve his game and his equipment. Big Charlie agreed and brought the putter home one night.

Over the years, Little Ben has been abducted twice – the first time was during bag transfers on a Delta flight, the second from his car parked in his driveway – benched, bent, kicked and, well, downright beaten up. Doesn't look worth a darn – barely did back then – but it was all about the feel. Little Ben was the club he leaned on.

Dave Marr used to tease Ben that he was going to have him written up for child abuse. "You're always chastising Little Ben," he'd say. "You have treated him so poorly."

The spike mark on the flange – yes, Ben stepped on him – used to serve as a guideline for long downhill putts. He filed him down one day, too, to dull the shine. The ragged, exposed edges just made him look all the more ragged.

Despite the repeated abuse, Little Ben only had two shafts from the time Ben picked him up until he walked off the sixth hole at Muirfield Village during his singles match against Eamonn Darcy at the 1987 Ryder Cup. Ben had three-putted and that just summed things up. Nothing had gone right.

He was holding Little Ben by the head instead of the shaft and, in a fit of frustration, he hit a buckeye laying on the ground. The putter hit it just right and the shaft snapped in two.

"Oh my God," Ben thought, "what a time for this to happen."

He hit it out of bounds off the tee at the seventh hole, then hit into a bunker and he conceded the hole before they ever reached the green. He was 3 down when walked to the eighth tee, where captain Jack Nicklaus asked him how it was going.

OK, Ben mumbled. "But I broke my putter back there."

Nicklaus just stared at him: "You did what?"

Ben hung his head like an 8-year-old who was in trouble for breaking a window with a wild swing. "I broke my putter."

Jack just shook his head. "Well, the way things are going, I don't blame you. Just do the best you can."

It wasn't the first time Ben's temper had gotten the best of him, rather the most recent. He was still hobbling on the toe he smashed against the oil drum at the 1980 Colonial.

Roger Cleveland designed a "replica" of Ben's 8802. This was Scotty's putter that Ben used in winning the 1995 Masters.

This time, Ben got a bit lucky. He didn't even have to putt on the eighth hole. Surprisingly, Darcy conceded a 5-foot par putt. The rest of the way Ben either used his sand wedge or 1-iron on the green, depending on the situation. Ben fought his way to a 1-up lead, but lost the 16th and 17th that eventually gave Darcy a 1-up win. On 18, Ben drove it into the stream left of the fairway.

Ironically, Darcy never knew what happened. At the 1988 British Open, Darcy said he thought Ben was using different clubs to counteract the speed on the greens.

"No, Eamonn," Ben said, "I'm not that good."

Little Ben's original shaft snapped the year after Ben got him. The re-shaft and re-grip lasted until that sixth hole. After the Ryder Cup, he even tried taking the snapped shaft to Austin jeweler Phil Shaw, who soldered the shaft together with a tiny band and replaced the old leather grip with a paddle grip. Ben used it to finish fifth at the '87 Tour Championship at Oak Hill.

But change was coming. At the 1987 U.S. Open at the Olympic Club, then USGA Executive Director Frank Hannigan gave Ben a heads-up that paddle grips would be banned starting in 1988. So Ben had Little Ben re-gripped.

Since '87, Ben has had the old 8802 re-shafted a couple dozen times, but he's never been the same. Neither has Ben's putting. The proof is in the numbers. That old dented, banged-up, abused club was in the bag for 17 of Ben's 19 wins.

After three-putting the sixth hole in his singles match with Eamonn Darcy at the 1987 Ryder Cup, Ben broke his putter in frustration and had to putt the rest of the way with his 1-iron (shown here) or his sand wedge. He lost to Darcy 1 up.

"It sounds crazy, but putting is all about feel," Ben said. "It's ridiculous, but I've never been able to get that feel back."

Three weeks before the 1995 Masters, Ben was making his way through the putters in a corner of Scotty's office. Scotty was always finding something to add his stash – a Ben Crenshaw designed Cleveland putter, another old 8802, anything vintage or Crenshaw – and Ben never walked into the office without throwing down some golf balls and fiddling with the latest additions.

This time, he picked up a black 8802 and went to work on the carpet. He was messing with Scotty's Cleveland Classic 8802 clone, too. Scotty told him to take them.

> 1985 was a year that for Ben was best defined by one word – life. ... He married Julie Forrest ... teamed with Bill Coore (to design golf courses) and Scotty became his business manager.

He did. All the way to Augusta, where the evening before the Masters, he lined up all three putters – Little Ben, Scotty's putter and the black 8802 – and practiced a little. It had been a long day. He and Kite were up before dawn to fly back to Austin for Harvey's funeral and they'd just returned, with Scotty joining them on the flight back to Augusta.

When Ben went with Sayers' putter and had two good rounds to start the Tournament, Julie immediately nicknamed it Little Scotty. Looking back, it was one of the pieces of that mystical week at Augusta. But hang on. More on that – as well as a 45-foot lag putt and some improbable Sunday birdies – a bit later.

As Ben was coming down the stretch in 1984, he was battling not just the course, but his history at the Masters at majors, period. He'd been close so often and he knew everyone in the game was pulling for him to win.

"If there was one thing going through my mind out there," he said after winning his Green Jacket, "it was how I didn't want to let everybody down again."

He didn't. But that 60-footer on the 10th hole, those decisions, those shots, didn't just put Ben in the major club. It raised everyone's expectations that there would be many more.

Ben thought there might be, but he knew how long it took to get that first one and golf wasn't going to make his second any easier. In fact, he was prescient after the win. "Golf is the hardest game in the world to play well," he said. "And as soon as you start thinking you're somebody special, it'll teach you a lesson."

Maybe a bunch of them.

So few come within the back nine of defending at Augusta National and Ben wasn't one of them.

Scotty and Brent both made their first trips in 1985 and they started the tradition of playing basketball at their rental house. Nothing serious, mind you. Just shooting baskets or playing HORSE to pass the time.

It wasn't a horrible year for Ben and Carl, just a get-it-done kind of year. They tied for 57th and nothing really stood out. At least not on the course.

As it would turn out, 1985 was a year that for Ben was best defined by one word – life.

The year threw Ben a serious health curve. At the same time, it brought him three more lifelong partnerships. He married Julie Forrest in November, teamed with Bill Coore to form a golf course design company, and Scotty became his business manager and later took over as his agent as well.

The divorce from Polly, followed by the win at Augusta, had taken a toll. In 1985, Ben was run down, tired. At first it didn't seem out of the ordinary and his friends and family chalked it up to stress. But the longer it went on, the more weight Ben lost from his already slender frame, the more concerned everyone became. And the more rumors flew.

He was missing more cuts than he made and he followed an opening 70 at the Masters with 76-77-79. He fell to 149th on the money list, making just under $26,000 for the year.

"The stress of the divorce and everything . . . it was ughhh," Ben said. "I felt run down, I lost weight and I was shaking all the time. I felt weak.

"It was the little shots that became the hardest. And that gave me even more stress."

Ben finally went to the doctors and he was diagnosed with Graves disease in December 1985. He had a tremendously overactive thyroid and there were three options – surgery, radiation or drinking radioactive iodine. He chose to drink radioactive iodine.

"They gave me something temporarily," he said. "I don't think it's a medication I could pass the test with today."

When Ben started the medication, doctors told him he'd start feeling like himself in a few months, and Julie made sure he stayed on track. By spring 1986, he was. He finished tied for 16th at the Masters and then, after sharing the lead with nine holes to go, he finished tied for sixth at the U.S. Open at Shinnecock Hills. The Open was exactly six weeks after he drank the iodine.

"He was a new man," Julie said. "I remember (the tie for 6th) felt like he had won a major. He was able to compete and he was back to being his old self physically."

Later that summer, he won the Buick Open.

Although he will be on synthetic thyroid for the rest of his life and has to be checked every six months, Ben has never felt better. And, in the fall of 2012, his numbers were the best they'd been.

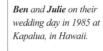

Ben and Julie on their wedding day in 1985 at Kapalua, in Hawaii.

* * * *

Romance was the last thing Ben had on his mind in 1984. His marriage was crumbling and he wasn't ready to think about a relationship. Until he met Julie.

They met at Riviera Country

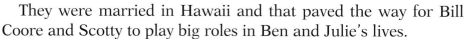

Top, **"The Boys,"** the Coore-Crenshaw construction team. Above, **Bill Coore** and **Ben** plot a course routing.

Club – on the 12th hole – but didn't have their first date for more than a month. The divorce was in motion and they dated long distance. Julie was in Los Angeles, then moved to Dallas to work for American Airlines.

In November 1985, they were married at the Kapalua International.

Julie didn't know anything about golf when they started dating. In fact, she watched him hit a couple of good shots and saw a birdie lip out. All she said was, "Lucky for you."

And when she learned he'd won the Masters? "Isn't that nice?"

Ben laughs now, but at the time he was shaking his head. It didn't take long for Julie to learn the game and jump into life on the road. Although friends were surprised about the relationship at first, Julie won them over when they saw how much in love they were.

"Marrying Julie," Ben said, "is the best decision I ever made."

They were married in Hawaii and that paved the way for Bill Coore and Scotty to play big roles in Ben and Julie's lives.

Scotty had been one of Ben's close friends since those elementary school days at Casis and it was natural for him to step into his role as manager/agent for Ben. They grew up in the same neighborhood, played Little League together starting at 10 and today they still live just a few blocks away from each other. Scotty knew golf, had the long history with Ben, and so working together made sense. He also signed on as the business manager/business development officer for Coore & Crenshaw, making it all a sort of family affair.

When Ben saw Rockport Country Club for the first time he saw

One of **Ben's** and partner **Bill Coore's** first projects was the **Kapalua Plantation Course** in Hawaii. It opened in 1991.

a touch of naturalness to the layout. It was interesting and well thought out. Canadian designer Rod Whitman, who worked with Pete Dye, suggested Ben meet the architect – Bill Coore, who was working with Pete's brother Roy at the time.

Ben had been thinking about designing for a while now. More and more players were jumping into course design and he'd been

> And when he did partner with [Bill] Coore, Ben knew it wouldn't be a distraction. He was right. He kept playing and winning. In fact, nine of his 19 Tour wins came between 1986 and 1995.

enthralled with it ever since he picked up Charlie Price's book.

"Jack (Nicklaus) had a big influence on me," Ben said. "I was fascinated he was getting into it. I enjoyed reading about it and seeing where they were working and what they did. I talked some to Jack and talked some to Arnold.

"But also, over the course of time and at different intervals, I would see Herb (Wind) and he would reinforce it. He told me, 'Someday you'll build courses.' "

Coore was starting to make a name for himself – he designed Rockport Country Club in concert with three-time Masters winner Jimmy Demaret – and he had his own little crew. He wasn't the least bit interested in a partnership, but Ben knew that he would need a partner to pursue designing.

Sand Hills Golf Club, in remote Mullen, Neb., opened in 1995 to rave reviews.

As fate would have it – and isn't that the story of Ben's life too – a potential client called both Ben and Coore separately to ask them to look at a piece of land for a project. Neither one of them got the job. In fact, the project never went forward.

But it did get Ben and Coore face to face and, a few months later, they formed a partnership. "I think Bill just said, 'This might work.' "

Houston Country Club thought so. The members hired Coore & Crenshaw to redo all 18 greens and Prairie Dunes members had them redo the first two greens at the Hutchinson, Kan., course. Their first two full designs were Barton Creek and Kapalua's Plantation Course in 1991, and they were followed by Sand Hills Golf Club in Mullen, Neb. They've now completed 24 new courses, including Friar's Head (Baiting Hollow, N.Y.), Bandon Trails (Oregon) and Austin Golf Club.

Their recent renovation of Pinehurst's No. 2 has gotten rave reviews and will get two major tests in 2014 when the course hosts the U.S. Open and U.S. Women's Open in back-to-back weeks.

"Bill's been a blessing," Ben said. "We've had occasional differences, but never anything cross. He's a very talented individual who can assess a piece of land very quickly.

"He's a master router. He can look at a topographic map and after we walk the property, he'll go back and study the map and he can lay out the directions of holes and how they fit together so fast it's incredible."

A shot here or there, a little more magic and Ben could have been wearing the Green Jacket again in 1987, 1988 or 1989. ... He tied for fourth in 1987, missing the playoff by a shot. He was fourth in 1988 and third – again a shot away from the playoff – in 1989.

Ben's job is shaping and playability. He looks at the contours, the greens and the bunkers so they fit proportionally.

"It's like (the partnership) with Carl," Ben said. "We just do it together."

Big Charlie and some of Ben's friends weren't too keen on his partnership with Coore. They were concerned that designing courses would be a distraction to his playing career, that he wouldn't be able to balance the two.

At the time, Big Charlie seemed to have a point. Ben's career had been a roller-coaster ride. And now he was adding something else to the mix?

Ben listened to what they had to say, but his mind was made up. It had been probably as far back at that first trip to Brookline when everything he had studied in books came alive. He just didn't know it.

That week in Boston was the moment when doglegs became natural routes across the property and bunkers went from minor annoyances to a window into the character of the architect and his design. It was the moment when Ben realized golf was more than just a game. It was becoming a passion.

It would be almost two decades until Ben took his first look at a pristine piece of land and saw a golf course taking shape in his mind, but the idea of designing – the dream of creating something – was there. Even at 16.

And when he did partner with Coore, Ben knew it wouldn't be a distraction. He was right. He kept playing and winning. In fact, nine of his 19 Tour wins came between 1986 and 1995.

"I respected their opinions," he said. "Whether or not I would have been a better player? Maybe so . . .

"But so far as being more balanced with my passions? I get so much out of architecture. It's something I can do for a long while. Longer than my playing career."

*   *   *   *

Bobby Jones always said it's never the caddie's fault. Never.

The player has the final word. He takes his caddie's thoughts into consideration, but ultimately, it's what he sees. He pulls the club. He hits the shot.

He makes the mistakes.

"If I needed advice from my caddie," Jones said, "he'd be hitting the shots and I'd be carrying the bag."

Yes, caddies make mistakes. Just think about that day at the 1983 Masters when most of them showed up late for tee times Sunday morning after that rain delay. Or dozens of other times when a caddie left an extra club in the bag or stepped in a line or gave a player a bad piece of advice.

"A caddie can make a dumb mistake and get chastised for it," Ben said, "but the player is the final arbiter."

But that doesn't stop Carl from kicking himself. To this day he hangs his head when he starts talking about the 1989 Masters. He tries to put it into perspective, he tries not to blame himself, but it never works.

If only he had checked the bag one more time. If only he hadn't left the bag to grab a bite to eat. If only …

Ben shakes his head.

"It was nobody's fault."

It was just another promising Masters week that wound up belonging to someone else.

As Carl would say, they came mighty close.

Three years in a row.

Three years, in fact, when they were in the final pairing on Sunday – all of them with a serious chance to win.

A shot here or there, a little more magic and Ben could have been wearing the Green Jacket again in 1987, 1988 or 1989. Maybe all three of them.

He tied for fourth in 1987, missing the playoff by a shot. He was fourth in 1988 and third – again a shot away from the playoff – in 1989.

"When you get that close to a major again and … ," Ben said, trailing off. "Well, it's really frustrating. Those were three really nice chances. You feel you put yourself into position and . . .

"Everyone who plays in a major championship wants to put themselves in striking distance and I did. I just didn't get it done."

Ben had the win in '84 and five other top-5s from 1983-91 and was hardly alone in his frustration. Both Seve Ballesteros and Greg Norman had incredible runs of close calls in the '80s, too. They both lost that playoff to Larry Mize in 1987, then Norman, along with Ben, bogeyed the 72nd hole to miss making the 1989 playoff between Faldo and Scott Hoch. Ballesteros had those two wins (1980, 1983) and five top-5s in seven Masters from 1980-89;

Norman had four straight top-5s from 1986-89, starting with 1986, when he shared second with Tom Kite.

Ben and Norman never discussed it. "It's the kind of thing you don't talk about," Ben said. "As players we're definitely aware of position and performances. Greg's record there goes into Tom Weiskopf territory. Tom finished second four times, Greg three times. They're both great players who could have and should have won the Masters."

> "There was never a day when I felt so wet," Ben said [about Sunday at the '89 Masters]. "You were grabbing everything. I even took my shirttail out. I thought the club was going to come out of my hands."

Larry Gatlin calls the Masters his spiritual spring cleaning. It's a chance to talk a bit and watch a lot of friends play a little golf, a gorgeous place where he feels God's hand. "I walk, pray, and I do it every year," he said. "It's a hallowed, spiritual piece of God's ground. If it's not spiritual, don't come."

But with that comes the gut twisting that goes along with watching friends like Ben come oh so close way too many times. Gatlin was there to celebrate both wins and commiserate during those close calls.

"You felt it because you know how he felt about Mr. Jones and how he felt – and still does – about the Tournament," Larry said. "Plus, back then, the golf course suited his game so perfectly. He's a right-to-left player and it's a right-to-left golf course.

Part of the "Team Crenshaw" brain trust (from left) **Knox Fitzpatrick**, **Ben**, **Larry Gatlin**, **Scotty Sayers** *and* **Mickey Holden** *at Augusta.*

"The only left-to-right dogleg is 18. The course fit his game and fit his eye. Spiritually, psychologically, mentally and emotionally, it fit him. He could go shoot 65 because the hole looked as big as a trash can."

But he could also come up just this short.

After winning twice on Tour in 1986, Ben opened 1987 with five top-6 finishes in his first eight events, one of them a playoff loss to T.C. Chen at Riviera. Then, three weeks before the Masters, he won the USF&G Classic in New Orleans.

That year, Augusta National played extremely hard. Ben opened with a 75 and was six shots behind leader John Cook, but rounds of 70 and 67 put Ben in the lead Saturday night. He struggled in the final round, but had a share of the lead standing on the 17th tee. He had just tapped in his ninth par in a row and was looking to make something happen. He hit a perfect drive, but he and Carl differed on the club for his approach shot.

Carl thought Ben should hit a wedge, but it was one of the rare times when Ben disagreed. He was thinking a little 9-iron and a birdie.

"For some reason, we just saw that shot differently," Ben said. "Obviously, in retrospect, he was correct. But it wasn't cross. We just disagreed.

" . . . It was one of those shots that was right in between clubs and you cannot put the ball past the cup with the pin on the right side. You just can't. I hit a pretty good shot, but I pulled it just slightly. It went just off the apron where the grass was sticky and I was chipping downhill.

"I took three to get down; that was a bogey. I'm sure in Carl's mind, he wanted me to hit the wedge, because you're going to be short of the cup and putting uphill. That made eminent sense."

Despite the bogey, Ben still had a chance to make the playoff, but the 15-foot birdie at 18 didn't fall.

Late that afternoon, he was in the interview room watching the playoff. Ballesteros had been eliminated on the first hole of sudden death and Ben watched him walk back up the hill.

Seve didn't come directly to the press building. He was so mad, he went straight to the Champions Locker Room, leaving Ben with a room full of reporters.

Together the reporters and Ben watched Mize make a preposterous shot of his own – a 140-foot chip-and-run – on the second playoff hole to beat Norman.

"I've told many people, if I'd listened to Carl (at 17), I might have been in that playoff."

Ben got off to another strong start at the beginning of 1988, winning the Doral Ryder Open in March and collecting four other top 11s. Ben and Carl were four back going into the weekend and, after a third-round 67, they were two back going into the final round and in the final pairing.

Again, it wasn't their day. Instead, they had a front-row seat for two of the best shots Sandy Lyle ever hit. While most point to Lyle's incredible bunker shot at the 18th that day, Ben's mind goes to

Larry Mize celebrates after he chipped in for birdie from 140 feet on the second playoff hole (No. 11) in the 1987 Masters. *Ben* missed making the playoff by a shot.

Lyle's incredible second shot at the fourth.

It wasn't just good. It was one of the best shots Ben has ever seen.

The flagstick was back-left and Lyle hit a 1-iron over the green, close to where the old water fountain used to sit by the fifth tee. He pulled a sand wedge, hit it short of the green and watched it trickle onto the collar, then the green and disappear.

Ben was one shot behind Lyle before that miracle chip and it took him until the 15th hole to close the gap and get back within one again.

"It was," Ben said, "the most beautiful shot you ever saw. He saved at least two shots there. Conservatively.

"He was brute-strong back then. Those were the days he could hit a 1-iron 260 yards or more. He was obviously playing some of the best golf of his career too."

He was also getting a bit of good fortune that week, too.

Ben wasn't. He would follow that 67 with a lackluster even par and even when he did get within one down the stretch, nothing fell. Instead of putting pressure on Lyle, Ben had to settle for pars on the last three holes.

"A 72," he said, "is not what you want in the final round when you're in contention."

Lyle, meanwhile, was in control. He hit a 1-iron off the tee at 18 and pulled it just enough that it rolled into the first bunker. Lyle wasn't sure he could get it to the green. He had to finesse and power his approach shot, and he needed to make birdie to win.

He took the 7-iron and flipped it up

Disappointment in three consecutive years, top, 1987, below 1988, and right, 1989.

into the air. He barely took any sand, just picked the ball off the surface and watched it roll down 10 feet from the hole.

"I said, 'God Carl, look at this shot,' " Ben said. "It was unbelievable. It was well played. He deserved it."

Lyle became the first player since Gary Player in 1978 to birdie the 18th for the win.

Ben was disappointed. He knew he was right there and so capable of winning again.

"I just didn't do the right things," he said, "at the right times."

Team Crenshaw was grilling hamburgers at their rental house during the 1989 Masters when some guests came up the driveway. It was 9-year-old Augusta native Charles Howell III and his parents. They wanted to meet one of Charles' heroes and Ben was glad to oblige. After all, he remembered being 10 and looking up to the older players in Austin.

Ben was, once again, in the mix heading into Masters weekend. He was two shots behind co-second-round leaders Faldo and Lee Trevino. He was playing so well that by the time the sky fell in on Saturday afternoon and play was suspended, Ben had a four-shot lead over Faldo, Hoch, Mike Reid and Norman, who had actually completed his round. Ben was on 14.

Ben and Seve persevered through some difficult rainy conditions Saturday at the 1989 Masters.

"When they shut down play (rain and darkness) Saturday . . . I just wish we could have finished," Ben said. "I had a great rhythm.

"It's hard to start and stop. Hard to switch gears because you have to find that feel again. How hard? You have to search for it every day."

The showers stopped Sunday morning, giving Ben an opportunity to add to his lead. But after missing birdie putts at 14 and 15, he bogeyed 18.

By the time the field finished the third round, Ben had given back three shots and led Hoch and Reid by just one, Seve by three, Norman by four and Faldo by five.

The weather turned nasty again and when the leaders teed off in the afternoon, it was miserable. One minute it was raining hard, the next it was a trickle. You could see rain streaming off the television towers and play was slow – snails-pace slow. And at one point a half dozen different players led or shared the lead.

This time, it wasn't one shot or one decision that stood between Crenshaw and a second jacket. It was towels.

Carl still hasn't totally forgiven himself for that Masters. Towels were his job. Especially on a rainy day. But, as with everything else at Augusta, sometimes things just don't unfold the way you planned.

The rain made it all but impossible to hold a club, so Carl knew he would need extra towels. Instead of grabbing from the pile of standard towels, he went back into the locker room and got some really big, thick good towels for the final round. He put them in the bag and went to have lunch.

Carl swears someone saw him put the better towels in the bag and took them while he was at lunch. He never looked again until the round was underway and he reached for a towel. They were gone.

[After the 1989 Masters], Ben and Scotty were sitting in a Popeyes, waiting for their takeout order and watching the rain come down. … It wasn't a night to even try to put another disappointing loss into perspective. That would come with time. So would another chance.

"There was never a day when I felt so wet," Ben said. "You were grabbing everything. I even took my shirttail out. I thought the club was going to come out of my hands."

Carl kept digging in the bag, hoping he just misplaced at least one towel. Outside the ropes, Julie, Scotty and friend Martin Davis were feeling helpless. They could see what was happening, but weren't sure if they could give him a towel or not.

"We thought it would be a rules violation if he got help from outside the ropes," Scotty said. "We also figured if it were legal, the Club would have had towels at the tee box. It turned out the Club had put towels on the tees, but the supply had run out by the time the final groups came through."

Ben wasn't sure about the rule either. Could he ask Hoch to borrow a towel? He didn't ask until the 18th tee, when Hoch said he didn't think so. It turned he could have borrowed one.

He and Carl just pressed on, wringing out sweaters and shirts and hanging the one towel they had inside the umbrella.

Ben sighed. They had all been at tournaments where volunteers brought towels out to players during inclement weather, but not at this one.

Despite rain, Ben hit a 5-iron to seven feet at the 16th. The rain was coming down hard enough that water was dripping off his visor, so he threw it down and rolled in the first of two of the prettiest back-to-back birdie putts you'll see.

At 17, he skied his tee shot a bit and hit the Eisenhower Tree. Ironically, Hoch hit a tree too – on the other side of the fairway. Ben managed to get his 4-wood approach on the green, where he had a 40-footer for birdie and a share of the lead. The ball fell in the hole on the last turn and he went to the 18th tee tied for the lead with Hoch and Faldo.

"How I played 17 was a miracle because I had no feel left," Ben said. "We were both so wet. There wasn't a dry part on Carl, wasn't a dry part on me."

Up ahead, Norman had bogeyed the 18th, so one of three leaders was going to put on the jacket.

"Nick Faldo had a new putter going into the last day and he made one 100 feet long on the second hole," Ben said. "He putted beautifully that day and shot 65. It was well done."

Faldo's putt was the longest putt made in Masters history.

Norman closed with a 68, despite that bogey, for his fourth close call in as many Masters.

And Ben? After a perfect tee shot, his second shot was a solid 5-iron, but his right hand slipped off the club and the ball caught the front left bunker. His third was *this* close to being perfect.

"I just didn't have enough room to stop the ball," he said. "It hydroplaned and skipped past the hole."

Then, the 12-foot par putt that had to go in to get him into the playoff ran past. He knew it wasn't a good putt. He started walking the second he hit it.

"I just couldn't gain a feel," Ben said. "I just rushed it, I guess."

Ben was still miffed when he came into the interview room.

"I was trying to get over what (his miss) was self-inflicted," he said. "It was just total frustration that I couldn't hold the club. It was a golden opportunity . . . "

As he sat there talking, he watched the playoff along with the writers. When Hoch stood over his 2-foot putt at the 10th hole, Ben blurted out: "Hit it."

"It looked like he took a little more time over his short putt; he took a lot of time," Ben said. "I was shocked when Scott missed that little putt."

To this day, Carl can't think about that Masters without kicking himself over the stolen towels, but the win in 1995 did ease the burden he was carrying.

Those three Masters defined Ben's career at Augusta just as much as the two wins did. In losing, he learned. In coming close so often, he hoped there was another one in him.

He thought back to what Nicklaus said to his caddie Willie Peterson after he bogeyed the 72nd hole in 1977 and lost a chance to win his fifth Green Jacket. "Geez, that was too bad Willie."

Ben had wanted to be in the Clubhouse that night in 1989, celebrating a second jacket. Instead, he and Scotty were sitting in a Popeyes, waiting for their takeout order and watching the rain come down.

"It was pretty darned depressing," Scotty said.

Ben shook his head. He was really down. Three chances. Three mighty close calls.

"I just don't know," he said, "if I'll ever have another chance like this to win another Masters."

It wasn't a night to even try to put another disappointing loss into perspective. That would come with time.

So would another chance.

CHAPTER 5

A SECOND MASTERS WIN – FOR HARVEY

"I was so emotional, I wouldn't have been surprised if there were tears in my eyes. It was one of those great moments in sports."
– CBS broadcaster Walter Cronkite, on Ben's 1995 Masters victory

The old caddie shack was tucked back away from the course, but not too far from the Quonset hut that served as a pressroom until 1990. The caddie building was a one big room set with card tables for those all-day games, an old pool table, a waist-high gas heater, and a deep fryer that was always bubbling with something.

Players and caddies gathered at the old green picnic tables and ate southern pork chops and fried chicken off simple white paper plates. No club silver, no sturdy white china ringed in green with the Augusta National logo in the center. It was the best meal on the property during Tournament week and the line was long and steady.

Horace Avery – Ironman and Big Henry's brother – started early in the morning, serving up breakfast, and cooked all day. The aromas and the noise drew folks over for a hearty meal and they stayed a bit to talk, too.

"You couldn't keep Tim Simpson out of there," Carl said. "Dave Stockton . . . all the guys dropped by."

Ben would stop by to eat and catch up on the caddie grapevine – who was caddying for which player, who was playing at what tournament.

Prices were cheap, but there was still a credit book for those hoping a good week would pay a few bills. Sometimes, caddies who were just flat out of money would show up and, after they'd had two or three meals, someone would ask who they were working for that week.

Horace wielded a mean deep fryer and, as everyone will tell you, he was a much better cook than he was a caddie. He was kinda mean and would snap at people. But that didn't stop them from lining up to pay $1.50 for a pork chop or $2 for a chicken sandwich.

The caddies got a new house in 1994 that had a full kitchen, lockers that could be shared and a wall of honor filled with pictures of some of those legendary characters from Augusta's caddie pen.

Harvey Penick had a profound influence on Ben. Harvey gave Ben one last putting lesson a week before he passed away.

Ben and Carl study a putt during the 1995 Masters. Ben defeated Davis Love III by one stroke for his second Green Jacket.

The Club transformed the 18 acres of the old gravel-and-grass parking lot for members, media and players that bordered Washington Road into a perfectly manicured practice range in 2010, with two dogleg fairways where players can carve shots around trees to prepare. With that construction came a brand new spacious caddie house with plenty of lockers and facilities for everyone and big screen TVs.

The food is good in the caddie house – it's what the Club serves in other places during Masters week – but it's just not the same to Carl and some others. Grabbing a yogurt for breakfast instead of one of Horace's chicken sandwiches just doesn't seem right.

The Augusta caddies were spoiled by the good, cheap food, so paying their own way when they went out on Tour could be an adventure.

One day Carl and Sampson Marshall were in Palm Springs and they walked across the street from their hotel for breakfast. Marshall ordered one fried egg between two slices of bread. They served it up all neat in a brown paper bag.

"That'll be $5.15," the waitress said.

"What much?" Marshall asked, shaking his head in disbelief.

Carl wasn't sure what was coming next. "He put his money back in his pocket," Carl said, "left the bag on the counter and said, 'Eat it your damn self.' "

During those mighty close years, Carl's life took more than a few twists and turns. In 1987, he married his third wife – Debra – and they had two children. Debra had two more children from a previous marriage and Carl had a son and a daughter from his first marriage.

It was a constant struggle for Carl, who tried to split his time between his family, his job with Jack Stephens and Debra's schedule as a school nurse.

"I was still traveling with Mr. Stephens and it got to the point where my wife wanted me home," Carl said. "What it came down to was if I was going to work like that, Debra needed to stay home.

"It was hard on her with the children at home. I needed either more time to be at home or needed more pay to have someone help her. It just got to where I became the problem."

Carl was catching it from both sides. Someone – either Stephens or Debra – was always unhappy with him. He just wanted the pressure off his shoulders.

Stephens called Carl into his office in March 1990 and they talked about the problem. Stephens had remarried too and Debra was reaching out to his wife. It was uncomfortable.

> During those mighty close years, Carl's life took more than a few twists and turns. In 1987, he married his third wife – Debra – and they had two children.

"I think he was trying to figure out what needs to be done here," Carl said. "It was causing me all kind of hell."

So, they parted ways and it wasn't easy. Although stories floated around that they did not speak for years, Carl and Stephens did visit at the Masters each year.

Carl had to contribute to the household income, so he went out on Tour for several weeks at a time, picking up a different bag every week. Carl even called Scotty's office to ask if Ben and Scotty knew of anyone who needed a caddie.

Starting in late 1985, Tony Navarro worked for Ben for about four years, which meant four wins – the Buick Open and Tour Championship in 1986, New Orleans in 1987 and Doral in 1988. Navarro, one of the elite caddies who also caddied for Greg Norman (1992-2004) and Adam Scott (2004-11), was good on the bag. But Ben was struggling with his game in 1989 and he was frustrated. After missing the cut at the 1989 U.S. Open at Oak Hill, he and Navarro split.

Ben used Rob Kay, who caddied for Payne Stewart early in his career for a bit. Kay was on the bag for one of Ben's best – and worst days – at Firestone. The night before the opening round, Ben slept wrong on his neck and woke up with a serious crick in it. It was so stiff, he couldn't even look down the fairway to watch his shots.

"It hurt so much," he said. "I played one-handed. At Firestone. All I could do was hit it with my right hand."

*Caddie **Tony Navarro**, seated, worked for **Ben** on the PGA Tour from 1985-89.*

He shot 64 and swore he must have gotten it up and down at least 11 times that day. "It was a miraculous round."

Ben always had trouble at Firestone, but that year, he wound up in a playoff with David Frost, who got it up and down from the rough on the second hole of sudden death for the win.

"Merely," Ben said with his tongue planted in his cheek, "one of my eight playoff losses."

But by the time Carl got on Tour, the caddie grapevine said Ben would be looking for a new man. Rob was getting married and changing careers.

"Next thing I knew, the Tour was in New Orleans and Ben asked would I go to work for him at Colonial," Carl said.

He did. They won.

Despite an ugly 71st hole.

Ben and Curtis Strange were tied going into the final round and Ben threw out a 30 on the front nine to separate himself from the field and closed with a 66 to beat Nick Price, Corey Pavin and John Mahaffey by three. It was Ben's 15th Tour victory, his first win since the 1988 Doral Ryder Open and his second win at the iconic Fort Worth course where Ben Hogan won five times. But it was far from easy.

On that 71st hole, Ben pushed his 1-iron right and into the creek, leading to a desperate bogey. "It was a windy day and I completely messed up 17," he said. "I somehow hit a really good shot into the green and . . . I could have made a double. Instead, I made a bogey."

"Ben was kind about it, but truth is Debra was giving me hell," Carl said. "She was bothering Ben too." So, Ben and Carl ended the Tour partnership. But not the friendship.

It also had everyone buzzing. Could having Carl on the bag be what Ben needed?

The partnership made all the sense in the world theoretically. Ben and Carl were so good together at the Masters and everyone assumed they would be a killer team on Tour, too.

They weren't.

Ben had just three top 10s after winning Colonial, missed four cuts and didn't make the top-30 field for the 1990 Tour Championship at Champions.

"Missed it by a few 100 spots," he chuckled.

Jackie Burke was of one Ben's most vocal cheerleaders. He wanted him in the field and tracked his progress all fall. Burke knew it would come down to a good tournament in San Antonio – the cut-off date to make the field – for Ben to get in.

"I had gone down to see Jackie three weeks before the tournament," Ben said. "He knew I was getting deeper and deeper and he said, 'Hey, let's back off that cliff so you can be here.' "

Didn't work. Ben went into the H.E.B. Texas Open 29th on the money list and needed a top-5 finish there to make the Tour Championship field. He never had a shot. He shot 73-70, missed the cut by three shots and wound up 33rd on the money list – $29,747 behind the 30th and final place.

Still, he drove down to Houston to watch the tournament to hang out with Burke and see Jodie Mudd beat Billy Mayfair.

"Champions was in great shape," Ben said. "It was playing really fast. I remember Jackie saying – as only Jackie can – 'the only birdies you're going to see out here are in the trees.' "

Ben and Carl finished the year with top 10s at two unofficial money events, but it wasn't enough.

Not only were the results mediocre, Debra was still on Carl

about finances. She didn't really understand that caddies' incomes were tied to the player's success. Obviously, Carl cashed a big check after Colonial, but the rest of the checks that year weren't close to that number.

"She wasn't used to the ups and downs," Carl said. "She'd say we've got these two babies and you have to do your part."

In frustration, she reached out to Julie just as she had reached out to Stephens' wife, and that caused even more friction.

"Ben was kind about it, but truth is Debra was giving me hell," Carl said. "She was bothering Ben too."

So, Ben and Carl ended the Tour partnership.

But not the friendship.

In 1991, Carl was out in the yard at the house in Little Rock when he saw smoke coming from the kitchen. Debra had left something on the stove and gone into the other room to fix Carlisa's hair.

"I ran into the kitchen and it was burning bad enough to get everyone out of the house," Carl said.

There wasn't much to salvage. They would have to start over again, and Debra had been offered a job at Parkland Hospital in Dallas – the hospital where they took President Kennedy and Gov. Connally after they were shot in 1963. The Jacksons decided to move.

Carl continued to work part-time on Tour, but the problems persisted. They needed either two incomes so Debra could have some help with the children or Carl would have to make enough on his own so she could stay home.

He worked for a number of players, including Jim Thorpe, Stiles Mitchell, Donnie Hammond, John Wilson, Sean Murphy, Mike Donald and Brad Fabel, who, he said, was one of the best ball strikers he ever saw. "He could hit all the shots," Carl said.

Jackie Burke won the Masters and the PGA Championship in 1956. Together with *Jimmy Demaret*, they founded, built and co-owned Champions Golf Club, which hosted the 1967 Ryder Cup, 1969 U.S. Open and five Tour Championships.

They were all nice guys to work for and he loved to caddy, but there just weren't many top 10s, let alone a win, and that cut into his take-home pay.

"If I stayed out two weeks it was too much (for Debra)," he said. "I was half-heartedly on the Tour just trying to keep same income level."

In 1992, the Jacksons watched another house burn. This time, one of the children was playing with matches. They had to rebuild again.

The two fires destroyed most all of Carl's family pictures and keepsakes. He didn't even have a photo of his mother until his brother found one in 2012 and shared it.

"It's just," Carl said, "a part of life."

No matter what happened, Carl was committed to family. He wanted all six of his children to get the opportunities he didn't. He was determined that all of them would go to college and they did.

And, he didn't want the cycle of the dysfunctional family he grew up in to continue, so he and Debra found ways to juggle their jobs and responsibilities. Much of the time, it meant Carl was at home with the kids.

Meanwhile, Ben and Julie were raising their family in a quiet cul de sac in Tarrytown, about a half dozen blocks away from the Bridle Path home where Ben grew up.

> Family only enhanced Ben's game and passion for design. He and Bill limited the number of courses they would work on to two a year so each one got the attention it needed.

Ben couldn't get enough of fatherhood. Their first daughter, Katherine, was born in 1987 and Claire followed in the spring of 1992. Anna Riley, their youngest, was born in 1998.

Family only enhanced Ben's game and passion for design. He and Bill limited the number of courses they would work on to two a year so each one got the attention it needed. It gave them time for their families too.

On the course, Ben fell to 75th on the money list in 1991, but won once a year for the next four years.

Ironically, Ben's best finish in '91 was a share of third at the Masters. He eagled 15 on the final day to close within two of the lead, but parred the last three holes to tie Lanny Wadkins and Steve Pate, two shots behind winner Ian Woosnam and one behind runner up Jose Maria Olazabal.

Ben finished 46th the following year and missed the cut in 1993. He bounced back in 1994, winning in New Orleans the week before the Masters, which gave him a bit of momentum. He tied for 18th at Augusta that year, 13 shots behind Olazabal.

Ben visited *Ben Hogan* and *introduced him to his firstborn, Katherine Vail.*

"There wasn't much happening for me," Ben said of the Masters. "It was a dearth of golf ability. I don't think there was any reason for it. I couldn't get back into the area of contention in the Tournament."

Those so-so years never stopped him from thinking he could win there again. The Club had only tweaked a few things on the course at the time, and Ben knew if he had a good week, he had a darn good chance to not just contend, but win.

* * * *

Ben and Scotty and their families were having a quiet Sunday morning brunch at Cisco's in east Austin. The couples are close – they are godparents to each other's daughters. And, even though the Sayers girls – Samantha and Charisse – are a bit older than Katherine and Claire, they pretty much grew up together. So most Sundays when Ben was in town, the families would sit at the restaurant and talk about life and business.

Ben was on his way to New Orleans the next day to play his way to the Masters. Nothing much felt right. He tied for fifth at the Mercedes Championship and was third in Phoenix, but had missed the cut at Doral and THE PLAYERS Championship. In fact, he'd missed three cuts in his last five events and hadn't broken 70 in two months.

Maybe the worst stat of all was putting. Ben, always one of the best putters in the game, was ranked 69th. And if that wasn't enough, the big toe he smashed at Colonial was aching.

As they were finishing up, Ben said he was going to take the girls and go visit Harvey for a bit. They hadn't talked in a while and Harvey was struggling. He was frail. He had never quite recovered from a bout with pneumonia and was bedridden. That, coupled with the pain, was taking its toll.

Ben's Most Memorable Putts at Augusta

1. Birdie on #10 Sunday, 1984
Ben and Carl were hoping to two-putt, but Ben sank a 60-foot curling putt.

2. Two-putt par from front of #14 Friday, 1995
Carl called the first putt (45 feet) the hardest he's ever seen

3. Second putt (for par) on #14 Sunday, 1984
Ben had left his first putt 15 feet short and still on the upper shelf. Making the 15-foot putt gave him confidence to birdie #15 and seal the win.

4. Birdie putt on #17 Sunday, 1995
13-foot putt gave Ben a two-stroke cushion going to #18

5. Birdie putt on #16 Sunday, 1995
5-foot putt gave Ben a one-stroke lead

6. Birdie putt on #13 Sunday, 1995
20-foot birdie putt tied Ben for lead

7. Birdie putt on #17 Sunday, 1989
After Ben drove it into the Eisenhower Tree in the rain, he managed to get a 4-wood on the front of the green. His 40-foot birdie tied him for the lead.

8. Birdie putt on #12 Sunday, 1984
After bogey on #11, an unexpected birdie on #12 put Ben back into a tie for the lead.

9. Birdie putt on #15 Sunday, 1985
Birdie putt after laying up gave Ben three-stroke cushion

10. The next one

Harvey always offered his weathered hand to Ben – palm up – to shake and hold for a few minutes when they said hello as well as goodbye. This Sunday was no different.

"Harvey searched long and hard for his words and how and what to say to people," Ben said. "He would study the pupil once he held out his hand to shake it. He would study your countenance. Before the lesson began, he knew what kind of person you were."

As Harvey's wife Helen sat in the living room with Julie and played with Katherine and Claire, Ben and Harvey chatted about this and that, about how something was just a little off in Ben game.

Harvey knew what it was.

From his bed, he had watched Ben's weekly struggles and figured it out. A few days earlier, in fact, Austin Country Club member, pupil and friend Barbara Puett, who was one of the best female amateurs in the city, stopped by to visit and they talked about Ben.

"I need to get well," he told Puett, "so I can help Ben."

That Sunday afternoon, Harvey sent Ben to the garage to poke around for an old Gene Sarazen putter he kept in his bag, then watched Ben stroke a few imaginary putts next to Harvey's bed. Those hands had a magic to them anytime they gripped a putter – no pair of hands looked better.

He watched Ben swing and reminded him about feel. Harvey knew all Ben had to do was trust, and he reinforced that for about 30 minutes.

When Ben got up to leave, Harvey didn't hold out his hand. Instead, Ben put his hand on Harvey's and kissed him on the forehead.

"I love you Harvey," Ben said.

Harvey struggled to look up.

"I love you too, Ben."

The following Sunday night, Ben and Julie were in the Trophy Room at Augusta National, having dinner with Jack Stephens and Pat Summerall, when Club Maitre d' Arthur Williams handed Julie a note that said "Call Tom or Christy Kite."

She knew before she ever dialed Christy's number. She could feel it. Harvey was gone.

"I wasn't going to let Ben hear it on the phone," Julie said. "I called Christy and got the details, then I went in and pulled him aside.

"We went out on the porch and I told him. We stood there and

Club Maitre d' Arthur Williams handed Julie a note that said "Call Tom or Christy Kite." She knew before she ever dialed Christy's number. She could feel it. Harvey was gone.

cried. It was really bad for about 15 minutes, but then we regained our composure and went back in."

"I think all of us (who knew Harvey)," Ben said, "whenever we left Austin, we knew it could happen, and we hated the thought that we might be away."

It helped to have friends there who let Ben talk about how much Harvey had meant to his family and his game, how much he'd be missed. It may have helped, too, that he wasn't in Austin because he was away from the emotions there and was able to deal with his feelings by himself.

Everyone wondered how Ben and Tom would deal with Harvey's death. While they were making travel arrangements to Austin Wednesday morning to attend the funeral, those who knew them assumed Kite might be the one who handled it best; Ben, they thought, would get swept up in his emotions.

It was just the opposite.

Tom missed the cut. And Ben? He honored the man who guided his career with an unbelievable week and a Masters win from his heart.

Two of the greatest moments in Ben's life – his two Masters wins – began with emotional upheaval. There was the final decision to divorce Polly in the spring of 1984 and the pain of Harvey's passing in 1995.

Both life-changing events brought sadness, pain and relief; both grand moments were filled with tears of joy.

Ironically, they both came during Masters week.

Ben's emotions were in check Monday morning when he met Carl on the practice tee, but his game was still in shambles. Harvey's lesson, his reassurance to trust – and, as he always said, take dead aim – hadn't quite taken hold in Ben's mind. Something was still a little off with his swing.

It took Carl just a couple of swings to see that Ben was reaching at the ball. They played the first nine and as they were coming up the eighth hole, Carl knew he needed to get Ben off the course.

"I took my normal short cut and I look back and see him reaching

From left, **Tom Kite,** **Harvey Penick** *and* **Ben.**

for the ball again," Carl said. "I said out loud to myself 'Damn, it's like you're playing hockey back there.' "

When they got to the practice tee, Carl sat down on the ground and watched Ben hit balls for a couple hours. "If Ben swung wide he would have hit me on the knee," Carl said.

Carl knew how to fix the problems, but waited for the right time to make his suggestions.

It came the next morning.

Ben was hitting balls and Jackson said just two things – move the ball back a tad in your stance and tighten up your shoulder turn. Ben hit four balls and . . . that was all he needed.

Ben declared, as only a Texan can, that it was absolutely the best practice session he'd had in a long time. They'd known each other for so long and Carl saw a spark in those blue eyes, something he hadn't seen in a long, long while.

"Carl started the week off by crawling inside Harvey's body," Ben said. "That's the damn truth. He knew how poorly I'd played in New Orleans and understood what was going on. He was going to try to find a way to tell me.

"I don't know what my swing looked like. Probably like I was killing snakes."

The sun was just coming up when the private plane took off from Augusta's Daniel Field carrying Ben and Julie, Tom and Christy Kite, Chuck Cook and Terry Jastrow. They were headed to Austin to celebrate Harvey and lay him to rest.

Harvey had been watching the New Orleans tournament the afternoon he passed away and he was pulling hard for Davis Love III, who needed to win to get into the Masters field. Davis' father had been one of Harvey's pupils too, and that love extended to his son.

Ben and *Tom Kite* appropriately were pall-bearers at *Harvey Penick's* funeral just prior to the 1995 Masters.

Harvey was failing fast, but he hung on long enough to find out Davis won.

Davis was torn about flying to Austin. His dad died in a tragic plane crash in 1988 and he wanted to honor Harvey. Ben and Tom told him he needed to stay and practice.

Ben had played the first two rounds with Davis in New Orleans,

> (Ben) was trusting himself, his instincts and his heart. He was focusing. He knew he had a chance.

so Davis knew how badly Ben was playing and Ben knew Davis was at the top of his game.

"Ben told me, 'Look, you're playing great. You've got as much chance to win as anyone. You need to stay and practice,' " Davis said. "He was almost discounting his game. But what he told me … I knew that's what my dad would have told me to do, too.

"It was great that Ben went out of his way to ease my mind about my decision."

Austin was damp, dreary and gray, almost as if it, too, was mourning Harvey's loss. Ben, like everyone else, had been crying, but when his brother Charlie saw him at the chapel with the other pallbearers, he was surprised. There was a peace about his younger brother, a calmness that he didn't expect.

As they were leaving, Ben gave Big and Little Charlie big hugs and they saw the same spark in his eyes that Carl had seen the day before.

"I really think I'm onto something," Ben said, explaining what he and Carl had worked on.

When the limousine drove off, Charlie looked at Big Charlie. "I told Daddy, I don't think I've ever seen him with such conviction," Charlie said. "It's like he had new life in him."

Or maybe just a frail hand resting on his shoulder.

Ben and Tom got back to the course about 5:30 that afternoon and Davis was there waiting. He had just finished playing in the Par 3 Contest and wanted to know about the service.

He noticed that Tom was in a rush, while Ben seemed relaxed. He had those three putters – Little Ben, the black 8802 and Scotty's Cleveland Classic – with him and lined them up. He putted with each of them and talked over the pros and cons with Scotty.

"I figured he would practice with the others, then go back to Little Ben," Sayers said. "He always does."

Yet this time, he didn't.

Ben putted alone until the sun went down. He was interrupted only once. Tiger and U.S. Amateur runner up Trip Kuehne – in suits and ties – were walking around the grounds waiting for the Amateur Dinner to begin when they stopped by for a few minutes to visit.

Tiger asked Ben a few questions about putting. They talked about the contours of the greens and watched Ben putt a bit. Then they were off to the Clubhouse for the dinner.

It had been a long day and he was emotionally spent. Yet as he let the rhythm of his stroke take over, he lost himself in those marvelous greens, in those contours and slopes. He was trusting himself, his instincts and his heart. He was focusing.

The turning point that week came at the 14th hole on Friday. Ben had one of those scary-tough Augusta putts that moved every which way.

He knew he had a chance.

What he didn't know, but was beginning to feel, was that Harvey was there to guide him through one of the most mystical, magical Masters weeks in history.

"When you think about someone who meant so much to your life, you think about all the times and all the things he taught us – you try to absorb as much as you can," Ben said. "In a lot of ways, it was a very appropriate time for him to go. It was a week when he would be on everyone's mind."

Carl spent Wednesday at the course just visiting with friends and hanging out because he wasn't sure what to do. Even though he had seen the spark and was feeling good about this week, he wasn't sure how Ben would handle Harvey's service.

"I was just looking for anything, just to be in the feel of the

From left, **Phil Mickelson**, **Jose Maria Olazabal** *and* **David Frost** *jointly led the first round of the 1995 Masters.* **Ben** *was four strokes back.*

Masters," he said.

He was relieved and excited when he heard Ben had told his dad and brother that he and Carl had found something on the practice tee, that he was feeling good about his game.

The dreary rain moved east Thursday morning and settled on Augusta. It didn't bother Ben a bit. Neither did the fact that he was paired with 1991 British Open champ Ian Baker-Finch, who opened with a 79.

Ben benched Little Ben and put Scotty's putter in the bag. Something just felt right and the putts started to fall. After opening with rounds of 70-67, Julie nicknamed it "Little Scotty."

The decision paid off. Ben didn't three-putt once that week, a rare feat for anyone at Augusta.

Better yet, Ben was finding fairways.

"I was hitting a lot of shots with authority and making some putts," Ben said. "Nothing helps your confidence more than seeing yourself do what you're trying to do."

He bogeyed the first hole Thursday, but let it roll off his back. Again, there was a peace, a serenity and, most of all, an unwavering focus.

The only really hard moment came at the 13th hole, when Ben had to take a drop out of casual water. Baker-Finch's struggles had put them behind, but this delay caused rules officials to put them on the clock.

"When you get stopped like that, you don't have time to plead your case," Ben said. "You could say Ian was struggling, but it was impossible for them to know. They don't take that into account."

It was just another blip. Ben was playing the course. He was challenging Augusta National and she was pushing back.

Ben's opening 70 left him four shots behind Phil Mickelson, David Frost and Olazabal. Team Crenshaw celebrated that night with its annual barbecue. A couple dozen folks were there, including the eight other people staying in the five-bedroom rental house with Ben and Julie.

Ben was flying just under the radar. Jack Nicklaus had holed out for eagle, was one shot back after 18 holes and there were momentary thoughts of a seventh Green Jacket for the then 55-year-old. But the star was a young kid named Tiger Woods, who was making his Masters debut.

*Amateur **Tiger Woods**, playing in his first Masters, tied for 41st place with an aggregate score of 293 and received a Sterling Silver Cup as Low Amateur.*

The U.S. Amateur champ was something special and had everyone talking even before he opened with a 72. Only the fourth African-American to play in the event, he drew crowds with his length off the tee and his charisma.

That was all fine by Ben, whose focus was on the course, not who else was on the leader board or any wow factors. Plus, he was all talked out, so it was a relief to see other players in the media spotlight.

The turning point that week came at the 14th hole on Friday. Ben had one of those scary-tough Augusta putts that moved every which way. It was probably a three-putt, maybe four-putt if you really misread it – a 45-footer that had to skirt the crest diagonally and somehow stop near the hole.

Ben lagged it to 18 inches.

"It would take me 30 minutes to describe it," Ben said. "It was one of the hardest putts I ever had. It was diabolical. It could have gone wrong real easy."

But it didn't. Instead, it gave them the confidence they needed.

"That," Carl said shaking his head, "was the meanest putt I've ever seen."

Only those walking with him and friends who visited with Ben and Carl after the round even knew about it. Without today's expanded television coverage or a formal interview in the press building, it was just a number on a card and looked like just another two-putt par.

It was so much more.

Tiger had another solid round and quiet Jay Haas had thrown out a 64 to take the second-round lead. Ben was tied for fourth, two shots back. Tiger, Haas and Nicklaus, who had followed that opening 67 with a 78, got the headlines; Ben just focused.

It was still early, but Ben and Carl could feel something happening. Those little mistakes weren't piling up, they were being smoothed away. Nothing was bothering them.

"Ben was driving the ball," Carl said. "He was in a gear where everything was flowing with the driver. We've had times where he played good, then wham.

"But when you don't make a bogey on the back nine until the 72nd hole . . . that's focus."

Ben nodded.

"The most amazing thing is how we held our concentration the whole week," he said. "It was unspoken between us. We knew what had happened, but we had this thing that was positive and we were going to see how far we could take it."

*With **Ben** and **Brian** **Henninger** tied for the lead, five players were one stroke behind: (from left to top right) **Jay Haas**, **Fred** **Couples**, **Scott Hoch**, **Steve Elkington** and **Phil Mickelson**.*

*Prior to going to the Club for the final round of the 1995 Masters, **Ben** spent 40 solitary minutes on the driveway contemplating his round.*

They were playing their favorite golf course and their favorite tournament. Nothing else mattered.

"We were going to ride it out," Ben said.

When Ben shot 69 on Saturday, he left the course tied for the lead with Brian Henninger. Five players were a shot behind them – Mickelson, Haas, Steve Elkington, Scott Hoch and Fred Couples – and Strange, Norman and Love were lurking.

A reporter at the 18th green Saturday night asked Ben what it would mean if he could win this Masters for Harvey.

That Sunday, Harvey was on his mind too. Ben had the feeling he was with him. By late that afternoon, he was convinced his old friend and mentor was his 15th club.

"I'm trying *not* to think about it," Ben said quietly. "The simple truth is I'll carry Harvey in my heart until the day I die. He had such a profound influence on his players.

"… I think it was Kathy Whitworth who said he came close to being the perfect human being."

And the perfect teacher.

This one was tight and Harvey – not just his spirit but all those times he spent showing Ben how to be patient, prepared and take dead aim – were about to make the difference between another close call and another Green Jacket.

Team Crenshaw was giddy, but trying to keep everything in perspective. Yes, Ben and Carl had been in the final group in 1987, 1988 and 1989, too, and didn't win.

But this year? Something just felt different.

Maybe it was those bounces that kept going Ben's way. Julie called them "Harvey Bounces" and no one was arguing. Least of all, those who saw a certain bogey at the eighth hole Saturday take a miracle bounce out of a bunker. Or even that putt at 14 on Friday.

Whatever it was, whatever magic was happening, people weren't just seeing it. They were feeling it.

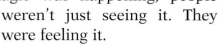

Charlie had missed the 1984 win and wasn't going to miss another. Julie had called him Saturday night and he took the first plane out Sunday morning. He wasn't missing this one.

Ben's Sunday tee time wasn't until 2:41 p.m., and when Charlie pulled into the rental house driveway, Team Crenshaw was having a pine-cone chipping contest. The first thing Charlie noticed was how calm his little brother was.

*The hardest thing about leading the Masters is the afternoon tee time on Sunday. Here, **Team Crenshaw** – left to right, **Charlie Crenshaw, Scotty** and **Julie Sayers**, **Julie** and **Pat Oles**, **Mary Beth Ryan** and **Ben** and **Julie** – pose for a shot after spending the morning chipping pine cones on the lawn.*

"He just looked at me with a smile and said, 'Let's go see what happens.' He just got in that zone."

They were all talking when suddenly Ben stopped in mid-sentence and walked down the driveway. He stood there alone for 40 minutes.

Ben thought about the day that was in front of him. He thought about Harvey. He allowed himself to be still and silent, to let that peace he'd been feeling all week wash over him.

"I said a silent prayer," he said, looking back on that day. "I prayed for strength, no matter what the outcome."

His voice cracked as he tried to finish the thought and he paused to wipe away the tears. Seventeen years later, his emotions were about to get the best of him again.

"I prayed to accept whatever the day would bring."

He struggled with the words, then excused himself and walked away to regain his composure. Ben had thought about that moment so many times over the years, but this was the first time in a very long while he allowed himself to feel it.

That Sunday, Harvey was on his mind too. Ben had the feeling he was with him. By late that afternoon, he was convinced his old friend and mentor was his 15th club.

And one more little thing. The spirit of Bobby Jones played a

*Brian Henninger entered the final round tied for the lead with **Ben**. Henninger shot 76 and finished eight strokes back, in a tie for 10th place.*

cameo in the day too.

When Preston Piermattei, the man who helped Ben coordinate his wardrobe for the Bobby Jones clothing company, stopped by and suggested Ben think about wearing a shirt designed by Jeff Rose with images of Jones from all four tournaments during his 1930 Grand Slam, Ben didn't need much convincing. The shirt played enough of a role that when Ben captained the 1999 Ryder Cup, he used a similar look for the Sunday team shirts – that one with Ryder Cup images. The design went 2-0.

*The great sportswriter **Herbert Warren Wind** followed **Ben** in 1995. It would be Herb's final Masters.*

Carl was in front of the Clubhouse earlier than he needed to be Sunday morning. He was anxious. Everyone in contention always is because they have more time on their hands than they need.

"When they finally show up, Ben gets out of the car and his body language is so calm, it was reassurance," Carl said. "There was nothing there to say Ben was too pumped up, too excited."

Ben pulled his first two drives Sunday morning and still managed to open up a two-shot lead on Henninger, who bogeyed the second and third holes. He saved par on the first hole and made birdie at No. 2 with a Harvey Bounce that popped his drive off a pine tree and toward the edge of the rough rather than allowing it to bury itself deep in the azaleas. From there he wedged to eight feet.

"We made birdie from there and that's when I started to believe it was going to be our week," Carl said. "Everybody who's going to win the Masters knocks in a few long putts or chips in and he wasn't getting those. Ben's breaks were just coming in other ways."

Ben bogeyed the fifth hole, but stiffed it at the sixth, then saved par from the bunker at the seventh.

CBS' Jim Nantz had been watching the magic unfold as he prepped for his first Masters Sunday as the anchor of the network telecast. He knew something special was happening. He'd felt something similar at the first Masters he worked for CBS – Nicklaus' unbelievable win in 1986.

"We came on the air just as Crenshaw was about to hit out of that bunker," Nantz said. "The mental resilience that man had to have that week was just immense.

"Not only do I think 999 people out of 1,000 would crack under the same circumstances, but I think they would have done so Thursday."

Not Ben. He birdied the ninth hole and he and Carl headed to the second nine.

They didn't say a word to each other on the walk. They didn't have to. They were in position and it was time, as they always told each other, to reach deep. It was their signature thought.

*Jack Stephens, right, had a profound influence on **Ben** and **Carl's** lives.*

"We knew this was the time," Carl said. "It was happening without us saying it. I could see that fire in his eyes. He was reaching as deep as he could."

Love and Norman teed off 45 minutes ahead of Ben, and both had hot rounds. Love closed with a 66 and was the leader in the Clubhouse as Ben was playing 15; Norman's 68 left him two shots back.

Ben and Carl shared a big old hug and walked off the green. Charlie, Julie and the rest of Team Crenshaw were all crying as Ben walked into the scoring tent.

Herb Wind was walking in Ben's gallery in '95, too, wearing his signature tweed jacket, tie and cap. It would be his last Masters, but oh what a way to finish off a career. Wind had followed Ben's entire career, they shared a hero in Jones and, heck, Wind gave that famous corner its name – Amen Corner. Of course, he never told Ben that. It wasn't Herb's way.

Quiet, unassuming and an incredible historian and observer of the game, Herb and Ben conducted a tour of the great courses in the British Isles for about a dozen people one year in the early 1980s. They toured Open rotation courses like St. Andrews and Hoylake and took side visits to courses very seldom found on America's radar – places like North Berwick.

"We would play a round, then listen to Herb tell stories at night," Ben said. "I'd chime in when I could. The sheer breadth of his knowledge came through."

Wind had been there in 1984 and he was right there again fascinated by the way the day was unfolding, thrilled to see his old friend in the hunt once again.

Ben pulled his 5-iron approach to the 13th and had an awkward little chip. He came up 20 feet short, then sank the putt for birdie. "In my mind, I stayed on pace with what I needed to do," Ben said. "If I made a 5 there, I'd be giving one back."

He didn't look at a leader board until he was walking up to the 15th green and heard a roar at the 18th green. It was Davis finishing his round.

He and Ben were tied.

"When I made par (at 15), that's not what I needed," Ben said. "I needed one stroke better from there to the house."

If there was ever a done deal, that was it. At least on that Sunday.

Warren Stephens had dropped by the Jones Cabin to spend a few minutes with his father, who was relaxing before he made his way to Butler Cabin for the traditional Chairman's presentation of the Green Jacket to the winner.

"I hadn't been able to see him much that week and thought he might be having a little quiet time," Warren said. "Dad and I are talking and I'm about to leave when they bring Davis, his wife, his mother and his caddie in to wait for a possible playoff."

Warren got the high sign from his dad. He wasn't leaving.

When they landed, the entire UT Tower was lit up orange in Ben's honor – a tradition usually reserved for important state holidays and Longhorn national championships.

"I have to sit down and watch Ben play 15, 16, 17 and 18," Warren said. "Davis is a terrific guy and I wish he would win the Masters, but I didn't want him to win that one. I wanted Ben to win. I felt like I couldn't say a word."

Ben hit a perfect 6-iron with just a hint of a draw to the 16th green. "I didn't have to do anything to the shot," he said, "I didn't have to manufacture any part of it." Ben made the putt.

Ben was up by one.

Helen Penick was in Austin, watching with friends and sipping Champagne – a 1983 Dom Perignon that Simon & Schuster, the publishers of Penick's books, had sent to Harvey for his 90th birthday.

Ben hit a 9-iron to 13 feet at the 17th and made another improbable left-to-right birdie putt. He was up by two shots with one to play.

This wasn't a dream.

At that point, Davis turned to Mr. Stephens and said, "Ben's going to win." With that, his wife Robin, brother Mark and mother Penta went to pack the car and Davis headed to the press building to do an interview before Ben finished.

Carl saw the ball dive in and he knew what was coming. As they walked onto the tee, he knew Ben was going to turn and say, "What do you like off this tee?"

He didn't have to ponder this one. To borrow a line from Darrell Royal – Carl knew Ben had to dance with what brung him.

"I just responded, 'Put a good swing on it. You've been doing it

*Carl and Ben joined the list of golf's iconic photographs (from left): **Bob Jones** at the conclusion of the 1927 British Open at St. Andrews; **Ben Hogan** at the 72nd hole at the 1950 U.S. Open at Merion; **Jack Nicklaus** on the 71st hole of the 1986 Masters; and **Ben Crenshaw** and **Carl Jackson** on the 72nd hole of the 1995 Masters.*

all day,' " Carl said.

Ben's heart was pounding as he smacked that 4-wood off the 18th tee. He was playing the kind of golf most players only dream of. How could one man be so lucky? I couldn't believe it.

The patrons were screaming and cheering and congratulating him. He was getting caught up in the moment.

"I started walking down the fairway and that's when I started breaking up," Ben said.

Then he heard Carl's voice and felt Harvey's hand on his shoulder. Ben stopped and pulled himself together. He had a few more shots to play.

He wasn't in great shape when his 8-iron approach came up short. But he had this Tournament.

Ben thought back to those days when Harvey had him chipping under a bench. It wasn't just a drill. It was a lesson in how to play a shot with imagination, a lesson in the focus and passion it would take to learn to love the game, not just play a shot.

Harvey was gone, yet he wasn't. The kid with the amazing grip and endless imagination on the greens had just taken decades of little lessons and talks and wrapped them into one unbelievable week – and the perfect tribute to an incredibly special man.

"With his help, I had the most uncluttered mind you could come across," Ben said. "It was all simple and easy to understand, just like Harvey."

Ben chipped to 10 feet.

Could this be another one of those 18th-hole disasters? No way.

Two putts later, the ball disappeared into the hole.

Ben's shoulders started to shake and he dropped his putter by his side. He pushed his cap off and it fell on the ground as he cradled his face in his hands and sobbed. The tears streamed down his cheeks.

"I can't function," Ben said. "I'm down on the ground and I

hear this soft little voice – 'Buddy, are you alright?' "

Carl put his hands on Ben's shoulders to steady his old friend.

"I tried to do what I could for him. I wanted to tell him anything to make him feel better," Carl said. "So I told him I loved him. And I had goose bumps everywhere."

> Ben started the coffee and went to buy newspapers as he did every morning and was stunned when he saw the story had made every front page in the state of Texas. He grabbed them all.

The image is one of the most iconic in the game. Right up there with Nicklaus' putt at the 17th green in 1986, or Ben Hogan's 1-iron at Merion, or Jones on the crowd's shoulders on the 18th green at the 1927 Open at St. Andrews, to name a few.

The thanks goes to CBS executive producer Frank Chirkinian.

"The greatest thing I ever did," said Chirkinian, who passed away in 2011, "was not cutting away to the heroes shot, where the crowd goes wild. I stuck with Ben."

Ben and Carl shared a big old hug and walked off the green. Charlie, Julie and the rest of Team Crenshaw were all crying as Ben walked into the scoring tent.

Legendary CBS broadcaster Walter Cronkite was watching from above – actually, from the second row of the media tower on the 18th hole. It was his first Masters and, even though he didn't know Ben, they shared several things in common. Cronkite grew up in Houston, went to the University of Texas and he left his junior year (1935) when he went to work as a sports reporter. Plus, he had grandchildren living in Austin.

And, yes, he was blown away.

"He and Penick had me all wrapped up," said Cronkite, who died in 2009. "I was so emotional, I wouldn't have been surprised if there were tears in my eyes. It was one of those great moments in sports."

Carl was at the edge of the green when Chris Mazziotti, Henninger's caddie, told him to grab the flagstick. He hadn't thought about. Everything was moving fast.

Ben signed a few flags for Carl, then Scotty took him over to the Tournament office to get him an advance on his check. As they were driving over in a golf cart, Carl shook his head.

"I've waited 20 years for Ben to play that well," he said.

Scotty shook his head. "But what about 1984?"

Carl shook his head. No way to compare '84 to these last four days.

"It wasn't even close," he said.

Ben's winning 14-under 274 was a magic number. At that point, no one had ever shot 274 and lost a Masters. Only Nicklaus in 1965 and Raymond Floyd in 1976 – both finished at 271 – had shot a lower 72-hole total and only Ben Hogan in 1953 had equaled the 274.

Two years later, Tiger Woods shot 270 – a record that still

stands today – to win his first Green Jacket. But the 274 would last until 2001, when Tiger shot 272 to win his second jacket and David Duval finished second at 274.

The Gatlins were still crying when they congratulated Ben, but they couldn't stay long. They had to get on the road back to Myrtle Beach, but first they went over to Butler Cabin to pay their respects to Charlie Yates.

They headed to the porch to sing their traditional "Let the Lower Lights Be Burning" with Yates when Jack Stephens walked up.

"You are staying for the Champions Dinner, aren't you?" he said to Larry, Steve and Rudy. "You know, Ben would want you to and the members of Augusta National want you too."

Larry told him they were honored, but they didn't have jackets and ties. Stephens said, "You let me worry about that."

Within a few minutes, jackets and ties appeared out of thin air and the Gatlins were in the dining room singing "The Eyes of Texas" for Ben.

"You know," Stephens joked, "that 'Eyes of Texas' song isn't too popular with us folks in Arkansas." So the Gatlins ad-libbed "The Eyes of Arkansas." Everyone laughed.

Ben had gotten a chance earlier to call his dad. Big Charlie's legs couldn't handle the hills on the course any longer, but he watched every minute back home in Austin, celebrating along with everyone else.

During dinner, Ben got a message from Helen Penick: "Harvey and Helen send congratulations and love on this special day." Davis, who had flown home to Sea Island, called to congratulate him.

A police escort took them to the Augusta airport and the jet took off just before 11 p.m. that night and headed to Austin. On the way, he called Helen to say thank you.

When they landed, the entire UT Tower was lit up orange in Ben's honor – a tradition usually reserved for important state holidays and Longhorn national championships.

Julie and Ben laid the Green Jacket on the end of Katherine's bed before they fell asleep at 5 a.m. They were back up an hour later and getting Katherine off to school, where she took the jacket to show and tell.

Carl drove to Hilton Head and was on the tee at 7 a.m. Monday, caddying for John Wilson.

Ben started the coffee and went to buy newspapers as he did every morning and was stunned when he saw the story had made every front page in the state of Texas. He grabbed them all.

Julie was in the library when Ben came home with the stack of

*From left, **Steve Gatlin**, **Ben**, **Jack Stephens**, **Julie Crenshaw**, **Larry Gatlin** and **Rudy Gatlin** in the Augusta National Clubhouse after **Ben's** win in 1995. The Gatlin brothers were invited to serenade the members and the winner.*

newsprint. His voice was cracking as he tried to tell her what he was carrying.

By the time he got it out, tears were streaming down his cheeks. The past eight days … it was so hard to explain. So many emotions, so much sadness and loss, so much joy. So much to reflect on, so very much to celebrate.

> "I believe in fate. Fate has dictated another championship here, as it does so many other times. … I just played my heart out." – Ben Crenshaw

It wasn't something easily put into words, rather something no one but Ben and Julie could truly understand – an incredible week that would live in their hearts forever.

A dozen hours earlier, he had been surrounded by reporters who were looking for one quote that would put everything into perspective – that one tidbit that would explain how such a tragic loss would turn into such an improbable journey.

Those same long-weathered fingers that had placed Ben's hands on that little cut-down mashie so many years ago had somehow reached down and helped guide Ben through the week.

He had, as Ben said, crawled into Carl's body and found two little things that changed everything. He had intervened with a few of Julie's gotta-have-em bounces. He was the 15th club in Ben's bag.

He looked down and smiled as Ben just let go and played by instinct. All those marvelously simple thoughts he passed on over the years had come together in an unforgettable week.

The explanation was simple. So much of it was out of Ben's hands.

It wasn't the first time and it wouldn't be the last.

"I believe in fate," Ben said. "Fate has dictated another championship here, as it does so many other times.

"I don't know where I grew such confidence over a few practice days. I don't think I ever had a quicker transformation, but I just played my heart out."

Four years later, Ben was in the interview room at The Country Club late Saturday night getting peppered with questions. His Ryder Cup team was down by four points going into Sunday's singles and no team, to that time, had ever come back from that large a deficit. Reporters kept asking the U.S. captain the same question, just in different ways.

He paused for a minute, then looked straight ahead and shook his finger at the standing-room only crowd.

"I'm going to leave y'all with one thought and I'm going to leave," he said. "I'm a big believer in fate. I have a good feeling about this. That's all I'm going to tell you."

He got up and walked out.

The reporters thought he was certifiable.

The next day, they realized he wasn't.

Ben and Carl, middle, cross the Ben Hogan Bridge on the 12th hole on Sunday. Brian Henninger and his caddie walk on the far left and right.

Top row:

Left: *Three-time Masters winner* **Sam Snead** *and one of the time-honored traditions – signing autographs for patrons outside the clubhouse.*

Right: *Arnold Palmer and first wife* **Winnie** *with* **Jack Stephens** *during a ceremony to honor an Arnold Palmer water fountain.*

Middle row:

Right: **Davis Love III**, *with his brother* **Mark** *as his caddie, lines up a putt in the final round. Love finished his round and was tied with* **Ben**, *but eventually finished second.*

Bottom row:

Left: **Greg Norman** *closed with a 68 in 1995, but finished tied for third. It was the fourth time Norman finished either second or third at the Masters.*

Right: **Brian Henninger** *shared the 54-hole lead with Ben, but closed with a 76 and tied for 10th.*

Second Panel:

Top: **Ben** *blasts out of the bunker at the 7th hole and saves par on his way to a closing 68 and his second Jacket.*

Left inset: **Ben** *fist pumps after sinking an improbable left-to-right birdie putt at 17 in the final round that put him up by two strokes with one hole to play.*

Large photo: *Patrons file down the hill toward the sixth green.*

Right inset: **Ben** *came up short of the green on 18 and chipped 10 feet above the hole. With two putts he bogeyed the hole – only his fifth bogey of the week – but in doing so, won his second Green Jacket.*

1995 Masters

Large photo, left: Carl helps steady Ben on the 18th green as they share a hug after winning their second Masters.

Top row:
Left: Ben and Julie embrace as he walks off the 18th green.

Right: With Jose Maria Olazabal grinning, Julie tries on Ben's Jacket after the presentation.

Middle row:
Left: Jose Maria Olazabal, the 1994 champion, slips the jacket on Ben during the Green Jacket presentation.

Below: After the CBS cameras stopped rolling, Augusta National vice chairman Joe Ford, Ben and Jose Maria Olazabal share a moment in the Butler Cabin.

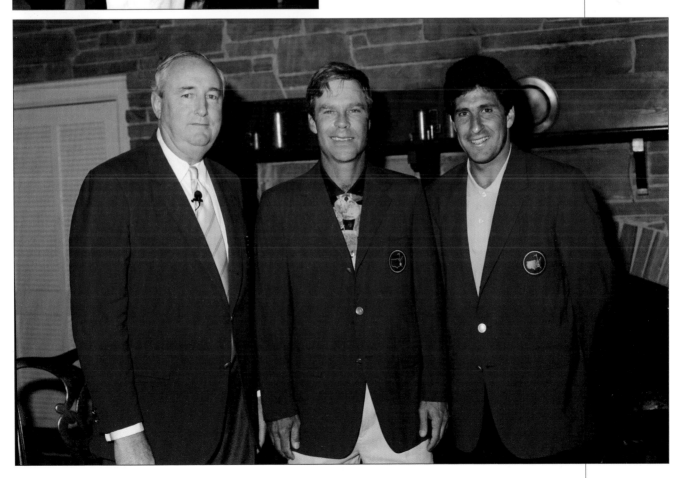

CHAPTER 6

BROOKLINE, ALOTIAN AND BEYOND

"I'm a big believer in fate. I have a good feeling about this. That's all I am going to tell you."
– Ben Crenshaw, to the media on Saturday night at the 1999 Ryder Cup

O ne day Big Charlie woke up and decided to put down his clubs.

Since he had a habit of playing on most any day that ended in Y, that meant he pretty much never went a day without a trip to the golf course. But he was almost 80 now and, while his mind was willing, his body wasn't.

His eyesight wasn't what it used to be, and those old knees that struggled to make the climb from Amen Corner to the Clubhouse couldn't take that 12-story elevation any longer. Nor could they shuffle around the smaller ups-and-downs on the property looking for what passes for a slightly flat area.

They could handle a little practice at Barton Creek CC or 18 leisurely holes in a cart, but it wasn't just that. It was those skills Harvey helped him refine over all those years. They just weren't there anymore.

The words had hardly gotten out of Big Charlie's mouth when Ben's head snapped to.

"What," he said, "are you talking about?"

Big Charlie smiled. "When your forward press is longer than your backswing, you gotta give it up."

All Ben could think at that moment was he sounded so much like Jimmy Demaret. And the memories of watching those two when he was growing up . . . well . . . like his dad and Jimmy and Harvey always said, you'll know when it's time.

But giving up the game and giving up lunch at the club with his buddies? They were entirely two different things.

Big Charlie's post-playing days revolved an awful lot around two stops each day – the market where he would search long and hard to find the perfect tomato and Barton Creek, where he would have lunch. Both of them made his face light up like a Christmas tree.

From left, **Big Charlie**, **Ben** and older brother **Charlie**.

You could find him at his same table at the club most every day eating the same thing – a cup of soup followed by a bowl of vanilla ice cream and a couple of chocolate chip cookies. People came and went, but the core group was almost always made up of Coach Royal, George Hannon, a few golf buddies whose forward-press-

Ben at the now famous late Saturday press conference, at the conclusion of the second day of play.

to-back-swing ratio equaled Big Charlie's, Brent and maybe Ben or Scotty. There were lots of stories and hardly ever a dull moment.

The gang started gathering at Austin CC in their younger days, then moved along to Onion Creek CC when Brent became the pro and to Barton Creek when Brent was hired there.

One day in early 1995, Scotty walked into lunch a little late. Ben had gone to practice and everyone else had scattered. Big Charlie was there alone, polishing off his dish of ice cream.

> [Ben] was leaving a meeting at Dallas-Forth Worth Airport and called his dad from Dallas with another little bit of news. PGA of America CEO Jim Awtrey had just asked him to be the 1999 Ryder Cup captain.

He and Harvey both loved vanilla. It was simple, they'd say. And it tasted really good. Enough said.

Ben was struggling with his game again and Big Charlie was fretting over it. When Scotty walked up, Big Charlie shook his head. The worry tumbled out.

"You know," he said, "no one ever remembers a golfer unless he's won at least 20 tournaments."

Ben had won 18 tournaments at the time and Scotty said he was pretty certain people would remember Ben even if he didn't win another tournament.

Big Charlie said, no. His son needed 20.

Scotty didn't want to argue, so he just let it go. When Big Charlie got an idea in his head, he was stubborn. And this time there seemed to be a hint of urgency in his voice.

It would take more than Scotty to convince him.

It took that memorable, mystical week at Augusta National.

A week or so after Ben's second Green Jacket and 19th career win, Scotty walked into the dining room again and there was Big Charlie polishing off his signature bowl of vanilla ice cream, with cookies on the side.

Scotty walked up to the table.

"Was that good enough for people to remember him?"

Big Charlie had a huge smile on his face.

"Yes," he said, "that'll do."

But Ben wasn't finished.

Two years later, he was leaving a meeting at Dallas-Forth Worth Airport and called his dad from Dallas with another little bit of news. PGA of America CEO Jim Awtrey had just asked him to be the 1999 Ryder Cup captain.

"Oh son, you don't know how much that means to me," Big Charlie said. "And . . . at Brookline."

"He was very emotional that I was being named a captain at Brookline, at a place where we had such a wonderful experience in 1968," Ben said. "His emotion was from a sentimental standpoint

The crowds at
The Country Club
*witnessed a historic
comeback and one
of the most dramatic
Ryder Cups in history.
The Americans won the
first six singles matches
on the final day to rally
from a 10-6 deficit.*

and that's what pleased him to no end. It was something we could share with each other."

Ben and Big Charlie got to share a lot during the next 19 months, and that meant everything.

Big Charlie had hidden something from Ben and Charlie for years – medullary thyroid cancer. He underwent two surgeries in the early 1990s – one at the Mayo Clinic, the other at Houston's M.D. Anderson – and the boys never knew. Even when he came back from Houston one year with bandages, he hid the truth when Charlie asked what happened.

"They got it all," Big Charlie said. "Don't worry about it."

They didn't. They figured it wasn't anything important. He'd tell them if something was wrong. He didn't want his boys worrying.

Finally, in the late '90s, the cancer came back and became more invasive. He was forced to come clean.

"You OK?" Charlie asked again.

"No son," Big Charlie said, "I'm not OK."

By that time, the cancer was in his voice box and doctors wanted to do surgery. Big Charlie declined.

He was sick, but for the better part of two years that didn't stop him from listening to all the decisions his son had to make leading up to the event. What he didn't get to share was the historic comeback Ben's team made in 1999 to beat the Europeans.

Big Charlie did undergo a couple of radiation treatments in 1999, but he wasn't handling it well and eventually went into hospice in March. Six weeks later, he passed away, but not before he heard about one last honor – the Francis Ouimet Scholarship Foundation had reached out to Ben and, a few weeks before Big Charlie died, the group gave out the first annual Charlie Crenshaw Scholarship.

Ben's game couldn't have been better the week he slipped on that second Green Jacket and he rode the momentum for a few more months. He finished fifth at the Memorial Tournament, tied for 15th at the British Open at St. Andrews and qualified for the '95 Ryder Cup team.

"Once you climb up those stairs and into that TV tower, you're history," Burke said. "You can kiss your golf career goodbye."

The following year, he missed the cut at the Masters, then, in 1997, finished 45th after closing with an 80. By that time, his game had entered another lull and the Ryder Cup captaincy gave him a focus off the course. But that wasn't the only change in Ben's life in 1997.

Ben began dabbling in television commentary with NBC when Demaret and Fred Raphael brought the Legends of Golf to Onion Creek CC. Demaret was involved in building the club and the tournament, which brought together the fifty-something legends of the game, some of whom hadn't played much, if at all, in recent times. The first event in 1978 paired 24 players into two-man teams for the 54 hole event. Gardner Dickinson and Sam Snead won the inaugural event, then, in 1979, Julius Boros and Roberto De Vicenzo beat Art Wall and Tommy Bolt in a six-hole playoff. The tournament was a hit and – boom – the PGA Tour saw the interest, a great opportunity and, in 1980, started what is now the Champions Tour.

Who better to talk about the legends of the game than Ben, the historian? He was a walking history lesson no matter which player or what subject. His stories had stories. The same went for a little foray into the booth for the first Skins Game in 1983.

Ben's tales added a depth to the broadcasts and, in 1996, CBS producers Frank Chirkinian and Lance Barrow convinced him to give it a try for real. They had signed him to a two-year contract and, after he would finish his round, he headed up to the booth to chat.

It was fun, yet, at the same time, a lesson in what he didn't really want to do.

It takes a Texan about 10 seconds to say hi. It might take Ben even a little longer. He kids about it, but it's true. And live television is a series of quick sound bites, not great, rich stories that take five minutes to tell.

"It was an experiment, no question about that," Ben said. "I've always referred to the area between 43 and 50 – I term it as no-man's land. You lose your competitive skills for the regular tour and you contemplate where you've been and what your future holds.

"I've observed so many other people in that situation. And if you'll look, a lot of times that's when you'll try your hand at announcing."

Jackie Burke has a slightly different spin on that time of life.

"Once you climb up those stairs and into that TV tower, you're history," Burke said. "You can kiss your golf career goodbye."

Harsh? Maybe. But Ben was 44, wasn't playing well and just hearing Jackie say that took the pressure off.

"It's there, but it was something I wasn't cut out at all to do live television," he said. "It moves too fast it's too quick in and out for me."

Ben knew it almost from the start, but it took a moment during the rainy final round of the 1997 PGA Championship at Winged Foot to force him into a decision. He was on the air, telling a story about Jackie Pung, who had lost a tournament to Betsy Rawls at Winged Foot in 1959. Pung had signed an incorrect scorecard and it bothered the members so much they collected enough money to give her a check for first-place money too.

Ben was barely into his story when producer David Winner's voice popped into his ear and told him to throw it back to the crew at 15. They did.

This wasn't going to work. Ben knew it, stood up, took off his headset and walked out. Jim Nantz tried to stop him so he could finish the story, but Ben declined and went down to watch Davis

Most Important All-time Putts at Augusta*

Jackie Burke Jr., 1956 final round, 17th hole
40-foot birdie highlights 8-shot comeback on final day – a Masters record

Ben Hogan, 1967 third round, 18th hole
25-foot birdie completes second-nine 30 at age 54

Jack Nicklaus, 1975 final round, 16th hole
40-foot birdie leads to one-shot win

Fuzzy Zoeller, 1979 final round, second playoff hole
8-foot putt clinches title

Jack Nicklaus, 1986 final round, 17th hole
18-foot birdie gives Golden Bear lead

Nick Faldo, 1990 final round, 2nd hole
100-foot putt is longest in major championship history

Mark O'Meara, 1998 final round, 18th hole
20-foot birdie to win first Masters

Phil Mickelson, 2004 final round, 18th hole
18-foot birdie catches lip and falls, giving Lefty his first major

Tiger Woods, 2005 final round, first playoff hole
15-footer to win fourth Green Jacket

Ben not included.

Love III win the tournament.

"I just walked out," he said, "and never went back . . . It was simple – I wasn't cut out to be an announcer."

Brookline had such a special place in his heart and, from the time he accepted Awtrey's request, his mind was focused on the team, the course and the task at hand. Seriously focused.

The foot he injured at the 1980 Colonial had become a chronic problem. He had broken the sesamoid bone on the bottom of his right foot when he came off the 16th green and kicked an oil drum in a fit of temper. It bothered him on and off and actually flared up in New Orleans the week prior to the '95 Masters.

Every year Ben and Julie stayed with the Bill Hines family, which had a fabulous cook named Raymond who made the richest crawfish etouffee. Unfortunately, it gave Ben gout from time to time, right in the joint where he kicked the oil drum.

"It seemed to bother me the most when I was on real soft turf like at Pebble Beach," Ben said. "The soft turf seemed to exacerbate the problem."

When he got to the Masters, the pain suddenly abated, but it never really disappeared. By 1997, it was so debilitating that just after the PGA, doctors removed that bone and the calcium deposits surrounding it. It was corrective surgery, but the damage had been done.

Even today, his foot is only about 50 percent what it was before the injury.

"It was something I had to do," he said. "It bothered me and it still does. I feel like I've lost the ability to push my right foot through the hitting area as I should, but that was a long time ago and it was a self-inflicted injury that's come back to haunt me.

"I don't know . . . in a lot of ways, I'm not the golfer I used to be. But I'm fine with that."

Ben with PGA of America Director of Media Relations Julius Mason at the Ryder Cup.

Ben's last PGA Tour top 25 came at the 1997 Kemper Open, where he tied for 19th. He was heading toward 50 and the Champions Tour and he wanted to spend more time with his young family, so his playing schedule was slowing down.

That said, the Ryder Cup captaincy couldn't have come at a more perfect time. Or at a better place.

Brookline had such a special place in his heart and,

Ben with his two co-captains, old friends Bruce Lietzke, left, and Bill Rogers, right.

from the time he accepted Awtrey's request, his mind was focused on the team, the course and the task at hand. Seriously focused.

Just 24 hours after he had accepted the job, Ben was coaching first base at Katherine's kickball game when his mind wandered to Brookline's 12th hole, which has an extra tall flagstick because it's hidden by the blind green.

He was contemplating how to play it when . . . suddenly Katherine is yelling at him.

"Dad, why didn't you tell me?"

She's been doubled-off. The pitcher caught a pop fly and Ben never saw it. He was lost in thoughts, forgot to tell Katherine to tag up and she was out by 30 steps. Scotty, the third-base coach, was staring at him and Julie was screaming from the stands.

"Earth to Ben."

It was already one of Julie's most repeated lines. It was about to become just short of a mantra.

With a lot of help, Ben had it all covered. He talked to former captains and had PGA of America Director of Media Relations Julius Mason and Senior Director of Tournaments Kerry Haigh on speed-dial to confer on-course and team logistics. He turned his day-to-day organization over to Scotty and Julie.

Ben pulled in close friends Bruce Lietzke and Bill Rogers to serve as assistant captains and he was the first captain to add caddies to his brain trust. Although Carl was his caddie at the Masters, he wasn't really considered because he had never caddied at a Ryder Cup, nor was he a Tour caddie. Instead, Ben chose his Tour caddie Linn Strickler and Tom Watson's longtime caddie Bruce Edwards.

"I wanted Bruce for his positive convictions and I wanted Linn to provide levity," Ben said. "All the players knew them and enjoyed being around them.

"I used them for newer eyes. They watch golf week to week. I thought maybe they could see something that somehow I or Bruce and Bill didn't see. I asked them to observe everyone – American and European – and get their thought on what they were looking like. What their body language was. It's what the caddies do all the time."

Ben knew what he wanted. And what he didn't want.

Today, the current trend for Ryder Cup captains is to tweak courses or set up holes to favor the home team. Ben didn't think that way when it came to The Country Club, a quirky old layout filled with elevation changes and small greens.

"It's a great test of golf," Ben said, "but one that needs knowing. You don't have to do much with The Country Club. What I really didn't want was some kind of impenetrable rough – a sort of choking off of the players' skills. I didn't think that would lend itself well to match play or for the spectators.

"I wanted it playable and exciting. You've just got enough to handle with the undulations and the character of the golf course. I thought that was plenty."

It was, honestly, one of the easy parts of a long two years.

The Ryder Cup captaincy was an honor and a great achievement, but no matter how much planning went into it, there were

> Going into the final day, history wasn't on America's side. No team had ever come back from a four-point deficit to win a Ryder Cup.

*The 18th hole at **The Country Club**, one of the most historic golf courses in America.*

unexpected twists and turns.

"I facetiously said it took years off my life and really it did," Ben said. "It took a great emotional toll on me and on Julie. We were both so wrapped up. There were so many minute details. When you're the captain in this country, you and your wife are the host and hostess. You have to think of everything."

And deal with controversies you never saw coming.

Heading into the 1999 PGA Championship at Medinah, Ben was focused on the makeup of his team. The top nine spots (in this order) were solid – David Duval, Tiger Woods, Payne Stewart, Davis Love III, Mark O'Meara, Hal Sutton, Justin Leonard, Jim Furyk and Phil Mickelson – but the 10th spot was up-for-grabs, which also meant he could have even harder decisions than normal when it came to his captain's picks.

The European team in a light mood at the opening ceremonies of the 1999 Ryder Cup.

But even that took a back seat heading into the actual tournament.

The issue of compensation to the Ryder Cup players had come up before and Tom Kite, who captained the 1997 team, had warned him it might come up again. Players had discussed among themselves the question of compensation from the PGA of America or, at the very least, designated charitable donations to charities of their choice, but now they were talking to the press. And the headlines were overshadowing everything else.

Ben wasn't totally caught off guard because of Kite's heads-up. What surprised him was how the topic exploded.

"It got so heated early in the week that I talked with several players and tried to sort things out," Ben said. "The PGA even called a players meeting to discuss it."

Later that fall, the PGA decided that each U.S. captain and player could designate $200,000 in donations. At the time, it was $100,000 to their university and $100,000 to a charity of their choice. Today, the amount is the same, split evenly between player development and a charity of the individual's choice.

Once play started that week, Ben went back to rounding out his team. Going into the final round, there was a chance either Bob Estes or Steve Pate could knock Jeff Maggert out of the 10th spot.

As it turned out, Maggert made the automatic list. Ben knew he was going to pick Tom Lehman, but there were about a half dozen others in the running for the final spot. He chose Steve Pate over Fred Couples, Lee Janzen, Steve Stricker and Jeff Sluman.

"Steve was playing the best golf of his life," Ben said. "He was focused, tough and feisty. And he had finished third behind Curtis Strange at the 1988 U.S. Open there."

> Ben came up with the idea to read Col. William Barrett Travis' letter from the Alamo. Everyone loved it. And, he had the perfect person to do it – close friend and then-Texas Gov. George W. Bush, who was running for president …

Ben had the perfect team, although no one realized that until the final day. Being in Boston, where the United States was essentially born with the Boston Tea Party in 1773, was amazing.

Even more so was the fact the event was at Brookline, the site of amateur Francis Ouimet's remarkable 1913 U.S. Open playoff win over British professionals Harry Vardon and Ted Ray, the two best players in the world at the time.

Everyone knew the story of how Ouimet, an American kid who grew up across the street from the course and had a 10-year-old caddie – a kid who took down the two greatest players of that day in one of the most improbable upsets ever.

What no one knew was another improbable moment was just around the corner.

The Americans were frustrated after Day 1. They hadn't played well and were down 6-2. They played better on Day 2, but were disappointed that Europe had a 10-6 lead.

"I saw some outstanding shots on our side Saturday," Ben said. "I thought the play was much closer than the point total."

Going into the final day, history wasn't on America's side. No team had ever come back from a four-point deficit to win a Ryder Cup.

Ben was grilled in the press room that night. Why had the Europeans mastered both the four-balls and foursomes and the Americans hadn't? What was wrong with his team? What about that 4-down history?

"The press wanted me to say, in effect, we didn't have a chance," Ben said, "and I wasn't going to say something I didn't believe . . . I really felt, in my heart, the matches were much closer than the margin and everyone was putting too much emphasis on that."

Two more reporters asked about the 4-down margin and Ben

*Sweden's **Jesper Parnevik**.*

*Left to right, **Scotty** and **Julie Sayers**, then-Governor **George W. Bush**, **Laura Bush** and **Ben** and **Julie Crenshaw** at the Texas Governor's Mansion on Dec. 13, 2000. The photo was taken just after Al Gore conceded the election and Bush made his acceptance speech as the incoming 43rd President.*

snapped. He had been rambling through the press conference. His mind was on his team.

Suddenly, he looked straight ahead and pointed his finger at the room of reporters.

"I'm going to leave y'all with one thought, and I'm going to leave. I'm a big believer in fate. I have a good feeling about this. That's all I am going to tell you."

With that, Ben got up and walked out the door.

Reporters looked at each other in disbelief. They thought he had lost it, that he was all but certifiable. He knew they wouldn't understand.

But his team? The players were watching in the team room and cheering. He said what they were thinking.

Ben always seems to find moments of clarity, as he calls them, over breakfast at Cisco's. The two-story turquoise building in east Austin has been the go-to spot in Austin for more than 60 years, dishing up migas and huevos rancheros and hot biscuits to everyone, including legendary politicians, athletes, football crowds and musicians in a packed house.

It's been a Crenshaw family favorite for, well, forever, dating back to when Ben and Charlie were kids. They still go most every Sunday morning.

"I don't think I could live without Cisco's," Ben said, "and Katherine, oh my gosh, when she was a little baby – like two years old – she got hooked on their hot sauce."

One summer morning in 1999, Ben and Scotty and their families were having breakfast – Ben loves the huevos rancheros – when Ben came up with the idea to read Col. William Barrett Travis' letter from the Alamo. Everyone loved it. And, he had the perfect person to do it – close friend and then-Texas Gov. George W. Bush, who was running for president and had a fundraiser scheduled in the Boston area during Ryder Cup week.

"Texans know about it, but some of the guys on the team, maybe they'd just heard of the Alamo," Ben said. "The letter is inspirational . . . really inspirational. It describes a clarion call for freedom and independence. This was a man facing death and a cry for freedom. He was going to fight for it even if meant dying for it, which he did."

The team was fired up Saturday night and players were rallying around Ben's walk-off point-and-stare.

> His team had a rare chemistry. It was the perfect blend of gritty players like Leonard and leaders like Lehman, Love, Sutton and Stewart, who was the heart and spirit of the team.

They weren't happy with NBC's Johnny Miller, who had suggested Leonard was playing so poorly, it might be better for him to watch at home. And Europe's Colin Montgomerie had said something Saturday night that really stuck in their craw – "You know we've won, don't you. It's silent. Great, and that's the best thing we can do – silence the crowd by outplaying them."

The U.S. team had a different take. Yes, it was over. But Montgomerie had the wrong team.

The team scarfed down P.F. Chang's for dinner and watched a 30-minute video by Mickey Holden, which Ben and Julie made sure was filled with clips of every player. Those were then interspersed with great shots, inspirational messages like George Scott's "Kick 'em in the ass" speech from "Patton" and John Belushi's "It's not over until it's over" rant from "Animal House."

When the video ended, Bush walked into the room and read the Travis letter.

"When he walked out, I said, 'You're looking at the next president of the United States,' " Ben said. "They were speechless."

It was just the spark they needed. Everyone in the room took turns speaking from his or her heart. And it was Robin Love who added the final exclamation point with a Harvey quote – "Take dead aim."

The next day was red, white and blue. The U.S. won the first six singles matches and seven of the first eight. In the ninth match, Leonard, the 1997 British Open champion, was struggling. He was 4-down to Olazabal and Davis, who had beaten Jean Van de Velde, 6 and 5, to earn the first point that day for the U.S., went to give Leonard a pep talk.

Rogers let Ben know Davis was there and Ben said, "Don't let anyone near Justin. Davis is the right person to be with Justin right now. That is one of the best decisions I made as the captain. Davis picked him up and the rest was history."

Leonard won four straight holes, and headed to the 17th tee all-square.

What happened next was a miracle. Fate. A moment frozen in time.

Leonard's perfect approach spun back and he had an incredible difficult up-and-over-the-ridge, 45-foot putt for birdie. The preposterous putt hit the back of the hole, fell in and the U.S. team spilled onto the green to celebrate. The putt had clinched at least a half point, which meant the U.S. was about to win the Ryder Cup. If Olazabal missed his 25-footer, the small gold trophy would officially belong to the Americans.

No one was comfortable with the premature celebration, but later that night the U.S. was dealing with a delayed controversy. The European team was upset with the Americans' celebration and the press was all over it.

Ben apologized, but it wasn't enough for many of the Europeans.

"In retrospect, it was totally emotional," Ben said. "It was an incredible time for us. At that place and in the way it happened … the way I like to look at it, if Justin Leonard had a remotely holeable putt the reaction would not have been anything like it."

When Leonard's putt careened into the cup, Ben kissed the 17th green. Later, he talked about his team's indomitable spirit.

"Today?" he said. "It's up in the trees. It's fate."

His team had a rare chemistry. It was the perfect blend of gritty players like Leonard and leaders like Lehman, Love, Sutton and Stewart, who was the heart and spirit of the team. A month later, Stewart died in a plane crash.

"It was just tragic that he left us so quick after that," Ben said. "His elation after having made the team and his fabulous win at

Payne Stewart and Michael Jordan share a light moment on Sunday.

Right, Captain Crenshaw, with Scotty Sayers driving, zig-zagged his way all over the course, guiding and encouraging his team during Saturday's matches.

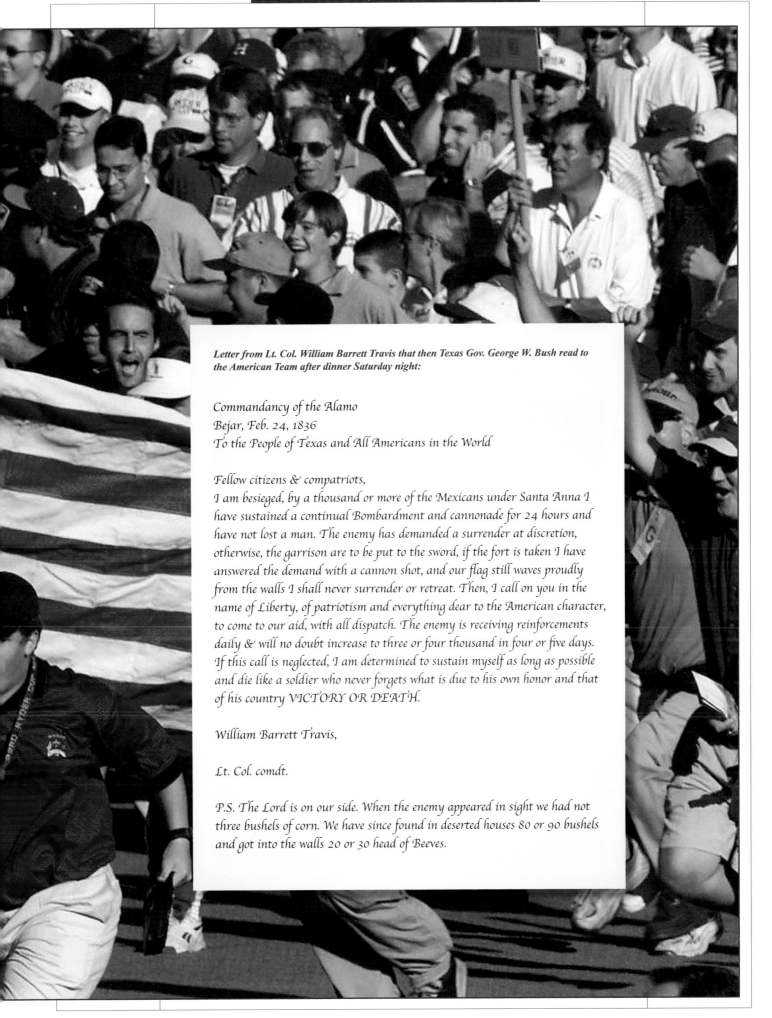

Letter from Lt. Col. William Barrett Travis that then Texas Gov. George W. Bush read to the American Team after dinner Saturday night:

Commandancy of the Alamo
Bejar, Feb. 24, 1836
To the People of Texas and All Americans in the World

Fellow citizens & compatriots,
I am besieged, by a thousand or more of the Mexicans under Santa Anna I have sustained a continual Bombardment and cannonade for 24 hours and have not lost a man. The enemy has demanded a surrender at discretion, otherwise, the garrison are to be put to the sword, if the fort is taken I have answered the demand with a cannon shot, and our flag still waves proudly from the walls I shall never surrender or retreat. Then, I call on you in the name of Liberty, of patriotism and everything dear to the American character, to come to our aid, with all dispatch. The enemy is receiving reinforcements daily & will no doubt increase to three or four thousand in four or five days. If this call is neglected, I am determined to sustain myself as long as possible and die like a soldier who never forgets what is due to his own honor and that of his country VICTORY OR DEATH.

William Barrett Travis,

Lt. Col. comdt.

P.S. The Lord is on our side. When the enemy appeared in sight we had not three bushels of corn. We have since found in deserted houses 80 or 90 bushels and got into the walls 20 or 30 head of Beeves.

Pinehurst . . . We miss him."

Ben carried so much away from that Ryder Cup, including graying hair, but one of his most prized possessions is a 12-inch bronze miniature of The Country Club's statue of Ouimet and his caddie Eddie Lowery that the caddies gave him.

"It's one of the most sentimental things I have," Ben said.

*   *   *   *

Carl won't tell the story.

He'll tease you a little, dangling former President Bill Clinton's name at you. He'll mention a golf shot. Then tell you to call Warren Stephens, who can describe the moment better than anyone.

It seems one day John Tyson of Tyson Foods invited the former president and Arkansas native's son to play a round with him at Alotian. Warren was in the group, which meant Carl was on the bag.

Everything was going along fine until they got to the 12th hole – a very tough par 4 – and Clinton missed the green right. The flagstick was way over to the left.

"It would be a hard shot for anyone," Warren said.

Let alone, a medium-to-high handicapper like Clinton. Carl was pointing to the spot on the green where Clinton needed to land the ball so he could have a nice attempt at par.

At that point, the former golfer-in-chief stepped over a line. He was eyeing the shot and the whole group heard him ask Carl how hard he should hit it. Then he showed Carl some practice swings.

"I think that is the worst thing you can do," Warren said. "I don't even know how you ask this. He asked, 'How hard do I hit it? Should I hit it like this or like this (showing different angles and force)?'

"I'm sitting there going: 'That's a no-win proposition.' He showed him where to hit it. You're the one who has to figure out how hard to hit it."

Clinton chipped it too hard and it went over the green.

"It's easy to do," Warren said. "I'll tell you, I've done that. You hit it a little too hard and it's gone."

The former president was not pleased.

"Clinton went off mouthing about 'Well, Carl you told me to hit it that hard and look where it went,' " Warren said. "We're all just standing there. No one is saying a word. He's an ex-president."

Carl was surprised, to say the least, but kept quiet. Just went about his business. As they walked off the green, Warren threw his arm around Carl and whispered in the ear.

"Well, Carl, now you can say you've had your ass chewed out by an ex-president of the United States, I guess," Warren said. "I don't know what to tell you. That silly son of a bitch shouldn't have asked you how hard to hit it anyway."

They got a good laugh out of it and Clinton didn't ask Carl another question the rest of the round.

He wasn't the first player to try to bully Carl. It was, however, the first ex-president.

It was a perk of the job to rub shoulders with the powerful folks he met over the years, but most of them were good times. The two Bush presidents – both 41 and 43 – were fun, and Dwight Eisenhower was amusing at times. Especially when it came to his tree.

> "I believed he had something up his sleeve. I saw an expression on his face. He was working on something. He put the right players in the right places."
>
> – Carl Jackson

This one? It was just another line to add to his list of interesting things that have happened in his life.

When it came to handling tough situations on the course, Carl didn't blink. It wasn't so easy at home.

Carl calls them stressful times.

Days when money ran low and bills piled up, when what might normally be just a little bump in the road became a mountain almost too steep to climb.

When he was little, those times were just life. The most stressful ones meant Margie would pack up the kids and they'd move in with relatives for a bit. Just until things got better, she'd say.

Carl broke the cycle when he went to work for Jack Stephens, but he still had those tough times. Money would get tight and, with six children, it was never easy.

Debra had seen the good times with two big paychecks – the 1990 Colonial and 1995 Masters – but she never quite found a way to balance the normal times with the great times. Whether it was Carl's job with Jack Stephens or part-time caddying or other ventures, she never felt Carl was holding up his part of the finances. And the strain showed.

After Carl parted with Stephens, Debra's career provided a steadier flow of income, so Carl became a part-time "Mr. Mom," part-time caddie. Weeks when he wasn't caddying, he would get the children to school, cook and take care of things at home.

Most often those stressful times, Carl said, meant: "I needed money. And when you've gotta have it, nothing good happens."

But 1995 was one big exception. His check from that second Masters win allowed Carl and Debra to leave the Dallas area and move to suburban Atlanta to start over yet again. There, they were just a few hours down I-20 from their relatives in Augusta. Debra had family in Atlanta and they were both working.

It was good for awhile, then it wasn't. Debra was working in nursing. Carl was taking care of the kids and caddying at the Golf Club of Georgia.

"We were working as a team and doing the best we could,"

Carl said. "Debra was high maintenance, which is OK, but I just couldn't live up to it."

So when a friend offered Carl a partnership in Diamondized Golf in 1999, they moved again, this time to Asheville, N.C. It didn't work out. The company's club coating process was too damaging to the ball and put too much spin on it for the pros.

A few months after the Ryder Cup, Carl started thinking about another Masters with Ben. But that's when life threw him a curve and *the* most stressful time hit. This time it wasn't about money. Carl was fighting for his life.

"It would have been nice if that had fit in and worked, but it didn't," Carl said. "And I didn't have the resume to go find a really good job."

There was always caddying and, since he was in North Carolina, he was able to share some of those long drives with old friend Tommy Bennett, who lived in the Raleigh-Durham area and was caddying part-time too.

That was a blessing until one night when Carl driving home in his Subaru SUV from the John Deere Classic. He was about half-way home when the car broke down.

"The money I had in my pocket was needed at home," he said. "I had to put a new engine in it and, until we could, we were down the extra car. For the first time, I was depending on someone to pick me up."

Like everyone else, Carl was a bit of a wreck as he watched the first two days of the 1999 Ryder Cup unfold. He was hurting for Ben when the team fell behind and fretting as the Americans left The Country Club down 10-6 that Saturday night since it looked like the U.S. would lose.

Then he saw Ben point his finger at the crowd and talk about fate at the press conference and he knew. He just knew.

"I'll never forget when he said that," Carl said. "That's Ben. It wasn't just wishful thinking. He believed what he said.

"I believed he had something up his sleeve. I saw an expression on his face. He was working on something. He put the right players in the right places."

Carl was smiling inside and out. Another Masters would be here before he knew it and, well . . . that always seemed to set even those stressful times right.

There's just something about the course. About the peaceful moments, about the beauty, about the memories. He grew up there and it's still so much a part of him.

"I still think about the rainy days and how after the rain you could go back out and smell the freshness of the sand," Carl said. "I remember the summers, how it would finally cool off about 10 or 11 at night . . . It's funny. Now, I can't sleep without an air conditioner."

As tough as some times were in the marriage, Carl said Debra did a marvelous job with the children.

"There were some things she didn't understand about golf, but she did a great job with the children, preparing them for school," he said. "I just needed more than I could make. A couple of good tournaments would have helped, but that didn't happen. It was life. And golf teaches you a lot about life."

A few months after the Ryder Cup, Carl started thinking about another Masters with Ben. But that's when life threw him a curve and *the* most stressful time hit.

This time it wasn't about money.

Carl was fighting for his life.

"My whole life I've worked with a big heart," he said. "I worked a lot of times when I didn't feel good or was in some kind of pain."

But this . . . Carl hadn't been feeling good for a while and then he started struggling to go to the bathroom. Debra kept a watchful eye on him until one Sunday afternoon in March 2000 when she looked at him and said they were going to the doctor right then. She knew a doctor who worked with her at a clinic and he was working weekends at the hospital.

The doctor examined him, then told him to go home and tell the kids he would be in the hospital for awhile.

Carlisa, Carl's youngest daughter, during her senior year in high school.

It was colon cancer. He needed to check into the hospital the next morning.

"I thought, 'Oh my god, you're close to death here,' " Carl said. "So we did what he said."

Ben called to tell Carl not to worry. He'd help him out. Not too long afterward, Warren called with the same offer.

"I remember saying I didn't know this was this serious," Ben said. "I want you to know we'll take care of you.

"From what he was telling me, he was obviously not feeling good about himself. The thing everybody – Debra, Warren, all of us – was concerned about was we didn't know if it had spread or if taking the section out would be a success."

Ben shook his head.

"We talked before the surgery and he was in bad shape. He said, 'Don't worry about me. Go play the tournament.' That wasn't possible."

The surgeons got the cancer, but had to do a colostomy. Debra knew what was coming. Carl didn't.

When he woke up in the hospital and realized he had to use a catheter and a bag, he saw it as an indignity. Then he thought about the cost, and the combination caused him to slip into a depression.

"Once I figured that out, I was about ready to die. I came apart," he said. "That's when I started thinking things, about the children. And Debra. They didn't need to be burdened. We had a lot of hospital bills and . . . I was kind of ready to go at one point."

So many of Carl's best moments have come at Augusta National, but another big one came in 2008, when he was inducted into the Arkansas Golf Hall of Fame.

Then, one morning, a doctor from South Africa was sitting by his bed when he woke up.

"I hear you're ready to go," she said.

Carl said yes, he figured he pretty much was. The financial burden would be too great for the family. But she talked him into trying a new chemo treatment that kept him in the hospital for a month.

It worked. Eight months later, doctors gave him the all clear. He had reconstructive surgery in December, and the bag and catheter were history.

"Ben and Warren were there for me and when you're that sick, you've got to have time to get well," Carl said. "They made that happen."

About six weeks later, Ben saw Carl out in San Diego, looking to pick up a caddie job for the week.

"What the hell are you doing out here?" Ben said. He couldn't believe Carl wasn't at home recuperating.

"He's a very, very strong man," Ben said. "I could tell he was still feeling the effects. I'd say he was 60-70 percent when I saw him. He was still hurting."

Everyone – caddies, players and even Tour officials – knew what he faced and wanted to help because, as Ben said, Carl had people to feed.

With Carl in the hospital in 2000, Ben called on Strickler, a walking dry-sense-of-humor quip known as "The Growler," to carry his bag at Augusta. They were a team on Tour for 13 years – Strickler also caddied for, among others, Curtis Strange and Greg Norman – but an anomaly at the Masters.

They couldn't walk a step without someone asking about Carl. And everyone – players, caddies and Augusta National Club staff and officials – wanted to know how he was doing.

"It was clear to them we were a team, we were always going to be a team," Ben said.

Strickler, who is irreverent and side-splitting funny in the same breath, wasn't offended. "If there was anybody who could take it, it was Linn," Ben said. "He knew the way I felt about Carl."

Ben and Linn struggled through several rain delays that year and missed the cut. On Saturday afternoon, Strickler – in typical "Growler" style – thought briefly of giving his Masters jumpsuit to a friend, but when he found out it would cost him or her $10,000 if a caddie didn't turn it in at the end of the week, he changed his mind.

The next year, Carl couldn't wait to get back to Augusta. If only the weather and Ben's game would have cooperated. Rain delays forced them to play almost 36 holes in one day, and Carl, who was only about 80 percent back, was struggling at the end. So was Ben as they shot 81-78 and missed another cut.

In fact, they've only made two cuts since 1997 – in 2006, when Ben was tied for 10th going into the weekend, but closed with 78-79 and 2007, when he closed 84-75.

"I was glad to be there," Carl said of 2001. "A little time before that, I thought I was never going to caddie there again. It was a testament to the good treatment I got to get me on the path to recovery."

During his recovery, Carl got deeper into Centurion Ministries, a group he had been involved with since his days in Little Rock, and was qualified as a Level I medical minister. He also spent a lot of time thinking about his family and the fact that he needed, as he called it, "an everyday job."

"It took me getting sick to understand how much they wanted me at home," Carl said. "Carlisa was playing basketball and running track and Jason was playing football and baseball and was on the wrestling team. They wanted me at their games and I could do that."

Warren called Carl frequently during his recovery. He was building Alotian and, when construction was well underway, he asked Carl to be the club's caddie master. It took Carl about a millisecond to accept.

He was so ready to go – "He said he couldn't be there any quicker than tomorrow," Warren said – and headed back to Little Rock a little early. That way, he had plenty of time before the course opened in September 2004 to find caddies and do yardage books. The clubhouse opened the following year.

"It was a blessing that I needed and I could be home with my wife and kids," he said.

Jason and Carlisa both attended private school – Episcopal Collegiate – and Jason went on to SMU. He walked onto the team and, eventually, coach June Jones gave him a scholarship. Carlisa will get her degree from Loyola-New Orleans in May 2013.

Carl's son, Carl Romeo Jackson, wife Cassandra and baby Jacob.

Carl and Debra ended the marriage in 2006. "When she wanted something, she wanted it then," Carl said. "We just got to a fork in the road, where, even though I had a job, I just couldn't make her happy."

When Carl took the Alotian job, Jack Stephens was still living in the same house and, every so often, Carl would see him at the club or drop by the house to visit. "He gave me the thumbs-up," Carl said. "He just kept saying how happy he was that I was there."

Stephens passed away in the summer of 2005, but Carl took the experiences and lessons he had learned from him years before and spun it forward. In 2009, he formed The Carl Jackson Foundation and Carl's Kids.

> In some ways, Ben is still recovering from the Ryder Cup. It was an incredible week and a majestic moment that took almost two years to plan. It enhanced his reputation as a historian and golf course architect.

Golf was his life and had been good to his family, so he wanted a vehicle to offer opportunities to kids who didn't have access to golf courses. Carl's Kids exposes kids to the game and everything surrounding it – players, caddies, golf pros, promotions and equipment companies. He has expanded it to include a summer-long program in Pine Bluff.

"It all goes back to my early years caddying at Augusta National and a lot of guys I grew up with who aren't around anymore," he said. "A lot of them could have been good golfers if they had been exposed to instruction. If those caddies learned to play as well as they did without instruction, how good could they have been with teachers? We learned it the caddie way, which meant some things we didn't do properly.

"We want kids to learn all the good points in life that golf teaches you. It teaches you to respect your fellow man. Even though you're competing, when you're playing a round you're respecting him and he's respecting you. And it teaches integrity."

Ben, Carlisa and Carl at Carl's induction into the Arkansas Golf Hall of Fame.

So many of Carl's best moments have come at Augusta National, but another big one came in 2008, when he was inducted into the Arkansas Golf Hall of Fame. Although he was honored in the inaugural class of the Caddie Golf Hall of Fame in 1999, the Arkansas honor was even better.

Ben and Scotty flew up to be there, and when Carl walked into the dinner, he noticed pictures of Jack Stephens and Byron Nelson on the wall. It added even more to the honor because Carl had caddied for Nelson during a practice round years ago.

"He made one of the best talks I've ever heard," Ben said. "It was heartfelt, proud and thankful."

Carl talked about growing up in poverty, about how Jack Stephens changed his life. He summed it up brilliantly, too.

"I know that I will meet my Lord and savior, and when I do, I'll see a lot of old friends. And Mr. Jack and I will be together again."

* * * *

He was simply a legend. A boy from Oklahoma who changed the

face of college football and left an indelible stamp on athletics at the University of Texas.

He drove defenses crazy with a little triple offense known as the wishbone. He brought three national football championships to Austin, created the iconic Longhorn logo and burnt orange.

He stood for integrity, and his legacy is summed up this way – the mark of a man is how he treats people who can never do anything for him. He transformed – with the help of buddies like Willie Nelson – Austin's sleepy music scene into the live music capital of the world.

And he always danced with what brung him.

You know him as Darrell Royal. Or maybe DKR.

But to those around him, the athletes and students whose lives – not just playing careers – he influenced for decades, the lifelong friends not just in Austin, but far and wide, he's simply Coach.

And to Coach, Ben was never just Ben. He was always Ben Boy.

Just where that started? Who knows? It was a term of affection for a old friend's son, a UT superstar, a distinguished alumnus, a Hall of Famer, a golf buddy and, most of all, his friend.

Ben Boy and Harvey were watching Coach on the practice tee one day when they noticed something was a little off. Coach was one of those practicers.

He'd stand there and hit balls so long you'd think he was trying to outdo another one of his UT athletes-turned-friend Tom Kite.

Harvey didn't need to see more than a couple of swings to know that someone had gotten in his head. Convinced him this would solve all his problems off the tee.

"Now Coach," Harvey said, "somebody's told you that if you could hook the ball you could get 15 or 20 more yards. Is that right?"

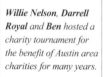

Willie Nelson, Darrell Royal and Ben hosted a charity tournament for the benefit of Austin area charities for many years.

Coach said, "Yes sir. That's right."

Harvey nodded. "Coach, that's not you. You should aim a little left and let the ball drift a little to the right."

Ben chuckled, recalling the moment. "In a way, he turned the tables and said, 'Coach, you've got to dance with what brung ya.' "

Over the years, Ben Boy and Coach played a lot of golf.

Ben Boy sat in on Coach's private pickin' sessions and they played in charity events together. He later joined them for the Ben Willie Darrell Tournament at Barton Creek, which benefitted east Austin youth.

"They formed it to have their friends all together to play golf,"

Ben said. "People came from everywhere: boosters, musicians, athletes and song writers. It was always a grand time."

Coach was at it again one day on the practice range at Barton Creek when Ben walked over and told him his swing looked pretty good.

> [Ben and Bill Coore] both enjoyed learning the intricacies and subtleties of the layout and tackled the project with enormous respect for Ross. They knew that, like Augusta, Pinehurst had those subtle undulations and you had to play similar little shots around the greens.

"Well, he said, Ben Boy it doesn't feel right," Ben recalled. "I gave him a couple of tips and then – I don't know what possessed me – I said, 'Coach, a good golf shot must feel like a good punt.' And the light went off."

Coach played quarterback, defensive back and was Oklahoma's punter in the late 1940s, and so Ben Boy and Coach spent the next 40 minutes taking about punting.

"I knew that's how he and his brother, grew up in Oklahoma," Ben said. "They didn't have anything but a football and they kicked it all the time.

"We related it to timing and the swing. I remember sayin', 'Coach, it must have been tough in that wind.' He said, 'Oh, Ben Boy, you had to drop it just right. You had to get your timing right.'"

Timing was indeed everything in punting, the golf swing, passing and, well, in life.

In some ways, Ben is still recovering from the Ryder Cup. It was an incredible week and a majestic moment that took almost two years to plan. It enhanced his reputation as a historian and golf course architect and, if he didn't say no from time to time to reporters, he wouldn't have a spare moment in the day.

As he eased in his 50s, Ben started playing on the Champions Tour, where he has had just 13 top-10 finishes and no official wins. He has had only three real chances to win – at the 2003 3M Championship, where he tripled the 15th hole in the final round and tied for fourth behind winner Wayne Levi at the 2007 U.S. Senior Open, where he finished second by three shots to Brad Bryant and at the 2008 Constellation Energy Senior Players Championship, where he bogeyed the final hole and tied for third.

In fact, his only win since the 1995 Masters was the 2009 Champions Tour Skins Game with Fuzzy Zoeller. And now that he's entered his 60s and is playing very little, he's pretty much run

*Ben and Julie's daughters – **Claire**, **Katherine** and **Anna Riley**.*

Coore & Crenshaw Golf Course Designs

ORIGINAL DESIGNS

Kapalua Plantation Course
Maui, Hawaii (1991)

Barton Creek
Austin, Texas (1991)

Sand Hills
Mullen, Neb. (1995)

Warren Course at Notre Dame
South Bend, Ind. (1995)

Klub Rimba Irian
Kuala Kencana, Indonesia (1996)

The Golf Club at Cuscowilla
Eatonton, Ga. (1996)

Talking Stick (36 holes)
Scottsdale, Ariz. (1997)

Chechessee Creek Club
Okatie, S.C. (2000)

East Hampton Golf Club
East Hampton, N.Y. (2000)

Austin Golf Club
Austin, Texas (2001)

Hidden Creek
Egg Harbor Township, N.J. (2002)

Friar's Head
Baiting Hollow, N.Y. (2002)

Old Sandwich Golf Club
Plymouth, Mass. (2004)

Bandon Trails
Bandon, Ore. (2005)

We-Ko-Pa "Saguaro Course"
Fort McDowell, Ariz. (2005)

Colorado Golf Club
Parker, Colo. (2006)

Sugarloaf Mountain
Lake Apopka, Fla. (2006)

Clear Creek Tahoe
Lake Tahoe, Nev. (2009)

The Dormie Club
Pinehurst, N.C. (2011)

Lost Farm at Barnbougle Dunes
Tasmania, Australia (2011)

Streamsong Resort
Fort Meade, Fla. (2012)

Bandon Preserve
Bandon, Ore. (2012)

Shanqin Bay
Hainan Island, China (2012)

Trinity Forest
Dallas (2013)

Cabot Links
Nova Scotia, Canada (2013)

9-HOLE ADDITIONS

Southern Hills
Tulsa, Okla. (1992)

Onion Creek
Austin, Texas (1996)

COURSE RENOVATIONS

Houston Country Club
Houston, Texas (1986)

Brook Hollow
Dallas, Texas (1993)

Riviera
Pacific Palisades, Calif. (1993)

Hot Springs "The Arlington Course"
Hot Springs, Ark. (1994)

Shady Oaks
Fort Worth, Texas (1995)

Onion Creek
Austin, Texas (1995)

Lakewood
Dallas, Texas (2003)

Prairie Dunes
Hutchinson, Kan. (2004)

Wykagyl
New Rochelle, N.Y. (2006)

Pinehurst No. 2
Pinehurst, N.C. (2011)

Maidstone Club
East Hampton, N.Y. (2012)

Shinnecock Hills
Southampton, N.Y. (2012)

Old Town Club
Winston-Salem, N.C. (2013)

out of chances.

"I'm plenty fine with the Masters being the last one," Ben said. "I wish I could have played better on the Champions Tour, but . . . it's obvious, the guys who have been successful as seniors have been 100 percent committed. And I don't think I ever was. But that's not an excuse.

"I played enough golf out there to do well and I just didn't do it … for a lot of different reasons."

The two biggest? Family and golf course design.

When he won the '95 Masters, Katherine was 7 and Claire was 3. Anna Riley was born the year before the Ryder Cup, and, well, Ben wanted to spend more time at home to watch the girls grow up and be part of their lives. Today, Katherine and Claire are both working in Austin and Anna Riley is finishing her freshman year at Austin High.

At the same time, Ben and Bill Coore found themselves in demand. They've either designed or renovated 24 courses since 2000 and just agreed to design the new Trinity Forest Golf Course, just southeast of downtown Dallas and Cabot Cliffs in Nova Scotia. In December 2012, they opened both Shanqin Bay (China) and Streamsong Resort, located between Tampa and Orlando.

Charlie Price's book introduced Ben to the world's great courses and, within a year or two, he was totally fascinated by design. He no longer simply played a course. He studied it. He took road trips from tournaments to see a course and fit in 18 holes – even on a busy week.

But it was Augusta that turned a fascination into a passion.

Bill and Ben at work on the Pinehurst No. 2 renovation.

"When I got there in 1972, I got a first look at what I was reading about," he said. "Everybody tries as journalists and students of architecture to describe the place, but you just can't. There's something that fails. When you see it in person, you think this is a creation."

That convinced Ben there is no substitute for laying eyes on a course, so he made as many side trips as he could. It turned into a lifetime of study.

"The more I'd travel, the more I'd see, the more fascinated I was," he said. "What is it about a hole that captures your attention? What it is about a setting that makes people stand up to think about how they're going to play the hole? What retains people's fascination?

"Those were the things I was discussing with and asking Herb and the others I looked up to. I'd pop out a name. Did you know so-and-so? He'd said, yes, I knew him. It might be Donald Ross. It might be (A.W.) Tillinghast. Herb knew them all."

Ben came to know them through those conversations, and that, plus history, has inspired some of his and Bill's designs.

There are those who believe Ross was a bit

> (The Pinehurst renovation) "… resembles what was there – a course encased in the sandy ground. It was basically islands of fairways encased in this beautiful sandy, barren ground. Now those areas illuminate the fairways." – Ben Crenshaw

miffed when he wasn't chosen to design Augusta National, so he turned Pinehurst No. 2, which he originally completed in 1907, into his lifetime project. Ross worked on the centerpiece course – one of eight courses at the resort – until he passed away in 1948. Ben and Bill have just renovated it in preparation for the 2014 U.S. Open and U.S. Women's Open championships.

The course was a gathering place for the rich and famous at the turn of the last century when they'd come south by train and stop over at Pinehurst to play those sand greens, which were replaced by grass greens in 1936. They loved it, and Ross' influence spread rapidly.

Bill grew up 40 miles away in Thomasville, N.C., and went to Wake Forest, so he knew Pinehurst well. But when they undertook the project, they turned to the Peter Tufts Library there, which has an impressive archive of old photographs and aerial shots. They also used Price's writings since he had been a frequent visitor over the years and lived there for most of the last decade of his life.

The sandy areas off the fairways had been covered with grass, turned into rough and had, Ben said, a monotone look. Bill and Ben re-defined fairways with irrigation lines, replaced 35 acres of grass with sandy areas covered with wire grass, other native plants and pine straw that don't need constant watering and reshaped some bunkers to their 1940s look.

"Hopefully people will see its restoration as a nod to its past in its native form," Ben said. "It resembles what was there – a course encased in the sandy ground. It was basically islands of fairways encased in this beautiful sandy, barren ground. Now those areas illuminate the fairways."

They both enjoyed learning the intricacies and subtleties of the layout and tackled the project with enormous respect for Ross. They knew that, like Augusta, Pinehurst had those subtle undulations and you had to play similar little shots around the greens.

"So it's anything but an unthinking process of how to play a delicate shot there because your imagination goes wild," Ben said. "I can do this or I can do that. Or should I do this or should I do that? Today, so many courses, you pull out a sand wedge and play that shot to the green, whereas at Augusta or Pinehurst, you're limitless

The 16th hole at the **Coore-Crenshaw** *renovated No. 2 course at* **Pinehurst**.

in your possibilities of what shots you can play."

And that makes all the difference in the world.

Ben was right. When George W. Bush walked out of the team room at Brookline that night, Ben said he would be the next president. Whether it was blind friendship or another one of his moments where clarity and fate collide . . . well, he was right. It just wasn't easy.

Ben and George W. had known each other for years – Bill Munn had introduced them at a Texas Rangers game – but after Ben married Julie, the couples became good friends. Laura and Julie hit it off just like their husbands did and the friendship grew deeper after the younger Bush was elected Texas governor in 1994.

They shared dinners at the Crenshaw house and Governor's Mansion and, although the Bush twins – Jenna and Barbara – were about five years older than Katherine, they all went to Camp Longhorn and attended Austin High. Jenna wound up as Katherine's counselor at Camp Longhorn.

Ben and Julie stood with Bill and Lynn Munn during Bush's first gubernatorial inauguration and . . . the rest is a blur. Bush beat popular and outspoken Gov. Ann Richards, and that launched his career. "It just catapulted from there," Ben said.

The Crenshaws hosted fundraisers at the house and entertained political heavy hitters like former Secretary of State Condoleezza

Rice and former Bush Chief of Staff Andrew Card. And when the 2000 elections was thrown into a recount in Florida . . . well, Ben had already been glued to the television for months.

"We're watching our friends go through this," Ben said. "My god, it was fascinating. I was literally a complete basket case. All of us were. All we'd do was watch the television."

And nothing was more riveting than the night the Florida Supreme Court ruled on the recount. Julie and Ben were having dinner at the Governor's Mansion and the governor got up during dinner and turned on the television to watch the decision.

"(Bush) doesn't watch TV," Ben said, "He just doesn't. When they announced the ruling . . . talk about quiet. He just looked at me and said, 'I've got to make a phone call. I may be playing a lot more golf with you.' Julie and I didn't know what to say or do."

Bush called Jim Baker, who served as Chief of Staff under Ronald Reagan and the elder Bush, and was also a close advisor to his son.

"What is our next step? What are we doing?" he said.

Baker replied, "We're going to fight it."

A month later, they were sitting with the Bush family during the inauguration. "It was the damndest thing," Ben said. "It made a huge impression on my life to watch a friend go through this."

In the next eight years, Ben and Julie visited the White House about 16 times – mostly around Christmas or in July. Ben even went with the president to Monticello in 2008 when he delivered a Fourth of July speech.

"I felt so humbled," Ben said. "And, in 2001, to watch him lead the nation after 9/11. . . . Some of the greatest moments of his presidency were how he led us through that and some of the things he put in place to keep the nation safe.

"I think about the criticism he's gotten since leaving office. I think about it a lot. I'm going to be a supporter of George Bush until they put me in the ground. He understood more than anyone that with any public office, you're going to get criticism – and a lot of it. And he bore it well."

Ben is friends with the elder Bush too. In fact, Ben and Julie spent a few days with the Bushes at their Kennebunkport home before the Ryder Cup. Ben and 41 played a little golf at Cape Arundel, they dined on Maine lobsters and relaxed. Barbara Bush – "She's a heartfelt, magnificent woman," Ben said – greeted Ben in her PJs that Sunday morning.

A few hours later, they were holding hands on the 90-minute drive to Brookline.

When Ben and Harvey were inducted into the World Golf Hall of Fame in 2002, an emotional night led to even more tears when Ben was introduced by both presidents on videotape.

"I was in real good shape after that," he said. "Oh, boy."

Ben and George W. don't see each other as often as they used to, but they do catch up and play golf when Ben is in Dallas or 41 comes to Austin.

What made them so close? The elder Bush, golf, politics and mutual old friends like Munn. They're all just a bunch of visit-ers.

"And he knows I'm his friend," Ben said, pausing. "Always."

*　*　*　*

Ben and Carl are sitting in Scotty's conference room telling war stories. Life is good. They've been chuckling and pointing and remembering things long forgotten for about 30 minutes when the subject turns to the secret to putting at Augusta National.

They look at each other and smile. Ben's hand moves through the air, following an imaginary line from the golf ball to the cup. Carl chuckles, thinking about all those putts he's seen come up short or wide or just flat nowhere close.

Most folks think everything breaks toward the 12th green. Players, long-time patrons, even members swear so many putts on the course pull toward that green.

Ben and Carl chuckle. Nope. Wrong.

They know the secret. They figured it out years ago and have, for the most part, kept it to themselves.

They call it The Pull.

"We've given it up to a couple of guys," Ben said, "and we're much more forthcoming than we use to be."

Think about Ben's preposterous 60-footer on No. 10 in 1984. Was that pulling to No. 12? Did that pull factor into Tiger putting it off the 13th green a few years ago? Or Ben's putt at the 71st hole in 1995?

"The slope of the green favors No. 12," Carl said, "but then The Pull grabs it a little and then throws it to the back."

They feel it starting at the first hole. In fact, only a very few areas on the greens there are not affected by it.

After a bit more prodding, Carl finally gives it up. Reluctantly would be an understatement.

"I picture the score board left of No. 11 green when I think about The Pull," he said. "Anywhere on the course, that's what I picture in my mind."

That's the way the course drains. Straight down to the low spot. Pappy must have figured it out decades ago when he was watching the construction crews.

"There's a lot of it on the course and it has an effect that's just uncanny," Ben said. "That's why we have so much fun looking at each other when people putt. That's how you learn.

"When you watch a putt that anyone else hits, you watch it and try to learn something. That's how you play tournament golf. We're reading everyone else's putts and thinking: what about if we had it?"

They both chuckled.

There is no mistaking their friendship and love for each other. As they sat talking about their 35 Masters together, they finished each other's sentences. They knew what the other was about to say before he said it.

> The respect and love between them ... that's easy to see. There's an ease out there when they're competing, an unspoken way they go about playing a course they revere.

Just last year, there was a rumor running around that Carl had died. Actually, it was another tall former Augusta caddie – Joe Collins. But that didn't stop folks from calling Scotty or Alotian to ask about it.

Carl picked up the phone and called Ben. "This," he said, "is Lazarus."

They laughed about that and so many other things that day. They talked together and separately about their friendship, their partnership and the love and reverence the patrons at Augusta have for them.

The key? It's simple. Teamwork. Without it, Ben might not have won two jackets and Carl might have walked away from Augusta.

Together, they are an iconic partnership. Ben and Carl. Carl and Ben. Never one without the other.

"(Teamwork) might seem like the simplest thing, but it was the most important," Carl said. "Over all those years, especially in the good years when the heat was on, every time Ben vented, I would settle him down by saying, "It's time to get to this next shot. It's the most important one. Every time he said OK. Every time."

Ben nodded.

"I would say it's unequivocal that I could not have done the things I did, the things I was able to do over there because of him," Ben said. "Just like he was saying, he handled me so well. The whole time. The whole time.

"He kept me in focus all the time. I know that there were times when I could have controlled my emotions a little better. They got me in trouble a million times."

Carl wouldn't have caddied for 51 years if Ben hadn't come into his life, if they hadn't formed that bond.

"I can't imagine a player I would have stayed with for so long," Carl said. "Ben exudes respect and love for so many people . . . that's really something to witness."

And Ben? He wishes he would have played better. For Carl.

Earlier that day, Ben was talking about how special their relationship was, how it was hard to imagine how they had come together so many years ago and, at one point, Ben was by himself and started talking about how there might not have been two Green Jackets without Carl.

"No question, it probably would have been harder," Ben said. "I do know the times I've played well over there – I've won or had the close calls – I know that he is the major part of that. So I'm saying I don't think I could have accomplished it without Carl."

He wiped away the tears and excused himself and walked outside to compose himself. This caught him off-guard. It was the second time that day.

"I have a hard time getting a hold of myself," he said. "I was out there thinking three words – love, kindness and respect. Carl is filled with Harvey-like kindness.

"This is what this man has given me. And this is what I have given him in return."

Carl has always considered himself an employee first, friend second. He doesn't let things go to his head. He remembers he's the caddie and Ben is the golfer.

The respect and love between them ... that's easy to see. There's an ease out there when they're competing, an unspoken way they go about playing a course they revere.

Yet every so often, they'll get a patron who doesn't understand why Carl does things before Ben asks, why he takes the lead when other caddies wait for instructions.

Not too long ago, one patron even felt as though he had to ask.

"Why," he demanded, "are you letting that caddie do this?"

The people around him shook their heads as if to say: "Get a clue." This is Ben and Carl.

Ben didn't break stride. He just looked up and – with eight simple words – silenced the guy.

"He can do whatever the hell he wants."

Carl and *Ben* *finishing at the 2011 Masters. It was Carl's 50th and Ben's 40th.*

Top row:
Left: *U.S. team member* **Jim Furyk** *and his caddie*
Mike "Fluff" Cowan *line up a putt.*
Right, *European fans cheer on their team.*

Middle row:
Left: **Captain Crenshaw** *watches intently.*
Right, *Europe's* **Miguel Angel Jimenez** *plays a shot.*

Left: *Europe's* **Padraig Harrington** *studies the line of
his putt.*

Above right: *European captain* **Mark James** *and
Ryder Cup rookie* **Sergio Garcia.**

Right: *U.S. fans cheer on their team in Brookline.*

Large photo, right: *American teammates and fans
exalt after* **Justin Leonard's** *improbable, 45-foot putt
on the 17th green on Sunday.*

Inset photo: **Justin Leonard** *and* **Jose Maria Olazabal**
*shake hands after their controversial match. Leonard
came from 4 down at the turn to halve the match.*

1999 Ryder Cup

Status	EUROPE	Hole	USA	Status
	WESTWOOD	F	LEHMAN	3 & 2
	CLARKE	F	SUTTON	4 & 2
	SANDELIN	F	MICKELSON	4 & 3
	VAN de VELDE	F	LOVE	6 & 5
	COLTART	F	WOODS	3 & 2
	PARNEVIK	F	DUVAL	5 & 4
ALL SQUARE	HARRINGTON	16	O'MEARA	ALL SQUARE
	JIMENEZ	15	PATE	3 UP
1 UP	OLAZABAL	14	LEONARD	
2 UP	MONTGOMERIE	13	STEWART	
	GARCIA	13	FURYK	4 UP
4 UP	LAWRIE	12	JAGGERT	

MATCH SUMMARY

		TOTAL
EUROPE		10
USA		12

Above: The scoreboard tells the story on Sunday: the wholly improbable U.S. comeback, the strongest and most dramatic in Ryder Cup history to that point.

Below: A celebratory U.S. team on the balcony of the Locker House at The Country Club.